Reading Shakespeare's mind

Manchester University Press

Reading Shakespeare's mind

Steve Sohmer

Manchester University Press

Copyright © Steve Sohmer 2017

The right of Steve Sohmer to be identified as the author of this work has been asserted by him in accordance with the Copyright, Designs and Patents Act 1988.

Published by Manchester University Press
Altrincham Street, Manchester M1 7JA

www.manchesteruniversitypress.co.uk

British Library Cataloguing-in-Publication Data
A catalogue record for this book is available from the British Library

Library of Congress Cataloging-in-Publication Data applied for

ISBN 978 1 5261 1327 6 hardback
ISBN 978 1 5261 3807 1 paperback

First published in hardback 2017

First published in paperback 2018

The publisher has no responsibility for the persistence or accuracy of URLs for any external or third-party internet websites referred to in this book, and does not guarantee that any content on such websites is, or will remain, accurate or appropriate.

Typeset in 10/12 Sabon by
Servis Filmsetting Ltd, Stockport, Cheshire
Printed in Great Britain by
Lightning Source

For Tully

such stuff as dreams are made on

In every man's writings
the character of the writer
must lie recorded

Thomas Carlyle, *Essays on Goethe*

Contents

List of figures	viii
Preface: impersonal Shakespeare	ix
PART I: Shakespeare, lovers, and friends	1
1 Joining the mice-eyed decipherers	3
2 Marlowe's ghost in *As You Like It*	15
3 The dark lady of *The Merchant of Venice*	53
PART II: Queen Elizabeth's *Twelfth Night*	75
4 *Twelfth Night* on Twelfth Night	77
5 Shakespeare's *Twelfth Night* wordplay	89
6 Shakespeare and Paul in Illyria	100
7 Nashe and Harvey in Illyria	110
8 M.O.A.I. deciphered at last	126
9 Beginning at the beginning	134
10 Tributes private and public	146
Epilogue: personal Shakespeare	172
Longer notes	175
Bibliography	189
Index	200

Figures

1 Julian and Gregorian calendars, 1601–02   79

2 *Farmer's Almanacke*, December 1601   80

3 Book of Common Prayer calendar, January   105

4 *Twelfth Night*, act 2, scene 5, from the Bodleian First Folio: digital facsimile of the First Folio of Shakespeare's plays, Bodleian Library, Arch. G c.7, http://firstfolio.bodleian.ox.ac.uk   128

5 Map of Tudor London   137

6 Book of Common Prayer calendar, November   142

7 Internal Twelfth Night calendar   143

8 Coat of arms of Argonise and Carey   160

9 The Hunsdon Onyx, Victoria and Albert Museum, British Galleries, room 57a, case 10, lent by the Trustees of the Berkeley Will Trust (author's photograph). Governors of the Victoria and Albert Museum, London   163

Preface: impersonal Shakespeare

In his *Essays on Goethe* (1828) Thomas Carlyle concluded, 'In every man's writings the character of the writer must lie recorded ... his opinions, character, personality ... are and must be decipherable in his writings.'[1] But four lines later Carlyle confessed he found William Shakespeare stubbornly enigmatic: 'Who knows or can figure what the Man Shakespeare was, by the first, by the twentieth perusal of his works?' Eighty years later in *The Impersonal Aspect of Shakespeare's Art*, Sidney Lee dismissed any 'critical test whereby we can distinguish Shakespeare's private utterances and opinions ... Where is the critical chemistry which will disentangle, precipitate, isolate his personal views and sentiments?'[2] Robert Browning, speaking as Shakespeare, sneered, 'Which of you did I enable Once to slip into my breast There to catalogue and label What I like least, what love best?'[3] Citing a multitude of such commentators, in 1991 Samuel Schoenbaum cautioned: 'if we try to get at Shakespeare's opinions by arbitrarily tearing passages from their context, we court hopeless perplexity'. Schoenbaum dubbed those foolhardy enough to try 'personalists' who 'ignore Shakespeare's dependence on written sources, rather than private experiences, for the material of his plays'.[4]

Despite Schoenbaum's warning, the twenty-first century has seen a remarkable run of intrusive biographies which attribute Shakespeare's opacity to crypto-Catholicism, wariness of tetchy censors, or a calculated self-distancing from the intrigues that roiled Tudor-Stuart England. These range from aggressive (Richard Wilson) to artful (Stephen Greenblatt) to measured (James Shapiro) to bizarre (Clare Asquith).[5]

The present book is not an attempt at biography. It proceeds from the modest assumption that Shakespeare's plays are more personal than we have recognized, that numerous characters and events he depicts were drawn from life, and that some of these may be recoverable.

I intend to explore aspects of William Shakespeare's plays and sonnets which scholars have overlooked or misinterpreted, thereby better to understand the plays and the man. I will sift for clues to his relationships with people who mattered: family, friends, colleagues, patrons, lovers, enemies. Sieving for these traces – in effect reading Shakespeare's mind – can be risky business; it is neither pure literary criticism nor objective historiography, though it must respect the rubrics of both. Rather, my investigations rely on a fundamental tenet of criticism: no author, his milieu and his times, are entirely separable from his works. Every *oeuvre* constitutes an autobiography of the writer – and in the case of a great writer, of an age.

In riddling his texts for the personal Shakespeare, of necessity I will engage with several cruces long believed inscrutable. Early readers have cautioned that some of my inferences may be received as doubtful and some of my interpretations exceptional. Not every reader will accept my solution to Malvolio's *M.O.A.I.* conundrum in *Twelfth Night*, or agree that 'Quinapalus' is an anagram of 'Aquinas' and 'Paul'. Opinion may bridle at the suggestion that Shakespeare wrote *As You Like It* to commemorate the seventh anniversary of the death of Christopher Marlowe and created the character of Jaques in the dead man's image. Readers reluctant to entertain Emilia Bassano Lanier as the 'Dark Lady' of the sonnets may find it difficult to accept her religious heritage and flawed marriage as the inspiration for Jessica in *The Merchant of Venice*. Even those who accept Gabriel Harvey as the model for Malvolio may balk at acknowledging Thomas Nashe behind the mask of Feste (and that of Touchstone) – just as some may shrug off my explanation for the vengeance-seeking steward filing suit against Viola's loyal Captain.

I am keenly aware that each of my inferences will admit three interpretations:

1. The parallels are merely coincidental, and any relationship between Shakespeare's text and actual persons living or dead is imaginary.
2. Shakespeare had the referent on his mind and it seeped into his text via subconscious activity.

3. Shakespeare intentionally created the connection, though he knew that only a handful of auditors would recognize it.

I will vigorously maintain the latter, that is, there are numerous passages in the plays which Shakespeare intended to be opaque to the mass audience but transparent to a coterie with specialized knowledge or personal connections.

This is *not* to suggest Shakespeare wrote in some arcane code decipherable only by fellow Rosicrucians, Freemasons, or anti-Petrarchanists. I am merely suggesting that events in a writer's life can and do inspire his choice of material and shape his language, sometimes in ways that only his intimates can recognize. This is hardly a radical notion. But I intend to press its boundaries. Those who seek affirmation of my views in current (or past) scholarly editions will not find reassurance; this book does not rehearse received wisdom but attempts to peer beyond it. Readers willing to restrain the impulse to pedanticism – that hobgoblin of progressive scholarship – may find that the solutions to Shakespeare's enigmas offered here are the best we have.

I owe sincere thanks to Professor Lisa Hopkins for encouraging my research on Christopher Marlowe and *As You Like It*, and to Ms Jocelyn Medawar, who gave me new insight into the play. As well, I owe an inestimable debt to my teachers, the late Dennis Kay, John Pitcher, Bill Carroll, the late Tony Nuttall, Gordon Kipling, and particularly Barbara Everett and the late Emrys Jones for instruction and inspiration.

Steve Sohmer
Paris, 21 July 2014

Notes

1 Thomas Carlyle, *Essays on Goethe* (London: Cassell, 1905), 78.
2 Sidney Lee, *The Impersonal Aspect of Shakespeare's Art*, address before the English Association, London, 11 June 1909 (Oxford: Oxford University Press, 1909), 7.
3 Robert Browning, 'At the "Mermaid"' (1876), in *The Works of Robert Browning*, Riverside Edition, 6 vols (Boston: Houghton, Mifflin), V.333.
4 Samuel Schoenbaum, *Shakespeare's Lives* (Oxford: Clarendon Press, 1991), 360–1. Schoenbaum apparently never wrote a play.

5 Richard Wilson, *Secret Shakespeare* (Manchester: Manchester University Press, 2004); Stephen Greenblatt, *Will in the World* (New York: Norton, 2004); James Shapiro, *A Year in the Life of William Shakespeare: 1599* (New York: HarperCollins, 2005); Clare Asquith, *Shadowplay* (New York: Public Affairs, 2005).

N.B. While this book was in production, the *New York Times* for 24 October 2016 reported: "The New Oxford Shakespeare edition of the playwright's works ... lists Christopher Marlowe as Shakespeare's co-author on the three *Henry VI* plays, parts 1, 2 and 3. It's the first time that a major edition of Shakespeare's works has listed Shakespeare's colleague and rival as a co-author on these works, the volume's general editor, Gary Taylor, said in a phone interview." Professor Taylor's announcement lends conviction to my suggestion below that young Shakespeare had closer relations with Marlowe than we have imagined. In chapter 2, 'Marlowe's ghost in *As You Like It*', I suggest the men had a mentoring and perhaps intimate relationship, and that **Shakespeare wrote his pastoral comedy in 1600 as a seven years' memorial to his "dead shepherd" who died in 1593.**

PART I
Shakespeare, lovers, and friends

1
Joining the mice-eyed decipherers

In July 1929, at the height of the Jazz Age and two months shy of his twenty-third birthday, William Empson was rusticated by Magdalene College – indeed, banished from Cambridge town – having been discovered in possession of prophylactics and/or engaged in sex with a woman.[1] But randy William had already composed and would shortly publish *Seven Types of Ambiguity*, which, alongside *The Meaning of Meaning* produced by his tutor I. A. Richards and collaborator C. K. Ogden, became foundational texts of the 'New Criticism', modern literary theory, semiotics, and the practice we know as 'close reading'. Ever since, literary scholars have parsed, deconstructed, interrogated, and endlessly re-interpreted passages of prose and poetry in a relentless quest for meaning, secondary (and tertiary) meanings, allusions, topicalities, metadramatic substrate, and authorial intentions (and tenure). By this declension, many have come to regard close reading as a modern innovation. It isn't. Subjecting a text to intensive scrutiny in order to discover recondite referents, insinuations, and/or connotations is hardly a new-found pastime. Close readers were the bugbears of writers of plays, prose and poetry during William Shakespeare's working lifetime as likely they were in Chaucer's and Euripides'. There is ample evidence, including vociferous complaints by Shakespeare's colleagues, their prosecutions and jailings, that their literary productions were closely audited and read, parsed, analysed, sifted to a fare-thee-well, curiously interpreted, and frequently misconstrued.

Elizabethan readers and auditors wished to come to grips with not only what their authors wrote, but what they thought – and that included not only what they said, but what they said they didn't say but did. Shakespeare and his colleagues were confronted by an avid but dissimilarly lettered public hungry for entertainment, information, and enlightenment and fully committed not only to hearing and reading their authors' texts, but to reading their minds. Below I'll reiterate furious protests against close reading by some of Shakespeare's writer-contemporaries. But bear in mind: Elizabethan authors were shrewd enough to recognize that protesting their innocence would only amplify the public's appetite for closely reading their works. Then as now, controversy made excellent publicity.

In his lifetime, Shakespeare was wise enough to avoid such growling; he never claimed that what wasn't there wasn't there, even when it wasn't. But his fellow actors and first editors, John Heminges and Henry Condell, *demanded* that we read between his lines. In the forepages of the First Folio they encouraged '*the great Variety of Readers*' to

> Reade him, therefore; and againe, and againe: And if then you doe not like him, surely you are in some manifest danger not to understand him. And so we leave you to other of his Friends, whom if you need, can bee your guides: if you neede them not, you can leade your selves, and others. And such Readers we wish him.[2]

When Heminges and Condell published these words Shakespeare was seven years in his grave and safely beyond the innuendos – but not the ken – of those whom Thomas Nashe had challenged as 'mice-eyed decipherers'.

During his life Shakespeare had been sufficiently wise to recognize that authorial disclaimers and protests of innocence would only excite notoriety and invite closer scrutiny. In fact, we seem to have only one repudiation from his lips – and that a markedly mild one, hardly more than a brushstroke – when he muttered in the Epilogue of 2 *Henry IV*, 'Oldcastle died martyr, And this is not the man' (Epi. 31–2).

Heminges and Condell declared that *post mortem* was high time to search Shakespeare's pockets, and that is exactly what I intend to do.

Close reading in a time of censorship

Among the Elizabethan public's motives for indulging in close reading – which as today ranged from curiosity to gossip-mongering to scholarly interest to prurience – one of the most

Joining the mice-eyed decipherers 5

tantalizing was their awareness of England's rigorous censorship of unofficial discourse on politics, the royal succession, foreign relations, religion, and certain personalities. Elizabethan England was a highly censorious arena, and dangerous for writers – playwrights particularly – who openly flaunted topicality. As Annabel Patterson notes in *Censorship and Interpretation*, 'governments fear the theater more than other forms of literature because of its capacity to stir up public opinion'[3] – presumably because books and other documents tend to be read in private, and the reader's opinion is, therefore, privately formed, whereas the experience of a play is shared with hundreds or thousands of spectators whose response to ideas laid before them is immediately detectable as 'the sense of the house'.

In one instructive act of censorship, on 12 November 1589 the Privy Council ordered the Archbishop of Canterbury, the Lord Mayor of London, and the Master of the Revels to

> consider of the matters of their the playing companies' comedyes and tragedyes, and thereuppon to strike oute or reform such partes and matters as they shall fynd unfytt and undecent to be handled in playes, bothe for Divinitie and State, comaunding the said companies of players, in her Majesties name, that they forbear to present and playe publickly anie comedy or tragedy other then suche as they three shall have seene and allowed, which if they shall not observe ... they shalbe not onely sevearely punished, but made incapable of the exercise of their profession forever hereafter.[4]

Modern scholars who regard this tri-partite commission as a lacuna of beneficence are naïve. Crossing the censors' intentionally vague and purposely ill-defined touchlines could invite a book burning (Nashe, Harvey, Marlowe, et al.), imprisonment (Jonson, Hayward, et al.), mutilation (Stubbes, Page), or even silence and ruin (Lyly, Nashe, et al.). Professor Patterson characterizes these ground rules as the 'cultural code' which embodied the 'hermeneutics of censorship' in Tudor-Jacobean England.[5] But the canons were sufficiently indistinct and the punishments sufficiently draconian to inspire prudence and self-censorship in any writer.[6] Patterson contends that 'the occasional imprisonment, however arbitrary, had exemplary or ritual force'.[7] Surely it was this arbitrary, even capricious, and therefore unpredictable enforcement which, as much as the severity of punishments, tended to snaffle writers.

A particularly curious (and worrisome) instance was the burning of certain books which touched neither 'Divinitie' nor 'State', ordered and effected on 1–4 June 1599 by the Archbishop of Canterbury, John Whitgift, and the Bishop of London, Richard Bancroft. They decreed 'that all Nashe's bookes and Dr. Harvey's bookes be taken wheresoever they be found, and that none of the said bookes be ever printed hereafter'. The order banned the printing of histories without Privy Council authorization, and the printing of plays 'excepte they bee allowed by suche as have aucthorytie'.[8] It is thought Nashe and Harvey were silenced as a consequence of the vitriolic pamphlet war they had waged since Richard Harvey's opening salvo in 1590.[9]

But exactly why the pair were cited and received the ultimate punishment (silencing) has never been satisfactorily explained. Charles Nicholl believes that Nashe was cited as *fons et origo* of the flurry of satirical books (which he was not), and Harvey as co-respondent.[10] But none of the transgressions proposed – 'licentiousness', 'offence against morality', 'pornographic', 'sexual subjects', homosexuality – is wholly persuasive.[11] (See 'Why the Bishops Burned the Books' in 'Longer notes' below for a more likely explanation.)

As the recent histories of Nazism and Stalinism spectacularly demonstrated, readers and audiences belaboured by a censorious regime are keen to read into any published or performed work an array of seditious propositions and arguments, concealed identities, innuendos, and insinuations. Such audiences are alert to any nuance, wink, hesitation, interpolation, or misquotation which might convey a political point. In Shakespeare's age this was equally true – and not only among auditors of so-called 'city plays' which engaged and dispatched the affectations and affectors of contemporary London society with tooth-edged, biting satire. Under the groaning of Elizabethan censorship, any play – any character – might be a carrack laden with contraband ideas and sentiments. Any scene or sub-plot might be an allegory masquerading as comedy.

This brings us to a critical point in our discussion: Elizabethan readers and playgoers had better memories than we do, and read books and attended plays with eyes and ears more keenly tuned to recognize secondary, esoteric, metaphorical, and otherwise veiled meanings. This is not easily grasped by modern citizens of free societies accustomed to forthright, uncensored modes of expression. In today's literature, cinema, and Internet entertainment, and in our print and electronic journalism, we expect bald, unmodulated frankness. Shakespeare's contemporaries didn't.

Unlike our unbuttoned society, Elizabethans knew there were rules against the staging of the sacraments or treating with matters of state. Playwrights who transgressed the latter prohibition – for example, Jonson and Nashe with *The Isle of Dogges* in 1597 – wound up fined, jailed, or in self-imposed internal exile. Eventually, there were rules against profanity and taking the name of the Lord in vain (1606), which is perhaps why in the Folio *As You Like It* (1623) Rosalind uses the Latinate euphemism 'Jove' when calling for divine witness: '*Ioue, Ioue,* this shepherd's passion Is much upon my fashion' (2.4.56). What we must recognize is that when Rosalind invoked 'Jove' Shakespeare's auditors heard 'God'.

For Shakespeare's first audiences, wringing recondite messages out of books and playtexts wasn't merely a pastime, it was a passion. In a sense, close reading was one of many word-games (such as anagrams) popular among lettered Elizabethans. They also encountered books and plays which openly drew on contemporary life and personalities, and presented them unmasked, unmuffled, and in the raw. When this occurred, the authorities could act quickly.

On 10 May 1601 the Privy Council complained to the Justices of the Peace of Middlesex

> that certain players that use to recite their plays at the Curtain in Moorfields do represent upon the stage in their interludes the persons of gentlemen of good desert and quality that are yet alive under obscure manner, but yet in sort as all the hearers may take notice both of the matter and the persons that are meant thereby.[12]

The practice provoked a stern rebuke:

> This being a thing very unfit, offensive, and contrary to such direction as have been heretofore taken that no plays should be openly showed but such as first were perused and allowed and that might minister to occasion of offense and scandal we do hereby require you that you do forthwith forbid ... them to from henceforth to play the same, either privately or publicly, and ... to take bond of the chiefest among them to answer their rash and indiscreet behavior before us.[13]

However, Arthur Kinney notes that living 'gentlemen could be played onstage if they were played favorably' and cites as evidence a letter from Rowland Whyte to Sir Robert Sidney dated 26 October 1599:

> Two days ago, the overthrow of Turnhout was acted upon a stage, and all your names used that were at it; especially Sir Fra. Veres, and he that played that part got a beard resembling his, and a watcher Satin Doublet, with Hose trimmed with silver lace. You was [sic] also introduced, killing, slaying, and overthrowing the Spaniards, and honorable mention of your service, in seconding Sir Francis Vere, being engaged.[14]

Professor Kinney goes on to say, 'It is tempting to find contemporary originals for Sir Toby Belch or Sir Andrew Aguecheek (*Twelfth Night*), Osric (*Hamlet*) or Oswald (*Lear*), but the only evidence we now have indisputably is Shakespeare's satire of the deceased Sir John Oldcastle in *1 Henry IV*. We still do not know why [the playwright risked doing that].'[15] If we are asking ourselves such questions four hundred years after the fact, wasn't the buzz of speculation among Shakespeare's auditors during their *après-théâtre* suppers loud and sustained? If occasions were plentiful, as we may infer they were, when recognizable Elizabethans were portrayed on stage for better or worse, should that not compel us to sift carefully for Shakespeare's inspirations for his characters? His first auditors – conditioned to see living persons portrayed on stage – did.

Authors protest close reading

Shakespeare's colleagues were not always flattered by the close attention paid to their texts. That could bring troubles unsought for. Thomas Nashe complained against close readers who (so he alleged) misinterpreted his works. In *Strange Newes* (1592), Nashe grumbled: 'Now a man may not talk [write] of a dog but it is surmised that he aims at him that giveth [exhibits] the dog in his crest [probably John Talbot, Ninth Earl of Shrewsbury, d. 1611]; he cannot name straw, but he must pluck a wheat-sheaf in pieces [probably Thomas Cecil, Earl of Exeter, 1542–1623].' Nashe caps his snarl at the impertinence of his misinterpreters, 'Intelligendo faciunt ut nihil intelligant' – they pretend understanding, but understand nothing.[16]

Nashe's indignation had not cooled when he produced *Christ's Tears over Jerusalem* (1593): 'I am informed there be certain busie wits abroad that seek to anagrammatize the name of Wittenberge to one of the Universities of England ... for not so much as out of mutton and pottage but they will construe a meaning of kings and princes.'[17] Devising anagrams was a favourite word-game of lettered Elizabethans – including Queen and courtiers – both as an amusement and recognized mode of esoteric discourse. I will show that Shakespeare played at anagrams to entertain the Queen in *Twelfth Night*.

Now Nashe locks horns with his most imaginative close readers:

> Let one but name bread, they will interpret it to be the town of Bredan in the Low Countreyes; if of beere he talkes, then straight he mockes the countie Beroune in France; if of foule weather or a shower of raine, he hath relation to some that shall raign next. Infinite numbers of these fanatical strange hieroglyphics have these new decipherers framed to themselves, & stretched words on the tenterhookes so miserably that a man were as goode, considering every circumstance, write on cheverel as on paper. For my part, I would wish them not to deceive themselves with the spirite of inspiration without proofe, or confound logic by making no difference betwixt *probabile* and *manifeste verum*.[18]

Nashe's '*probabile*' = 'probable, likely' rather than '*possibile*' = 'possible, perhaps' sharply undercuts his claims of innocence; it is either a slip of the pen or a provocation.

In *Nashes Lenten Stuffe* (1599) the satirist produced what may be his most conspicuous allegory. 'Ostensibly written as a panegyric to the city of Yarmouth and its chief product [herring], the work's rambling, stream-of-consciousness style soon yields to Nashe's legendary invective and devolves into a scathing critique of papists and court culture.'[19] Nashe brazenly challenged close readers to solve the riddles of his relentlessly riddling *Stuffe*: 'O, for a Legion of mice-eyed decipherers and calculaters vppon characters, now to augurate what I mean by this: the diuell, if it stood vpon his saluation, cannot do it.'[20] By issuing this challenge – and writing '*probabile*' rather than '*possibile*' – wasn't Nashe asking (if not begging) for ever more close reading which could only enhance his reputation as a social scold?

Another contemporary critic of society, Ben Jonson (1572–1637), complained in his preface to *Volpone, or The Fox* that close reading

> and (mis)interpretation of literary texts 'is now grown a Trade with many; and there are that profess to have a Key for the decyphering

of every thing: But let Wise and Noble Persons take heed how they be too credulous, or give leave to these invading Interpreters ... who cunningly, and often, utter their own virulent Malice under other Mens simplest Meanings.'[21]

Jonson decries these misinterpreters of minutiae who are

> so solemnly ridiculous, as to search out who was meant by the gingerbreadwoman, who by the hobby-horse man, who by the costardmonger, nay, who by their wares ... what great lady by the pig-woman, what concealed statesman by the seller of mousetraps [and, thereby] challenge the author of scurrility, because the language somewhere savors of Smithfield.[22]

Though Jonson raised several strenuous denials, it was no secret that his plays gleefully savaged the foibles of contemporary Londoners. Indeed, Jonson finally admitted that many of his characters had been drawn from life; in his *Apologetical Dialogue* (1616) he confessed, 'Now for the players, it is true, I tax'd [censured] them' – referring to his *Poetaster* written, as he put it, 'on' Marston.[23]

But Jonson also defended his practice by claiming – and a curious claim it is – that he had sufficiently disguised his living models so that no 'narrow ey'd Decipherers' could say with certainty who his victims were. That is: the targets of Jonson's vitriole – the living persons behind his masks – are both *sufficiently obscured* to be unidentifiable and *sufficiently obvious* to be recognizable. This is at best paradoxical, at least sophistical. And Jonson issued a blanket challenge: 'What Nation, Society, or general Order or State I have provoked? What Publick Person? Whether I have not (in all these) preserv'd their Dignity, as mine own Person, safe?'[24] Just as in the case of Nashe, wouldn't such a disclaimer – such defiance – provoke even more close reading?

Jonson went so far as to depict the alternative to his brand of vigorous, topical satire as an unwelcome return to the days when the stage was peopled not with characters, but with personifications of Virtue, Vice, and Everyman. He castigated

> those severe and wise Patriots, who providing [weighing] the Hurts these licentious Spirits [satirists] may do in a State, desire rather to see Fools and Devils, and those antick Relicks of Barbarism retrivd, with all other ridiculous and exploded Follies, than behold the Wounds of Private Men, of Princes and Nations.[25]

Jonson has offered his readers a prickly choice: either his genre of topical, satirical plays which lampoon the faults and transgressions of thinly veiled contemporaries – or a return to the desiccated Morality.

Clearly, the protestations of Nashe and Jonson could only inflame 'mice-eyed decipherers' and 'invading Interpreters' more finely to sift their works for topicalities and personalities. And they knew it. One can hardly ask for a more conclusive proof that Elizabethan literature was stuffed with topical, personal, cheeky, impertinent (and judgemental) portraits of living persons.

How the mice-eyed empower writers

More than a few years ago when I was in my salad days and bent on 'seeing the world', a Czech friend took me to a dingy club in Prague where a mob of dirty young people had assembled to listen to a dirty young band who played a brand of music we remember as 'garage rock' or 'garage punk' but that sounded like anarchy with a beat. One of their offerings was as dreary and downbeat as a dirge. In fact, it closed with a chant which can only be likened to Mongolian 'throat singing'. When it ended there was dead, absolute silence – as if the audience could not believe what they had heard. Then the room exploded with shouts and cheers, a mix of hysterical glee and seething rage. I didn't understand Czech. Even if I had, I don't think I could have grasped what I'd witnessed. Later, my host explained that the chant which so electrified the young *Máničky* ran:

> konečně jsem dnes pane K. rozuměl psovi
> konečně jsem dnes pane K. rozuměl psovi
> konečně jsem dnes pane K. rozuměl psovi

Roughly translated, the words mean 'Finally, today I understood Mr. K's dog.' Why should this phrase repeated three times electrify a crowd of young Czechs?

Because they all knew they were living under a repressive Communist regime – which is why that band, Plastic People of the Universe, had been debarred from performing in public. Everyone in that cold basement shared the everyday experience of living in a *dictatura*. And many knew the text to which the song referred: *Investigations of a Dog* (1922) by Franz Kafka, in which a dog tries to understand by logic and 'science' the mysteries of life to which other dogs seem oblivious. Mr. K's dog concludes:

> It was this instinct that made me – and perhaps for the sake of science itself but a different science from that of today, an ultimate science that prized freedom higher than everything else. Freedom! Certainly such freedom as is possible today is a wretched business. But nevertheless freedom, nevertheless a possession.[26]

One couldn't deliver a more explicit protest against the repression of the Gierek regime. Kafka provided the 'touchstone' text – a text which, though absent, was alive in the minds of performers and auditors alike. For Shakespeare's auditors that touchstone text was often the Geneva Bible.[27]

It is difficult for scholars in a free society to grasp how a violent censorious regime raises the consciousness of citizens who read books and attend performances. Though authorities have the power to repress free expression, their efforts have a double effect: readers and auditors learn to attend more closely to what authors and performers say. They come prepared. And eager to seize on every hint, allusion, or intimation which might have a social or political connotation. Censorship creates better readers and listeners. And that empowers writers to say what everyone thinks without saying it.

That Shakespeare – like Nashe, Jonson, and every writer living or dead – drew characters from life is hardly debatable. But the intelligent search for life behind the masks of Shakespeare's characters has been perverted by the rantings of conspiracy theorists, self-styled code breakers, creationists, anti-vaccinationists, and monomaniacs determined to appropriate Shakespeare to their personal cause or prove him their co-religionist. As to whether there are skeletons in Shakespeare's plays to be unearthed by literary archaeology, there's bountiful evidence that he and his contemporary dramatists (like all writers since Genesis) modelled many of their characters on lovers, friends, and enemies. Frances Trollope (1799–1863), a writer and social critic before her time who skewered Americans' manners in 1823 and Parisians' in 1835, said of the way she constructed her characters, 'Of course, I draw from life – but I always pulp my acquaintances before serving them up. You would never recognize a pig in a sausage.'[28]

Joining the mice-eyed decipherers 13

In the following chapters I will hazard the wrath of Nashe and Jonson, and join the mice-eyed in raking for the identities of lovers, friends, enemies, and benefactors whom Shakespeare ground up, spiced up, and served up. Though long obscure to us, they may have been perfectly transparent to those readers and auditors whom Gabriel Harvey dubbed 'the wiser sort' – *cognoscenti* with a knack for picking the pig from the sausage. And I will begin with Shakespeare's most elaborate and dramatic portrait, drawn of a man he may have admired as colleague, friend, and mentor.

Notes

1 John Haffenden, *William Empson*, 2 vols (Oxford: Oxford University Press, 2005), I.242–7. Given that the offences alleged were of a sexual nature, and therefore a violation of University regulations, Empson 'could no longer reside within the town bounds' (243).
2 John Heminges and Henry Condell, eds, *Shakespeare: The First Folio* (London: Jaggard, 1623), A3r.
3 Annabel Patterson, *Censorship and Interpretation* (Madison: University of Wisconsin Press, 1984), 14.
4 Quoted in E. K. Chambers, *The Elizabethan Stage*, 4 vols (Oxford: Clarendon Press, 1923), IV.306–7.
5 Patterson, *Censorship*, 52 ff.
6 An egregious and instructive contemporary occasion of censorship is the law against 'gay propaganda' passed by the Russian *Duma* on 11 June 2013; while it provides for lengthy prison sentences and hefty fines, nowhere does it specify what constitutes illegal propaganda.
7 Patterson, *Censorship*, 13.
8 Edward Arber, *A Transcript of the Registers of the Company of Stationers of London*, 5 vols (London and Birmingham, 1875–94), III.677–8.
9 In his *Theological Discourse of the Lamb of God* (London, 1590), Richard Harvey had attacked Nashe by name.
10 Charles Nicholl, *A Cup of News: The Life of Thomas Nashe* (London: Routledge & Kegan Paul, 1984). The eight other books burned were John Marston, *The Metamorphosis of Pigmalions Image* and *Certaine Satyres* and *The scourge of vilanie* (both London, 1598); Edward Guilpin, *Skialetheia* (London, 1598); Thomas Middleton, *Microcynicon* (London, 1598); John Davies, *Epigrames and Elegies* (London, n.d. [*ca.* 1599]), which included several of Marlowe's translations of Ovid's *Amores*; Ercole and Torquato Tasso, *Of Marriage and Wyvinge* (London, 1599) and *The xv ioyes of marriage* (London,

n.d. [*ca.* 1598]); and Joseph Hall, *Virgidemiarum*, 2 vols (London, 1597–98). Scholars still debate why *Caltha Poetarum* (London, 1599) by 'Thomas Cutwode' (Tailboys Dymock, fl. 1584–1602) received a reprieve.

11 Charles Ripley Gillett, *Burned Books: Neglected Chapters in English History and Literature*, 2 vols (New York: Columbia University Press, 1932), I.90; Lynda Boose, 'The 1599 Bishops' Ban and Renaissance Pornography', in Richard Burt and John Michael Archer, eds, *Enclosure Acts: Sexuality, Property, and Culture in Early Modern England* (Ithaca, NY: Cornell University Press, 1994), 191–9; Bruce Smith, *Homosexual Desire in Shakespeare's England* (Chicago: University of Chicago Press, 1991, 2nd edition 1994), 165.
12 Glynne Wickham, Herbert Berry, and William Ingram, eds, *Theatre in Europe: A Documentary History* (Cambridge: Cambridge University Press, 2000), 414.
13 *Ibid.*
14 Arthur F. Kinney, *Shakespeare by Stages: An Historical Introduction* (Oxford: Blackwell Publishers, 2003), 149.
15 *Ibid.*
16 Ronald B. McKerrow, ed., *The Workes of Thomas Nashe*, 5 vols (London: Sidgwick & Jackson, 1904–10, repr. Oxford: Basil Blackwell, 1958), I.261.
17 Alexander Bulloch Grosart, ed., *The Complete Works of Thomas Nashe*, 6 vols (London: privately printed, 1883–84), IV.5.
18 *Ibid.*
19 Henry S. Turner, 'Nashe's Red Herring: Epistemologies of the Commodity in *Nashes Lenten Stuffe* (1599)', *English Literary History* 68.3 (2001), 529–61.
20 Grosart, *Nashe*, III.218.
21 Ben Jonson, The *Works of Ben Jonson* (London: Hodgkin, 1692); Ben Jonson, *Epistle to the two universities, Volpone; or, The Fox* (London, 1605), 154.
22 Ben Jonson, *Bartholomew Fair* (London, 1605), 'The Induction', 374.
23 Jonson, *Apologetical Dialogue* (London, 1616), 128.
24 Jonson, *Epistle*, 153–4
25 *Ibid.*
26 Franz Kafka, *The Complete Stories* (New York: Schocken E-Books, 1971), 345.
27 Citations throughout are from *The Geneva Bible* (London, 1599).
28 *ca.* 1848. Sabine Baring-Gould, *Early Reminiscences 1834–1864* (New York: Dutton, 1922), 128.

2

Marlowe's ghost in *As You Like It*

In 1767 Edward Capell recognized Phebe's breathless exclamation in *As You Like It* 3.5,

> Dead Shepheard, now I find thy saw of might,
> 'Who ever lov'd, that lov'd not at first sight?' (82–3)[1]

as a nod from William Shakespeare to Christopher Marlowe and his *Hero and Leander* (2.176).[2] In 1925 Leslie Hotson's discovery of documents related to Marlowe's violent death revived interest in the poet's presence in the play.[3] In May of the same year Oliver W. F. Lodge identified Touchstone's 'it strikes a man more dead than a great reckoning in a little roome' (3.3.12–13) as a glance at the Coroner's Jury's verdict on Marlowe's homicide and an echo of his 'Infinite riches in a little room' (*The Jew of Malta* 1.1.37).[4] Six weeks later Paul Reyher connected Touchstone's remark 'When a man's verses cannot be understood …' (3.3.10–12) to the suppression of Marlowe's translation of Ovid's *Amores*.[5] Ever since the 1926 Cambridge edition of Quiller-Couch and Dover Wilson declared that Lodge's suggestion 'carries conviction' commentators have variously embraced or disputed these inferences.[6] And there the record of Marlowe sightings in *As You Like It* has rested until now.[7]

In this chapter I suggest that Christopher Marlowe is not merely an occasional visitor to Shakespeare's anti-pastoral comedy; rather, that in the interval 1599–1600 Shakespeare wrote *As You Like It* as an emphatic (if discreet) memorial for Marlowe; that Shakespeare created the character of Jaques in the image of Marlowe; and that Shakespeare himself may have taken the part of Jaques in performance. I will suggest that the playwright did so in observance of the seventh anniversary of Marlowe's death in 1593 because the 'seven years' mind' for a decedent was regarded as a significant occasion. Towards this end I will show that the text of *As You Like It* contains more appearances of the word 'seven' and its variants than any other Shakespeare play.[8] I will also offer evidence that Elizabethans regarded seven as a 'perfect' and holy number, and a cycle of seven years as particularly auspicious. Furthermore, I will propose that in the character of Touchstone Shakespeare sketched a thumbnail of his and Marlowe's sometime collaborator Thomas Nashe (d. 1599–1600). Finally, I will suggest that Shakespeare provides the date of his own arrival at London and his first encounter with the 'University Wits' who dominated the Elizabethan theatrical scene. I will also offer some admittedly speculative inferences regarding Shakespeare's motives.

I recognize that the above may strike the reader as a series of extraordinary conjectures; there is no proof that Shakespeare had even met Marlowe. My reading of the play entails that Shakespeare not only knew Marlowe and recognized his many qualities, faults, and vanities, but valued him as an inspiration and, perhaps, a mentor. If my inferences are correct they will dramatically alter our approach to *As You Like It* and show it to be a more personal play than we have realized.

I ask only that judgement wait until I have stated my case.[9]

Why 1600?

Christopher Marlowe was killed on 30 May 1593. Scholars date the composition of *As You Like It* between 30 June 1599 and 4 August 1600.[10] The date *a quo* is thought to be set by an exchange between the Clown, Touchstone, and Celia in 1.2:

> *Clo.* The more pittie, that fooles may not speak wisely, what wise men do foolishly.
> *Cel.* By my troth thou saiest true: For, since the littlewit that fooles haue was silenced, the little foolerie that wise men have makes a great shew ... (85–9)

Commentators receive this as a reference to the banning on 1 June 1599 and subsequent burning of satirical books ordered by Bishops Whitgift and Bancroft.[11] Among other items, the flames consumed works by Nashe and Gabriel Harvey, and Marlowe's translations from Ovid's *Amores*.

Marlowe's ghost in As You Like It

The date *ad quem* is fixed by an entry in the Stationers' Register on 4 August 1600 which describes *As You Like It* as 'to be stayed', that is, the manuscript was to be withheld from printing until further notice. Therefore, the play could have been on stage in May 1600, the seventh anniversary of Marlowe's death.[12] But why would the seventh anniversary of one's death be particularly significant – significant enough to move Shakespeare to create a tribute to Marlowe? And given Protestants' rejection of the existence of Purgatory in favour of a judgement to heaven or hell at the moment of death, why commemorate the anniversaries of the dead at all?

On the anniversaries of the dead

Jacobus de Voragine's *The Golden Legend*, written *circa* 1275 and first printed in Genoa *circa* 1470, became one of the most popular, widely read and most often reprinted early books; during the *incunabula* period it appeared in more editions than the Bible. William Caxton printed the first Englished *Legend* in 1483, and it had run through more than a dozen editions before William Shakespeare was born.

In his chapter on the 'The Commemoration of All Souls' de Voragine records that

> the church is accustomed to observe three manner days, that is the seventh day, the thirtieth day, and the anniversary ... The trental is kept, which is in three dizains [units of ten], that they [the deceased] may be purged of all such things as they have sinned in the Trinity and breaking of the ten commandments. The anniversary is observed, that they come from the years of calamity and maleurty [unhappiness] unto the years of perdurability. *And like as we solemnise every year the feast of a saint to their honour and our profit, right so we observe the anniversary of them that be dead unto their profit and our devotion* [my emphasis].[13]

Pre-Reformation English referred to prayers on the seventh day as a 'week's mind', and those on the thirtieth as a 'month's mind', and those repeated on the anniversary of a death were the 'year's mind'. These obsequies were often bought and paid for by the decedent; one student of wills and legacies left by Englishmen of means in the later Middle Ages discovered that 'merchants preferred a one-, three- or seven-year endowment for anniversary masses, and endowments for more than ten years were unusual'.[14] Clive Burgess, who pored over the wills of late medieval Bristol, discovered a 'plethora of intercessory services commissioned to benefit souls in Purgatory'; some decedents had requested seven years of anniversaries (obits) beginning one year following their death; others, perhaps more mindful of their sins, subscribed for obits in perpetuity.[15] The Reformation swept away this practice.

Elizabethan Protestants – for whom Purgatory had ceased to exist – no longer believed that *post mortem* prayers would profit the dead whose souls had immediately gone to heaven or hell.[16] Marking the anniversary of a loved one's death, perhaps first commended to early Christians by Tertullian (AD 211), remained then as now a rite of respect for the deceased and a salutary exercise for the living. This tradition of annual commemorations, commonplace in early Tudor England, may have lost its standing in the liturgy but remained bright in living memory in Shakespeare's time. But why was the *seventh* anniversary of a death considered particularly significant?

The perfection and power of seven

No number – not three nor thirteen – has been so laden with mystical significance in so many cultures and religions over so many centuries as seven. Annemarie Schimmel argues that seven has

> fascinated humankind since time immemorial ... The 7 ages of man, cited by Shakespeare, were known in antiquity, and in a pseudo-Hippocratic book 7 is called the number of cosmic structure ... Solon used the [seven] stellar spheres to divide human life into 7 periods of 10 steps each ... Such ideas were widespread all over the western world, and in the seventeenth century Sir Thomas Browne wrote that *every seventh year brings some change in life*. [my emphasis].[17]

Thomas Browne (1605–82) described his book *Pseudodoxia Epidemica or Enquiries into very many received tenets and commonly presumed truths* (*The Epidemic of False Beliefs*, sometimes called '*Vulgar Errors*') as an effort to correct erroneous 'Received Tennents, And commonly presumed Truths'. In more than 100 chapters and scores of subheads he ruthlessly debunks old wives' tales from the belief that mandrakes howl when cut to the belief that elephants have no joints, that 'a Badger hath the Legs of one

Marlowe's ghost in As You Like It

side shorter than the other', and that 'Jews stinke'. *Pseudodoxia* was a popular book that ran through six editions between 1646 and 1672; it provides a veritable gazetteer of the superstitions and delusions common among Elizabethan and Jacobean men and women of all classes, which ranged from the blatantly racist to the utterly disarming (the rose of Jericho, supposed to flower annually on the day of Christ's nativity, is revealed as a well-intentioned though mischievious monkish canard).

Thumbing through Browne also reveals how deeply the mystical allure of seven was woven into the psyche of Shakespeare's contemporaries. Browne's enumeration of seven's primacy and powers runs to several pages – from the seven days of Creation to the seven descendants of Cain to the Pleiades and man's precarious sixty-third ($7 \times 9 = 63$) year – the 'great Climacterical and dangerous year' – to which Browne devotes an entire chapter (chapter XII). Browne endorses the custom by which 'the daies of men are usually cast up by Septenaries [groups of seven years], *and every seventh year conceived to carry some altering character with it*, either in the temper of the body, mind, or both' (177, my emphasis). So it well might take seven years for the soul to be thoroughly quit of the body.

The principal source of Elizabethans' superstitions about the dominion of seven was the Old Testament, which – excepting the racy bits of the Song of Solomon – they read through once each year. Dr Schimmel epitomized some of the Old Testament appearances of the magic number which Elizabethans encountered annually, beginning with the six days of Creation and Sabbath. Then, in the

> seventh generation after Adam there appears Lamech, who lives for 777 years and should be avenged seventy-sevenfold (Gen. 4:24). The 7 steps leading to Solomon's Temple correspond to the 7 stories of the Babylonian temples. Noah's dove stays away for 7 days, and the flood prepares its arrival for 7 days; the Euphrates is divided into 7 brooks. During the sacrificial expiation in ancient Israel, blood was sprinkled 7 times, and a 7-day sacrifice was celebrated when Solomon's temple was inaugurated. (*Incidentally, the idea that the soul needs 7 units of time to free itself from the dead body can also be found in other parts of the world ...*) [my emphasis].[18]

This may account for the ritual observation of the 'seven years' mind' as obsequies for the dead. The New Testament is dotted with sevens: Christ on his cross utters seven last words; the Book of

Revelation, a potpourri of numerology, includes a lamb with seven horns, Christ holding seven stars in his hand, the notorious Seven Seals, letters to seven churches, and the seven trumpets that will sound on Judgement Day.

One assessment of the perfection and holiness of seven – exactly contemporaneous with Shakespeare's writing of *Julius Caesar* – can be found in *A New Treatise of the Right Reckoning of Yeares, and Ages of the World, and mens lives* (1599) by Robert Pont (1524–1606).[19] In his preface Pont explains, 'there is a marvelous sympathie of periodes of times, in reckoning by sevens, & by Sabbatical yeares, and of the manifold mysteries of the number of seaven' (ii). He begins his treatise:

> In the beginning (as the Spirite of God recordeth by Moyses) after that the Lord in sixe dayes, had created the Heaven & Earth, with all the furniture thereof, Hee rested upon the seventh day; Therefore hee blessed it, and hallowed it. This is also repeated in the fourth Commandment, for the perpetuall observation of that day; and because the number of seaven, by that reason is a sacred number, and most meete for al kinde of reckoning. *It was ordained also in the lawe, that amongst the people of God, everie seventh yeare should be holden [held] holy* ... (7–8, my emphasis)

Clearly, Pont was not just speaking for himself, but for the beliefs of a multitude of his contemporaries.

While we may never be entirely certain of any writer's motives, the time-honoured practice of remembering the anniversaries of a friend's death – coupled with the imputed power of seven – may have led Shakespeare to create his elaborate encomium for Christopher Marlowe in 1600, for Raleigh to have responded to Marlowe's 'Passionate Shepherd' in the same year, and for Heminges and Condell to publish the First Folio in 1623 to commemorate the seventh anniversary of Shakespeare's death.

Whatever Shakespeare's motive, his play is brim-full of sevens.

The recurrence of 'seven' in *As You Like It*

The rather common word 'seven' and its variants 'seventh', 'seventeen', and 'sennights' appear more often (thirteen times) in *As You Like It* than in any other Shakespeare play. More than one of the memorable speeches exploits the number seven. Of Jaques' 'Seven

Ages of Man' Marjorie Garber writes, 'The choice of seven for the ages of man was a popular one in Shakespeare's time, although some experts contended that there were three, or four, or six. But seven was the number of the planets, and the virtues and vices, and the liberal arts, and so on.'[20] Garber also cites the echo of Jaques' 'Seven Ages' in the final scene of the play: 'Jaques' portentous seven ages of man speech has its amusing and subversive pendant in Touchstone's account of the seven degrees of the lie.'[21] Harold C. Goddard notes without comment that in 4.1 Jaques enumerates 'seven different types of melancholy'.[22]

Among explicit appearances of 'seven', Rosalind declares in 3.2, 'I was seuen of the nine daies out of wonder, before you came: for looke here what I found on a Palme tree' (170–2). Again in 3.2, Rosalind employs 'seven' twice when she speaks of Time that 'trots hard with a young maid, between the contract of her marriage, and the day it is solemnized: if the interim be but a sennight, Time's pace is so hard, that it seems the length of seuen year' (304–7). Variants of 'seven' appear twice in Old Adam's speech in 2.3:

> From seauentie [sic] yeeres, till now almost fourescore
> Here liued I, but now liue here no more
> At seauenteene yeeres, many their fortunes seeke
> But at fourescore, it is too late a weeke ... (71–4)

There are many other manifestations of 'seven' only glanced at by commentators (or wholly overlooked) which I will enumerate as I illustrate allusions in Shakespeare's text to Christopher Marlowe.

The 'Dead Shepheard' of *As You Like It*

There can be no argument that *As You Like It* contains at least one explicit nod to Marlowe, Phebe's declaration to the 'Dead Shepheard' and her quote from his recently published *Hero and Leander* (1598).[23] This raises a curious question: why address Marlowe as 'Dead Shepheard'?

The scholarly consensus seems to hold that Phebe's epithet is a wink at what may have been Marlowe's best-known (though unpublished in his lifetime) poem 'The Passionate Shepherd to his Love' (*ca.* 1592, published 1599).[24] Its popularity is validated by Raleigh's mocking response, 'The Nymph's Reply to the Shepherd', published in 1600. But Phebe raises more questions than she answers. Would an Elizabethan audience casually have accepted a rural shepherdess quoting Marlowe? Imagine an Okie girl in the 1930s – Rose of Sharon Joad in John Steinbeck's *The Grapes of Wrath* – suddenly spouting a couplet by Yeats; wouldn't that blink readers' eyes and whet the nibs of critics? Literacy was uncommon among Elizabethan women generally and rural women in particular. Wouldn't an Elizabethan audience be surprised by a shepherdess who can read and write? And how could Phebe come by a quarto of *Hero and Leander*? However, if Phebe is speaking for the playwright, 'Dead Shepheard' assumes a deeper coloration.[25]

Some scholars have suggested that Marlowe had a hand in Shakespeare's earliest history plays, the *Henry VI* trilogy.[26] Robert A. Logan believes that Shakespeare composed *Titus Andronicus* and *Richard III* 'close to the time Marlowe wrote *The Massacre at Paris*, a period during which he and Marlowe were known to be working side by side in London (1590–93)'.[27] If these inferences are valid Marlowe may have supplied the role of inspiration, mentor, and/or collaborator early in Shakespeare's literary career. Both men arrived in London during the same period and their backgrounds were uncannily similar. Marlowe and Shakespeare were born within weeks of each other in Canterbury and Stratford-upon-Avon, comparable towns some distance from London. Both men had fathers named John, and both fathers were leather-workers: John Marlowe a shoemaker, John Shakespeare a whittawer. The great divergence in their lives came with Marlowe's higher education at Cambridge (MA 1587) and the explosive success of his *Tamburlaine, Part One* that same year.

When Shakespeare arrived in London (I will suggest that in 5.1 he gives the date as 1589) an early acquaintance may have been Thomas Nashe. Gary Taylor argues that Nashe was the author of Act 1 of *1 Henry VI*.[28] Did Marlowe also have a hand in this and other texts? The excessive violence of *Titus Andronicus* certainly owes something to Thomas Kyd's *Spanish Tragedy* (*ca.* 1582) or other contemporary works in the genre such as George Peele's *The Battle of Alcazar* (*ca.* 1588); indeed, Peele is suggested as co-author of Shakespeare's Roman bloodfest.[29] But Titus' extravagant language at his entrance in 1.1, 'Hail, Rome, victorious in thy mourning weeds …' (86–112), surely resonates with *Tamburlaine*'s 'high astounding terms'.

By 1589 Marlowe was a celebrated playwright with *Tamburlaine 1* and *2* under his belt; he may have been writing *The Jew of Malta* or *The Massacre at Paris* when Shakespeare arrived in London.[30]

Why might Marlowe have taken an interest in young Shakespeare? Any answer must be wholly speculative. But we can be confident that the men came from similar backgrounds, that Shakespeare was ambitious to become an actor and playwright, and that he was 'a prettie wit', and perhaps bisexual (Sonnets 18 ff.).[31] Anne Righter speculates that Shakespeare's honorific for Marlowe as a 'Dead Shepheard' was a 'purely private rite of memory'.[32] I take it as one poet's expression of gratitude to another.[33]

Encountering a passionate shepherd

A previously unrecognized indicator that Marlowe's ghost haunts the text of *As You Like It* appears in one of Shakespeare's gambols – perhaps the best of all his in-jokes. As Rosalind, Celia, and Touchstone enter the forest, whom do they encounter? Silvius, who with his very first line reveals himself as a passionate shepherd: 'O Corin, that thou knew'st how I do loue her' (2.4.20). In case we missed his joke, seventeen lines later Shakespeare's Corin gives us a nudge: 'if thou has not broke from companie, Abruptly as my *passion* now makes me, Thou hast not lou'd' (37–9, my emphasis). For those who have still missed the passionate shepherd connection Shakespeare crosses the T with Rosalind's rhyming couplet:

> Ioue, Ioue, this Shepherds *passion**
> Is much vpon my fashion.
>   (56–7, *my emphasis)

By introducing the passionate shepherd Silvius – and by the repetition of 'passion' – Shakespeare is preparing us to encounter Marlowe among the oaks and brambles of the Forest of Arden. This brings us to another key question.

Was Marlowe the model for Jaques?

Though he renders an insightful appreciation of *As You Like It*, for James Shapiro the character of Jaques[34] remains 'something of an enigma. He has a significant presence in the play (speaking almost a tenth of its lines), but no effect on it. He changes nothing, fails to persuade or reform anyone.'[35] One could say as much for Sir Oliver Mar-text and Audrey's would-be suitor, William (I will suggest that all three roles constitute a miniature *roman à clef*). Shapiro's Jaques is 'melancholy, brooding, and sentimental, and some have seen in him a rough sketch for Hamlet; others find him little more than a self-deluding, jaundiced, one-time libertine.'[36] Jaques will shrug off his enigmatic wrapper as we assess more than a dozen qualities that the Libertine of Arden has in common with Christopher Marlowe.

1. Jaques a poet

As 1 Lord describes Jaques mooning over the pageant of a wounded deer, Duke Senior asks: 'But what said Iaques? Did he not moralize this spectacle?' To which 1 Lord replies: 'O yes, into a thousand similes' (2.1.43–5). Moralizing in similes is what poets do, and Marlowe was a past master.[37] In 2.5 Jaques displays his poetical bent by reciting a verse he has authored as a stanzo for Amiens' first song:

> If it do come to passe,
> that any man turne Asse:
> Leauing his wealth and ease,
> A stubborne will to please,
> Ducdame, ducdame, ducdame:
> Heere shall he see, grosse fooles as he,
> And if he will come to me. (45–50)

With this doggerel Shakespeare presents Jaques as unmistakably a poet, and one with an attitude. The first thing we learn about Jaques is that he is a poet as Marlowe was.

2. Jaques thinks like a playwright

The 'Seven Ages of Man' speech smacks of the ruminations of a playwright. It begins:

> All the world's a stage,
> And all the men and women, meerely Players;
> They haue their Exits and their Entrances,
> And one man in his time playes many parts,
> His Acts being seuen ages. (2.7.140–4)

Here we have 'stage', 'Players', '*Exits*', 'Entrances', 'playes', 'parts', and 'Acts' in a single breath, a cascade of the language of the theatre. Jaques continues,

> At first the Infant,
> Mewling, and puking in the Nurses armes:
> Then, the whining Schoole-boy with his Satchell

> And shining morning face, creeping like snaile
> Vnwillingly to schoole. And then the Louer,
> Sighing like Furnace, with a wofull ballad
> Made to his Mistresse eye-brow. Then, a Soldier,
> Full of strange oaths, and bearded like the Pard,
> Ielous in honor, sodaine, and quicke in quarrell,
> Seeking the bubble Reputation
> Euen in the Canons mouth: And then, the Iustice
> In faire round belly, with good Capon lin'd,
> With eyes seuere, and beard of formall cut,
> Full of wise sawes, and moderne instances,
> And so he playes his part. The sixt age shifts
> Into the leane and slipper'd Pantaloone,
> With spectacles on nose, and pouch on side,
> His youthfull hose well sau'd, a world too wide,
> For his shrunke shanke, and his bigge manly voice,
> Turning againe toward childish trebble pipes,
> And whistles in his sound. Last Scene of all,
> That ends this strange euentfull historie,
> Is second childishnesse, and meere obliuion,
> Sans teeth, sans eyes, sans taste, sans euery thing. (144–67)

What playwrights write is dialogue. And each of Jaques' ages is characterized by a speaking voice: the infant 'Mewling', the schoolboy 'whining', the lover 'Sighing … a … ballad', the soldier 'Full of strange oaths', the justice 'Full of wise sawes, and moderne instances', the pantaloon's 'bigge manly voice, Turning againe toward childish trebble', and the last act mere babble. This is the diction of a playwright analysing the particular requirements for writing dialogue for each of these characters.

3. Jaques a social scold

1 Lord says of Jaques,

> Thus most inuectiuely he pierceth through
> The body of Countrie, Citie, Court,
> Yea, and of this our life, swearing that we
> Are meere vsurpers, tyrants … (2.1.58–61)

Social criticism is what playwrights do. Jaques tells us this is a role he relishes. Then he announces his ambition to become a fool. What is a fool? An amalgam of social critic and entertainer.

> The Wise-mans folly is anathomiz'd
> Euen by the squandring glances of the foole.
> Inuest me in my motley: Giue me leaue
> To speake my minde, and I will through and through
> Cleanse the foule bodie of th'infected world,
> If they will patiently receiue my medicine. (2.7.56–61)

In Jaques' succeeding speech, 'Why who cries out on pride …' (70–87), he proclaims that the follies he'll castigate are so common among society that he'll easily escape censure, an important consideration for any Elizabethan playwright wishing to keep his career and fingers intact. This speech also contains Shakespeare's wink at a line from his *2 Henry VI* which Marlowe cribbed in *Edward II*. Jaques declares: 'What woman in the Citie do I name, When that I say the City woman beares The cost of Princes on vnworthy shoulders?' (2.7.74–6). Shakespeare's Margaret had mocked the ambitious Eleanor, saying, 'She beares a Dukes Reuenewes on her backe' (1.3.78), before Marlowe's Mortimer sneered at the baseborn Gaveston, 'He weares a lords reuenewe on his back' (1.4.406).

4. Jaques a traveller

Marlowe's travels were controversial if not notorious. The fellows of Cambridge were inclined to deny his MA because they suspected Marlowe's intention to convert to Roman Catholicism and join the English recusant college at Rheims. It took a rare intervention by the Privy Council on 29 June 1587 to secure Marlowe's degree in respect of his prior 'faithful dealing' and 'good service' to the Queen.[38] It may well be that Marlowe had travelled to the Continent as a spy for Walsingham's secret service.[39]

Shakespeare drops two tantalizing hints that Jaques may have travelled abroad. The first appears in 2.5 when Jaques demands more song of Amiens: 'Come, more, another stanzo: Cal you 'em stanzo's?' (15). One is struck by the appearance of 'the fashionable Italian name for a verse, first recorded by the *Oxford English Dictionary* (*OED*) in Greene's *Menaphon* (1589), and first used by Shakespeare in *LLL*'[40] Here Shakespeare uses the word twice for emphasis. Later, Rosalind calls after him:

> Farewell Mounsieur Trauellor: looke you lispe, and weare strange suites; disable all the benefits of your owne Countrie: be out of loue with your natiuitie, and almost chide God for making you that

countenance you are; or I will scarce thinke you haue swam in a Gundello. (4.1.30–4)

Her 'Gundello' reference (modern: gondola) winks at Italy; it appears unlikely that Marlowe had travelled that far, though Robert Greene certainly did.[41] In an effort to blend in while abroad, Marlowe-the-spy may have adopted local fashions and patterns of speech. To insinuate himself among recusants abroad wouldn't a spy be wise to repudiate his country and 'chide God' for having been raised a Protestant in the shadow of Canterbury Cathedral? On his return from Europe, Marlowe – ever the faddist and dandy (*viz.* his putative portrait in Corpus Christi College, Cambridge) – may have affected his speech and attire, or lampooned Englishmen who did.

It is also noteworthy that Rosalind's description of an Italianate Elizabethan traveller is an unmistakable echo of Nashe's portrait of Gabriel Harvey during his encounter with the Queen at Audley End in *Have with you to Saffron-Walden*: 'the Italian that wore crowns on his shoes, and quite renounced his natural English accents & gestures, & wrested himself wholly to the Italian punctilios, speaking our homely island tongue strangely, as if he were but a raw practitioner in it, & but ten days before had entertained a schoolmaster to teach him to pronounce it.'[42] Below I will suggest that Nashe, in the person of Touchstone, is another lurking presence in Shakespeare's greenwood.

5. Jaques an atheist

One of the most baffling passages in *As You Like It* appears in the verse Jaques claims to have 'made yesterday in despite of my invention':

Ducdame, ducdame, ducdame:
Heere shall he see, grosse fooles as he,
And if he will come to me. (2.5.40–1)

Hearing this, Amiens says, 'What's that *ducdame*?' and Jaques replies, ''Tis a Greeke inuocation, to call fools into a circle' (48–52).

The elusive meaning of '*ducdame*' has been endlessly debated. In his edition of 1765 Dr Johnson thought that Sir Thomas Hanmer 'very acutely and judiciously read *duc ad me*. That is, bring him to me.'[43] The *Variorum* follows this remark with two pages of risible if well-intentioned guesses.[44] In fact, Hanmer and Johnson came close to the truth. The correct solution can be found in Jaques' explanation that his (obvious) nonsense word is a 'Greek inuocation, to call fools into a circle'. This may be a wink at the the *Collecta* or *Oratio ad collectam*, a form of invocation for gathering the faithful which dates from at least the era of Leo the Great (AD 440–61); it summoned believers to join the procession into the church to celebrate the Eucharist. The rite is commonly known in both Catholic and Anglican liturgies as a 'Collect', spelled as the common word for 'gather' but pronounced *käl' likt* or *käl' lekt*.[45]

Marlowe was formally schooled in Anglican ritual. He went up to Cambridge in 1581 on a scholarship established by Archbishop Matthew Parker for students preparing to enter holy orders.[46] After completing his education, instead of taking the cloth Marlowe became infamous as an atheist. Jaques, whom Shakespeare endowed with Marlowe's erudition and attitudes, has fashioned *'ducdame'* by anagrammatizing the Latin *'duc ad me'* into a nonsense word he characterizes as a 'Greeke inuocation' to gather the foolish together. In fact, his *'ducdame'* parodies the Collect which conveys the priest's welcome to congregants as they arrive, and sets the theme for the day's religious service.[47] But why does Jaques claim his Latinate anagram as *Greek*?

Because Elizabethans believed the anagram was a Greek invention, the brainchild of the poet-librarian Lycophron (third century BC) and his circle. In his *Arte of English Poesie*, George Puttenham cites Lycophron's as the earliest examples of the form.[48] When Jaques says 'Greek', Shakespeare is saying 'anagram'.

Jaques's assertion that his 'Greek' Collect draws 'fools into a circle' is an atheist's scathing mock of the rite of Communion and its believers. In *Twelfth Night,* Sebastian will spurn the agrammatizing Feste as a 'foolish Greek' (4.1.16; see the discussion below).

Moments later Jaques delivers another odd pronouncement: 'Ile go sleepe if I can: if I cannot, Ile raile against all the first borne of Egypt' (2.5.53–4). Delusional or over-imaginative Oxfordians take this as a reference to the Seventeenth Earl's bouts of insomnia. Rather, it is Jaques' glance at the original railer against the children of Egypt, Moses: 'And all the first borne in the lande of Egypt shall die, from the first borne of Pharaoh that sitteth on his throne, vnto the first borne of the maide seruant that is at the mille, and all the first borne of beastes' (Exodus 11:5). Jaques is declaring that he intends to carry on 'invectively' against usurpers, that is, against the rich and privileged of society – particularly the hereditary aristocracy whose wealth and power derived from being first-born into an Elizabethan society which observed the law of primogeniture – precisely the law which frustrates Orlando, and which Shakespeare's *cognomen* for the exiled Duke Senior emphasizes.

6. *Jaques a beast*

Scene 2.7 opens with Jaques nowhere to be found and Duke Senior speculating, 'I thinke he be transform'd into a beast, For I can no where finde him, like a man' (1–2). This is another of Shakespeare's in-jokes. Marlowe's nickname was 'Kit', which *OED* cites both as an abbreviation for 'Christopher' and as slang for a beast – 'a cat or any small, furry animal (particularly the young of a fox)'. Shakespeare's logic runs: Kit:= Christopher; kit:= beast ∴ Christopher ↔ beast.

7. *Jaques a reprobate*

When Jaques appears in 2.7 he reports the discovery of a fool in the forest, Touchstone. This sends him into a paroxysm of railing which begins:

> I must haue liberty
> Withall, as large a Charter as the winde,
> To blow on whom I please, for so fooles haue:
> And they that are most gauled with my folly,
> They most must laugh: (47–51)

Jacques proclaims his ambition to be a social scold, as Nashe was, and predicts that his auditors will find his Jeremiads hilarious even as they recognize themselves as the butt of his humour. But Jaques' demand elicits a stern rebuke from Duke Senior, one which reveals a personal backstory that we could not have guessed:

> Most mischeeuous foule sin, in chiding sin:
> For thou thy selfe hast bene a Libertine,
> As sensuall as the brutish sting it selfe,
> And all th'imbossed sores, and headed euils,
> That thou with license of free foot hast caught,
> Would'st thou disgorge into the generall world. (64–9)

Curiously, the Duke's denunciation has no precedent in the play. We've received no prior hint that Jaques has led a disreputable life – but Marlowe did. He was frequently in trouble with the law, having been

> arrested on 18 September 1589 for his part in the killing of William Bradley by his friend Thomas Watson, and on 26 January 1592 for coining in Flushing in the Netherlands; on 9 May 1592 he was bound over in the sum of £20 to keep the peace towards Allen Nicholls, Constable of Holywell Street, Shoreditch, and Nicholas Helliott, beadle, and to appear at the General Sessions in October; and on 15 September 1592 he was arrested for fighting in the streets of Canterbury with a tailor named William Corkine.[49]

Marlowe was also under caution from the Privy Council at the time of his death.

The Duke's censure can be read as an indictment of Marlow's profligate and (by Elizabethan standards) perverse lifestyle. In point of fact, shortly before Shakespeare began writing *As You Like It*, Marlowe's memory had been desecrated in two publications, one in 1597 by Thomas Beard, a puritan divine, and the other a year later by Frances Meres, both citing the poet's 'Epicurisme and Atheism'.[50] Perhaps this is why Shakespeare was so discreet in framing his tribute to Marlowe (sufficiently discreet that no scholar has detected it in four hundred years). Though the dead man's plays continued to hold the stage throughout Shakespeare's career, Marlowe-the-man had become an object of controversy, scorn, and derision.

8. Duke Senior breaks the fourth wall

Scene 2.7 includes both Jaques' 'Seven Ages of Man' speech and a response, Amiens' song 'Blow, blow, thou winter winde'. But first Duke Senior delivers a remarkable declaration which seems to breach the fourth wall of the theatre and involve the playhouse audience and London itself in the drama: 'This wide and vniuersall Theater Presents more wofull Pageants then the Sceane Wherein we play in' (138–9). Shakespeare is asking his auditors to receive what follows in a context far broader than the narrow stage on which the actors stand.

This is Jaques' cue; indeed, he completes Duke Senior's shortened line with 'All the world's a stage' and the so the great speech begins. As it ends, Orlando enters bearing Adam – a mere eight lines suffice to set him to meat – after which Amiens' song follows:

> Blow, blow, thou winter winde,
> Thou art not so vnkinde, as mans ingratitude
> Thy tooth is not so keene, because thou art not seene,
> although thy breath be rude.
> Heigh ho, sing heigh ho, vnto the greene holly,
> Most frendship, is fayning; most Louing,meere folly:
> The heigh ho, the holly,
> This Life is most iolly.
> Freize, freize, thou bitter skie that dost not bight so nigh
> as benefitts forgot:
> Though thou the waters warpe, thy sting is not so sharpe
> as friend remembred not.
> Heigh ho, sing, &c. (175–94)

Dusinberre notes that 'Amiens' song recapitulates the Duke's opening speech in 2.1, bringing Act 2 ... to a harmonious finale.'[51] But perhaps the song has a more important metadramatic function. If Amiens' song is read not as a bookend for the Duke's opening speech but as a reply to the dramatist in Jaques' 'Seven Ages' speech, Amiens' lyrics could be read as a dirge for Marlowe. Its principal theme is 'mans ingratitude'. Could this be a glance at Marlowe's homicide? Was the ingratitude the Privy Council's? Did they (or certain of their members) sanction Marlowe's death even though he had done the Queen good service as a spy? Then there is the matter of false friendship: 'Most friendship, is fayning'. Surely the men who murdered Marlowe were friends who proved false. Is Shakespeare hinting at the name of one false friend with 'Freize, freize, thou bitter skie'? The man who stabbed Marlowe was Ingram Frizer; his name was pronounced 'Freezer', and variously spelled in legal documents 'Frezer' and 'Ffrezer'. The words 'benefitts forgot' could refer to Marlowe's 'good service' to the Queen ignored by his killers. Or it could refer to maimed funerary rites; Marlowe was buried on the day after his death in an unmarked grave in an out-of-the-way church in an out-of-the-way suburb, hardly a fitting interment for the greatest English poet since Chaucer.[52]

This is a poser. Could Amiens' song be Shakespeare's meditation on the questionable death and hugger-mugger burial of Christopher Marlowe, and an indictment of his killers and their masters? Certainly, Duke Senior's shattering of the fourth wall encouraged auditors to relate Jaques' speech and Amiens' song to the 'vniuersall

Theater' – the wider world – perhaps to a tragic event in the life of the London theatre.

9. Jaques a homosexual

Curiously for a 'libertine', Jaques takes no interest in any of the female characters of the play. Indeed, only two characters seem to catch his fancy. The first is young Orlando, with whom he briefly fences in 3.2 before offering an invitation: 'You haue a nimble wit ... Will you sitte downe with me?' (268–70). Rebuffed by Orlando, Jaques declares, 'The worst fault you haue, is to be in loue' (274), that is, Orlando should be faulted for being in love with a woman (fault = female genitalia).

Jaques' second interest is Rosalind disguised as Ganymede, namesake of Zeus' toy-boy in Marlowe's *Dido, Queen of Carthage*. She will tersely blow off Jaques in 4.1 (see the discussion below). If Shakespeare were to write a play remembering the homosexual Marlowe, what better vehicle could he choose than the story of a girl pretending to be a boy pretending to be a girl teaching a boy to woo him or her?[53] One can see how, in the mind of a playwright, the ghost of Marlowe and the adventures of Rosalind-Ganymede could easily cohabit *As You Like It*.[54]

10. Jaques a spy

As noted, some scholars reckon that Marlowe served as an agent for Elizabeth's spymaster, Walsingham, and that the association may have led to Marlowe's death.[55] Marlowe's three companions in the room at Deptford were all sometime operatives or fellow travellers of the spy service.[56] In *As You Like It* Shakespeare touches on this aspect of Marlowe's career so lightly that scholars have never recognized it.

The moment comes in 3.3, a scene rife with allusions to Marlowe's life and death. Touchstone, courting Audrey, laments his rusticated circumstances:

> *Clo.* I am heere with thee, and thy Goats, as the most capricious
>   Poet honest Ouid was among the Gothes.
> *Iaq.* O knowledge ill inhabited, worse then Ioue in a thatch'd house.
> *Clo.* When a mans verses cannot be vnderstood, nor a mans good
>   wit seconded with the forward childe, vnderstanding: it strikes a
>   man more dead then a great reckoning in a little roome: truly, I
>   would the Gods hadde made thee [Audrey] poeticall. (5–14)

Agnes Latham's (undervalued) note on this exchange deserves reconsideration. She recalls that Ovid, exiled among the Getae, complained that in their barbarous country his verses were not understood.

> 'A hearer rouses zeal, excellence increases with praise, and renown possesses a mighty spur. In this place who is there to whom I can read my compositions?' (*Ex Ponto* 4.2.15–38) ... Cf. Nashe, *Pierce Pennilesse*, 1592: 'Ouid might as well have read his verses to the Getes that vnderstood him not'. (1.180)[57]

Latham has noticed that Touchstone's Ovid 'among the Gothes' isn't directly referencing the Latin poet's *Ex Ponto* as other commentators have supposed.[58] Rather, Shakespeare is remembering the predicament of Ovid as expressed by Nashe in *Pierce Pennilesse*. Shakespeare links Nashe with Touchstone via their identical references to Ovid.

Overhearing Touchstone's moan, Jaques-Marlowe, hidden and spying, grumbles, 'O knowledge ill inhabited, worse then Ioue in a thatch'd house', a glance at the story of Philemon and Baucis in Ovid's *Metamorphoses*; the exiled Roman poet was frequently at the sharp end of Marlowe's and Nashe's pens.[59] On the instant Touchstone delivers one of the play's putative references to Marlowe: 'it strikes a man more dead then a great reckoning in a little roome' (12–13).

The irony of Touchstone's allusion to the homicide of Marlowe being overheard by the ghost of Marlowe hovering a spy in the underbrush is breathtaking.

Moments later, Sir Oliver Mar-text enters, a character Shakespeare endows with a name unambiguously linked to Nashe via his *Marprelate* texts. It's difficult to discover the dramatic function of this scene; in return for her favours Audrey could have demanded a proper marriage to Touchstone without the intervention of either Mar-text or Jaques. Likewise, the scene in which William comes seeking Audrey's favour and is rebuffed by Touchstone (5.1) appears to have no dramatic function. One can't justify either scene – or the intrusion of the characters Mar-text and William – by arguing dramatic necessity. What, then, are the functions of the Mar-text and William scenes?

I suggest that the former illustrates episodes in Marlowe's and Nashe's careers while the latter is autobiographical. Scene 3.3 shows us a spying Jaques-Marlowe overhearing Touchstone-Nashe's 'great reckoning' lines, and Clown-Nashe brought face to face with a Mar-text. Below I will suggest that 5.1 functions to introduce a bumpkin named William (Shakespeare) and give us the date of his first encounter with London's theatrical scene.

11. Jaques a melancholic

Scene 4.1 begins with (homosexual) Jaques courting the 'boy' Rosalind-Ganymede: 'I prithee, pretty youth, let me be better acquainted with thee' (1–2). Lifted from its context, surely this is an archetypal Elizabethan pick-up line.

Brushed off by Orlando in 3.2, Jaques – the notorious 'libertine' and sinner who inexplicably ignores Celia, the play's only available female – now tries his luck with the play's other boy-figure. But canny Rosalind is miles ahead of him. She replies, 'They say you are a melancholy fellow ... Those that are in extremity ... are abhominable fellowes, and betray themselues to euery moderne censure, worse then drunkards' (3–7).

Her response, which seems to echo Duke Senior's indictment of Jaques – even though Rosalind wasn't present when the Duke spoke – is framed to shield herself while revealing the personality of Jaques. One could argue it is *precisely* the Duke's and Rosalind's indictments of Jaques which made the Jaques-Marlowe connection transparent to Shakespeare's first auditors.[60] Righter was particularly struck by these censures: 'one almost wonders if they were intended to evoke the image of Marlowe for the playgoers at The Globe'.[61]

Within a breath Jaques does his best to make himself sound interesting and even exotic:

> I haue neither [1] the Schollers melancholy, which is emulation: nor [2] the Musitians, which is fantasticall; nor [3] the Courtiers, which is proud: nor [4] the Souldiers, which is ambitious: nor [5] the Lawiers, which is politick: nor [6] the Ladies, which is nice: nor [7] the Louers, which is all these ... (10–14, my enumeration)

Jaques lists seven forms of melancholy – while writing *As You Like It* the number seven is inextricably bound up with Marlowe in Shakespeare's mind – none of which is his. Jaques has 'a melancholy of mine own' (the melancholy of a poet?) which he couches in terms meant to make him sound interesting.[62] He says it is 'compounded of many simples, extracted from many obiects, and indeed the sundrie contemplation of my trauells, in which by often rumination, wraps me in a most humorous sadnesse' (15–18). Travellers were not so common then as now and, if not vagabonds, might be people worth knowing. But Rosalind is ahead of Jaques again and turns his travels against him: 'A Traueller: by my faith you haue great reason to be sad: I feare you haue sold your owne Lands, to see other mens; then to haue seene much, and to haue nothing, is to haue rich eyes and poore hands' (19–22). As noted, Marlowe's travels had almost cost him his MA. For want of money he was arrested for counterfeiting in the Netherlands. Indeed, if his homicide was related to his spying his travelling may have cost him his life.

As Orlando arrives, Rosalind sees off Jaques with her evocative reference to a 'Gundello'. But not before Jaques-Marlowe pronounces what is unmistakably a playwright's benediction (or curse): 'Nay then God buy you, and you [Orlando] talke in blanke verse' (28–9) – which Orlando pointedly does not do for the balance of the scene. Even after Jaques has left the stage, Marlowe is still lurking in Shakespeare's mind and is again memorialized when Rosalind rehashes (and debunks) the tale of *Hero and Leander* (91–9).

As to Jaques' characterization of his personal form of melancholy, the phrase 'compounded of many simples' may be what it appears to be – a figure of speech. But it could also be a glance at Marlowe's use of recreational substances. 'Simples' were medicinal herbs, tobacco being one. The Frenchman Jean Nicot described its medicinal properties in 1559 (hence 'nicotine'), and Raleigh popularized smoking in England in the 1570s. By his own admission Marlowe was an enthusiastic user of tobacco (and boys). The infamous 'Baines Note' quotes Marlowe as saying 'all they that loue not *Tobacco* & *Boies* are fools.'[63] Numerous alcoholic drinks were 'compounded of many simples'; for example, gin, a medieval invention, is distilled with juniper berries (hence the Dutch *Jenever*). Whether Shakespeare's phrase 'many simples' is a glance at Marlowe's use of psychoactive substances is a nice question; Herodotus (484–425 BC) noted that the Scythians – Tamburlaine's tribe – enjoyed the use of a drug, apparently cannabis.[64]

12. Jaques no music lover

To qualify for a Parker Scholarship, Marlowe had to demonstrate an ability to sing plainsong at sight and, perhaps, the wit 'to make a verse'; Riggs speculates that Marlowe had learned music at a school organized by Archbishop Matthew Parker 'adjacent to Eastbridge Hospital where Canterbury pilgrims had lodged before the Reformation'.[65]

Marlowe may have had unpleasant memories of his musical education. Shapiro notes that 'Marlowe had hated jigs, and said so in the prologue to *Tamburlaine the Great*, where he announces that his play rejects "jigging veins of riming mother wits And such conceits as clownage keeps in pay."'[66] Perhaps this explains why Jaques scorns music in 2.5 and again in 4.2. In the former scene Jaques' stanzo for Amiens' song is a double parody; it sends up the greenwood song itself and simultaneously lampoons Duke Senior's band of merry men. In 4.2 Jaques equates music with noise as he demands the Forrester's song: 'Sing it: 'tis no matter how it bee in tune, so it make noyse enough.' (8–9). It comes as no surprise when in 5.4 Jaques shuns the nuptial festivities, proclaiming, 'I am for other, then for dancing meazures' (191). The 'meazures' that Marlowe favoured were poetical.

13. Jaques an old gentleman.

In 5.1 Audrey appears to refer to Jaques when she complains, 'Faith the Priest was good enough, for all the olde gentlemans saying' (3–4). In 1600 Marlowe (and Shakespeare) would have been thirty-six years old – not old by our standards. Then again, age is relative; how old is Audrey? The age of consent was then fourteen for boys, twelve for girls.

Does Audrey's reference to 'olde gentleman' suggest Shakespeare himself played the part of Jaques?[67] From playhouse in-jokes in the texts, I've suggested that Shakespeare played Caesar in 1599 and Polonius in *Hamlet*, both older men.[68] There may be another inside joke here: Shakespeare officially became a 'gentleman' on 20 October 1596. Did Shakespeare's tribute to – and admiration for – Marlowe run so deep that he himself played Jaques? Or was taking the role of Marlowe a reflection of Shakespeare's emulation?

14. Jaques offers seven blessings

Jaques' career follows a curious arc in the final act of the play. First, Orlando delivers a not-very-oblique allusion to Marlowe's *Faustus*. He explains that Rosalind-Ganymede, though 'forest-born', was tutored 'Of many desperate studies, by his vnckle, Whom he reports to be a great Magitian. Obscured in the circle of this Forrest' (5.4.32–4). Surely, 'desperate studies', 'great Magitian', and 'Obscured in the circle' are echoes of Faustus, who had yearned to be a magician and had many 'desperate thoughts'. These lines are Jaques' cue to speak, and his text is an impious biblical lampoon: 'There is sure another flood toward, and these couples are comming to the Arke' (35–6).

Moments later, Touchstone engages in a veritable fugue on the word 'seven'. He begins by enumerating the seven proofs of his qualifications as a courtier:

> I haue [1] trod a measure, I haue [2] flattred a Lady, I haue [3] bin politicke with my friend, [4] smooth with mine enemie, I haue [5] vndone three Tailors, I haue [6] had foure quarrels, and [7] like to haue fought one. (44–7, my enumeration)

Then he briskly moves to his quarrel 'vpon the seuenth cause' which exhausts the next fifty lines – with 'seuenth' repeated four times in eighteen lines. First, Touchstone enumerates the possibilities of a 'lye, seuen times remoued':

> I did dislike the cut of a certaine Courtiers beard: he sent me word, if I said his beard was not cut well, hee was in the minde it was: this is call'd the [1] retort courteous. If I sent him word againe, it was not well cut, he wold send me word he cut it to please himselfe: this is call'd the [2] quip modest. If againe, it was not well cut, he disabled my iudgment: this is called, the [3] reply churlish. If againe it was not well cut, he would answer I spake not true: this is call'd the [4] reproofe valiant. If againe, it was not well cut, he wold say, I lie: this is call'd the [5] counter-checke quarrelsome: and so to [6] lye circumstantiall, and the [7] lye direct. (69–81, my enumeration)

Then Touchstone again specifies the seven degrees:

> I will name you the de-grees. The first, the Retort courteous: the second, the Quip-modest: the third, the reply Churlish: the fourth, the Reproofe valiant: the fift, the Counterchecke quarrelsome: the sixt, the Lye with circumstance: the seauenth, the Lye direct .... (90–5)

As if we hadn't heard enough sevens, Touchstone adds one more:

> I knew when seuen Iustices could not take vp a Quarrell, but when the parties were met themselues, one of them thought but of an If; as if you saide so, then I saide so: and they shooke hands, and swore brothers. (96–100)

There's another seven yet as Jaques offers seven blessings to the principals:

> [to Duke Senior] you to [1] your former Honor, I bequeath your patience, and your vertue, well deserues it. [to Orlando] you to [2] a loue, that your true faith doth merit: [to Oliver] you to [3] your land, and [4] loue, and [5] great allies: [to Silvius] you to a [6] long, and well-deserued bed: [to Touchstone] And you to [7] wrangling, for thy louing voyage Is but for two moneths victuall'd … (184–9, my enumeration)[69]

So the run of sevens which began with Jaques' 'Seven Ages of Man' speech in 2.7 concludes with a barrage of sevens in 5.4. Given the many traits shared by Jaques and Marlowe – indeed, there's hardly a trait of Jaques not shared with Marlowe – would it not be remarkable if Shakespeare *didn't* have the seventh anniversary of his shepherd's death in mind as he wrote *As You Like It*? Not incidentally, both Jaques and Touchstone make exactly seven appearances in the play:[70] Jaques in 2.5, 2.7, 3.2, 3.3, 4.1, 4.2, 5.4; Touchstone in 1.2, 2.4, 3.2, 3.3, 5.1, 5.3, 5.4. Readers reluctant to accept Shakespeare's cascade of sevens in *As You Like It* as occasioned by the seventh anniversary of Marlowe's death are invited to supply a more satisfactory explanation.

15. Jaques seeks redemption

The final beat in the career of Jaques which deserves consideration is his turn towards redemption. When he learns from Jaques de Boys 'The Duke hath put on a Religious life, And throwne into neglect the pompous Court', our Jaques determines to seek out the Duke. 'To him will I: out of these conuertites There is much matter to be heard, and learn'd' (182–3). What accounts for Jaques' sudden interest in the contemplative life?

I believe it is a mark of Shakespeare's affection for Marlowe that he allows his melancholy libertine finally to express a desire to seek the keys to salvation. As Marlowe himself wrote in *Dr Faustus*, 'Never too late, if Faustus can repent' (2.2.84). And Shakespeare's fondness is made palpable by Duke Senior entreating, 'Stay, Iaques, stay' (192). Jaques leaves the stage headed for an 'abandon'd cave', an image tantalizingly suggestive of a hollow grave. Shakespeare has endowed his Jaques with more than a dozen traits of Christopher Marlowe. But in the end he must recognize that Marlowe cannot return from the green world to the city and court. His only future is to be hidden within earth.

Enter William

No commentator has offered a persuasive explanation for the presence in the play of Audrey's would-be wooer, the bumpkin William of 5.1. It is possible this character has an important though never recognized function: to give us the date of William Shakespeare's arrival in London and the beginning of his association with the Elizabethan theatre scene. In his dialogue with Touchstone William confirms that he was born 'i'th Forrest heere' (23), that is, the Forest of Arden, the namesake of which is in Shakespeare's Warwickshire.[71] William admits he is not 'Learned' (38–9), that is, did not attend university. Most significantly, William is 'Fiue and twentie' years old (20). Shakespeare was baptized on 26 April 1564. My inference is that William's age dates Shakespeare's first encounter with university wits, perhaps in the person of Nashe, and the world of London theatre to his twenty-sixth year, the interval from April 1589 to April 1590. Touchstone may be an effigy of Shakespeare's sometime collaborator, Nashe, the 'little wit' who likely died silenced and broke while Shakespeare was writing *As You Like It*. Shakespeare may be remembering Nashe for providing his first encounter with London's theatrical world.

Of all the new insights to *As You Like It* offered in this chapter, this is the most fundamental to our understanding of the arc of Shakespeare's career: if my inference is correct, by his own testimony William Shakespeare was twenty-five when he encountered London's theatrical set. If so, this autobiographical note reduces the interval of his 'lost years' from seven to four. And it places him in London at the very moment when professional theatre was coming into its own. Young Shakespeare was, so to speak, present at the Creation.

Marlowe's fame, Shakespeare's tribute

As usual in Shakespeare's plays, minor characters may comment on the main action and perhaps suggest the playwright's personal point of view. One minor but extraordinary character in the forest is Phebe ('the bright one'), who not only falls in love with

Rosalind-Ganymede on first sight but justifies herself by quoting Marlowe's *Hero and Leander*. How many of Shakespeare first auditors (and more recent ones, for that matter) have actually met a shepherdess who could quote Marlowe? Surely this must have struck Shakespeare's audience as at least a *trifle* out of the ordinary.

Phebe is Shakespeare's discreet but shining tribute to Marlowe as a poet of enduring importance and popularity. That her 'Dead Shepheard' is Marlowe is widely agreed. And he certainly had been dead for seven years. But why 'Shepheard'? As noted above, the answer could be this simple: perhaps Marlowe's best-known poem was 'The Passionate Shepherd to his Love', which appeared in 1599, shortly before Shakespeare began writing *As You Like It*. But there could be more significance to Phebe's tribute – if she is speaking for the playwright. Did Marlowe act as mentor, guide, and even protector (shepherd) when the twenty-five-year-old William arrived in London in 1589, encountered Nashe, and embarked on a theatrical career? In 1587 Marlowe had arrived in London with the manuscripts of *Tamburlaine 1* and Ovid's *Elegies* under his arm (perhaps *Dido*, too). Did Shakespeare do likewise in 1589? And did his scratchings and other notable gifts catch the eye of Marlowe? Were the pair friends, colleagues – perhaps even lovers? We may never be able to answer these questions with confidence. But if the portrait of William in 5.1 is autobiographical, then his fleeting appearance (he speaks a mere tem lines) is pregnant with meaning. Not incidentally, dating Shakespeare's arrival in London to 1589 fits well with received chronologies of his plays.[72]

The arrival of an ephemeral William (Shakespeare) in a district populated by so many sophisticates and *literati* sublimates the play from an anti-pastoral comedy into a personal memoir – one remembered with the greatest possible fondness, not only for the men behind the masks of Jaques and Touchstone, but for the naïve bucolic in homespun who stumbles into their midst. Is this Shakespeare fondly recalling the innocent he was when he arrived at the threshold of the world of the theatre? If so, it is a snapshot for the ages.

And if Marlowe had meant little to Shakespeare, would he – seven years after Marlowe's death – have been moved to construct such an elaborate, affectionate tribute to the man as we discover in *As You Like It*?

On the character of Touchstone

The view of rustic life which Touchstone expresses in his dialogue with Corin (3.2) smacks of Nashe's reflections upon his own period of rustication in Great Yarmouth after the *Isle of Dogges* fiasco of 1597 as recorded in his newly published *Lenten Stuffe* (1599).[73] Flashes of Nashean wit and cynicism illuminate several passages of Touchstone's dialogue, including his encounter with William:

> I am ... He sir, that must marrie this woman: Therefore you Clowne, abandon: which is in the vulgar, leaue the societie: which in the boorish, is companie, of this female: which in the common, is woman: which together, is, abandon the society of this Female, or Clowne thou perishest: or to thy better vnderstanding, dyest; or (to wit) I kill thee, make thee away, translate thy life into death, thy libertie into bondage: I will deale in poyson with thee, or in bastinado, or in steele: I will bandy with thee in faction, I will ore-run thee with policie: I will kill thee a hundred and fifty wayes, therefore tremble and depart. (5.1.46–57)

Touchstone sounds very much as though he is reciting a passage of Nashe. Indeed, 2 Lord describes Touchstone as 'the roynish clown' (2.2.8), using a rare adjective not otherwise found in Shakespeare but present in Nashe's *Strange Newes* (1592), in, 'clownish and roynish jeasts' (1.3.9–10).

Shakespeare's much-discussed excursion on the silencing of wit in 1.2 may be a nod to Nashe as well as Marlowe. The principal victims of the bishops' bonfire were Gabriel Harvey and Nashe, and the small stature of the latter may be remembered in the repetition of 'little wit' and 'little foolery'. Remembrances of Nashe pop up here and there in the text of *As You Like It*; Touchstone's 'This is the verie false gallop of Verses' (3.2.110) echoes *Strange Newes*: 'I would trot a false gallop through the rest of his ragged Verses' (1.275.7–8). And Shakespeare's admiration for Nashe may be summarized in an exchange between Jaques and Duke Senior at 5.4.102–5:

> *Iaq.* Is not this a rare fellow my Lord? He's as good at any thing, and yet a foole.
> *Du.Se.* He vses his folly like a stalking-horse, and vnder the presentation of that he shoots his wit.

Surely, a man must be of short stature to be able to shoot *under* the belly of a horse.

William Shakespeare at thirty-five

Everyone knows there is something different about Shakespeare's plays after 1599. I have suggested elsewhere that *Julius Caesar*, written to open the Bankside Globe in midsummer 1599, is the fulcrum on which Shakespeare's career turns.[74] It may be that graduating to housekeeper from playwright-for-hire – and having, in effect, his own theatre to work in – brought a feeling of liberation to the writer in Shakespeare. Or it may have been that he entered a period of profound religious doubt. What is certain is that a new maturity of vision and perspective coupled with intense skepticism begins to emerge in his plays.

It is possible that Shakespeare wrote *As You Like It* as a companion piece to *Julius Caesar* and that these were among the first plays presented at the Globe. In *Caesar* Shakespeare poses a colossal question: could a man with the initials J.C. really become a god? Or did his 'power' extend only to the superstitious?[75] In *As You Like It* the playwright pays a long-outstanding debt to his dead shepherd on the seventh anniversary of Marlowe's death. Taken together, these two plays mark Shakespeare's debut as a writer of skeptical views and bristling social commentary.

As You Like It embodies not only Marlowe's ghost but his spirit, that is, many of his attitudes toward the follies of Elizabethan convention, law and society. Marlowe was nothing if not an iconoclast who defied convention.[76] Shakespeare's *As You Like It* is one of his most seditious plays; Michael Hattaway noticed 'the play interrogates matters of gender, rank, and the social order'.[77] In fact, it slaughters any number of Elizabethans' sacred cows.

One of the play's targets is so-called 'agnatic' primogeniture, the medieval custom by which the estate of a deceased father passed *in toto* to the senior male descendant.[78] Orlando is its victim, and Jaques intends to make a career of railing against the rich and privileged – those 'first borne of Egypt'. Another of Shakespeare's targets is the Enclosures Controversy expressed in the plight of Corin, a peasant turned into a laborer by a non-resident capitalist landlord.[79] The long-simmering controversy would burst into open rebellion in Shakespeare's home county of Warwickshire in the so-called Midlands Revolt of 1607.[80] As for the bucolics of Arden, instead of writing sonnets, blowing reed pipes and discoursing like university professors as they did in popular *Eclogues* and the plays of Lyly, in *As You Like It* they are hard-working, poor and embittered. They don't own their flocks or farms, but share-crop or shepherd for (low) wages. Touchstone's anti-pastoral argument *contra* Corin (3.2.13–82) debunks the genre of pastoral romantic comedy, once so popular on the Elizabethan stage.

Though Shakespeare's play ends in marriages, along the way he derides the solemnity of the wedding ceremony in both the mock marriage of Ganymede and Orlando (4.1.114–27) and the Touchstone-Audrey-Martext episode. Shakespeare also belabors the sanctity of wedlock through repeated banter about cuckoldry and horns, and Rosalind's description of a wife's unruly behavior (4.1.39–46). In 4.2 a deer is given a funeral – another sacrament slighted. All this is pure Marlowe. Shakespeare debunks blood sports with his description of the weeping deer (2.1.33–43), Duke Senior's doubts about the legitimacy of hunting (2.1.21–4), and the foresters' song about horns (4.2.14–19). In going hunting, aren't the Duke and his men unlawful poachers? With a quotation from Marlowe's *Hero and Leander* Shakespeare debunks love at first sight by putting the line into the mouth of Phebe, who has just fallen in love with a woman dressed as a boy. All this is social commentary with a vengeance.

But the play's *most seditious* theme may be the unspoken question it raises: is flesh merely a garment? In the Geneva Book of Job, Elizabethans read, 'Thou hast clothed me with skin and flesh, and joined me together with bones and sinews' (10:11). That is to say, the 'me', the self, exists apart from flesh and bone. In *As You Like It* Shakespeare presents a girl, Rosalind, disguised as a boy named Ganymede ... the paramour of Zeus in Marlowe's *Dido, Queen of Carthage* ... acting as the romantic surrogate of a girl ... to teach a boy how to make love to her ... er, him ... er, well, whoever turns you on. If a person is not flesh and bone but the soul, what possible difference can the gender of one's lover make? To judge from Marlowe's predilection and the possible range of Shakespeare's own sexuality, not much. Shakespeare's admiration for and vindication of Christopher Marlowe shines out like golden thread in the fabric of *As You Like It*. Marlowe's ghost and spirit whisper among the branches of the Forest of Arden. Shakespeare's tribute to his 'Dead

Shepheard' is a glowing exemplar of the devotion of one poet to another. And to a man whom Shakespeare owed much, and may have felt he owed everything.[81]

Notes

1 Throughout this chapter, original spelling in *As You Like It* (First Folio 1623) is taken from David Bevington's online edition: www.internetshakespeare.uvic.ca. Modern lineation from Juliet Dusinberre, ed., *As You Like It*, The Arden Shakespeare, Series 3. (London: Bloomsbury, 2006).
2 Edward Capell, ed., *Mr. William Shakespeare his comedies, histories, and tragedies, set out by himself in quarto, or by the players his fellows in folio, and now faithfully republish'd from those editions in ten volumes octavo; with an introduction*, 10 vols (London: P. Leach for J. and R. Tonson, [1767–68]), I.64.
3 Leslie Hotson, *The Death of Christopher Marlowe* (London: Nonesuch, 1925).
4 Oliver W. F. Lodge, 'Shakespeare and the Death of Marlowe', *Times Literary Supplement*, 14 May 1925, 335.
5 'The jester's words might in the end be a veiled protest (veiled because delivered by the clown) against the burning on June 4, 1599, by order of the Archbishop of Canterbury and the Bishop of London, of copies of one, or more, of the surreptitious editions of Marlowe's translation of the *Elegies of Ovid*.' Paul Reyher, 'When a Man's Verses cannot be Understood', *Times Literary Supplement*, 9 July 1925, 464.
6 Sir Arthur Quiller-Couch and J. Dover Wilson, eds, *As You Like It*, The New Shakespeare (Cambridge: Cambridge University Press, 1926), 103–5. Ridley grudgingly drew the same conclusion: '[I]t is fair to say that Dr Hotson's discovery of the circumstances of Marlowe's death, in a quarrel over "le recknynge," taken together with the line from *The Jew of Malta*, Infinite riches in a little room ... have a direct reference to Marlowe ... Finally, besides the obvious Martext-Marprelate connection ... there are some fairly certain allusions to Nashe's *Strange Newes* (1592) ...' M. A. Ridley, ed., *As You Like It*, The New Temple Shakespeare (London: J. M. Dent and Sons, 1934), viii–ix. Among current scholarly editions, Brissenden takes exception: 'The comic context here does not suggest such an allusion.' Alan Brissenden, ed., *As You Like It*, The Oxford Shakespeare (Oxford: Clarendon Press, 1993), 174n. Dusinberre is equivocal: 'often taken to refer to Marlowe's death in 1591 [sic] in a Deptford inn ... However, the great reckoning may be a scatological joke – Hanmer emended to "reeking" – with little room a euphemism for a privy', an impossible notion. Dusinberre, *As You Like*

It, 266n. Apparently of no opinion, Hattaway directs the reader: 'For summaries of those who take the line to refer to the mysterious death of Christopher Marlowe at Deptford, see Knowles [Variorum Edition], 188–90.' Michael Hattaway, ed., *As You Like It*, The New Cambridge Shakespeare (Cambridge: Cambridge University Press, 2009), 163n.
7 Richard Wilson argues that Marcade, messenger of death in *Love's Labour's Lost* – perhaps written in the months immediately following Marlowe's death – remembers Navarre's servant Mercury in *The Massacre at Paris*, and perhaps Marlowe's identification with that equivocal god. Richard Wilson, '"Worthies away": The Scene Begins to Cloud in Shakespeare's Navarre', in Jean-Christophe Mayer, ed., *Representing France and the French in Early Modern English* (Newark, DE: University of Delaware Press, 2008), 95–7.
8 Citations from Martin Spevack, *The Harvard Concordance to Shakespeare* (Cambridge, MA: Belknap Press, Harvard University Press, 1973). I am deeply indebted to Ms Jocelyn Medawar, a devoted, enlightened Shakespearean and teacher at the Harvard-Westlake School in Los Angeles, both for calling my attention to appearances in the play of 'seven' which I had not previously noticed, and for inspiring my son, David, with a love of the subject.
9 I'm indebted to Professor François Laroque for reading an early draft of this chapter and offering wise and helpful counsel.
10 The earliest appearing in Edmond Malone's chronology of the plays in Johnson's and Steevens' edition of 1778, V.307. James Shapiro has written a thoughtful appreciation of *As You Like It* into his study of Shakespeare's *annus mirabilis*, 1599. Yet he seems to believe Shakespeare dashed off this play and others: 'In the course of 1599 Shakespeare completed *Henry the Fifth,* wrote *Julius Caesar* and *As You Like It* in quick succession, then drafted *Hamlet*.' James Shapiro, *A Year in the Life of William Shakespeare: 1599* (New York: HarperCollins, 2005), 4. Even from a playwright of Shakespeare's unique capabilities, this would require an (improbably) Herculean effort. As Verity notes, 'One may with justice ... be loth to use the word "haste" in connection with a work which for many readers is the high-water mark of Shakespeareian [sic] comedy.' A. W. Verity, *As You Like It*, The Pitt Press Shakespeare for Schools (Cambridge: Cambridge University Press, 1899, repr. 1932), xiii.
11 Richard McCabe, 'Elizabethan Satire and the Bishops' Ban of 1599', *Yearbook of English Studies* 11 (1981), 192.
12 'Marlowe never mentions Shakespeare, nor would Shakespeare allude to Marlowe until the turn of the [seventeenth] century, when his mighty rival had been dead for seven years.' David Riggs, *The World of Christopher Marlowe* (London: Faber and Faber, 2004), 281.

13 Jacobus de Voragine, *The Golden Legend*, ed. F. S. Ellis, 6 vols, Temple Classics (London: J. M. Dent, 1900, reprinted 1922, 1931), VI.57–8.
14 Jenny Kermode, *Medieval Merchants: York, Beverley and Hull in the Later Middle Ages* (Cambridge: Cambridge University Press, 2002), 131.
15 Clive Burgess, '"By Quick and by Dead": Wills and Pious Provision in Late Medieval Bristol', *English Historical Review* 102.405 (1987), 837–58.
16 Martin Luther's *Small Catechism* (1529) taught that 'We should pray for ourselves and for all other peoples, even for our enemies, but not for the souls of the dead' (*Small Catechism*, St Louis: Concordia, 2008). Likewise, John Calvin declared the practice of praying for the dead ungodly in his *Institutes of the Christian Religion* (1536). Even so, the first Anglican Book of Common Prayer (1549) had included a prayer for the dead. Morgan Dix, ed., *The Book of Common Prayer 1549*, facsimile (New York: Church Calendar Press, 1881), 217. Beginning with the edition of 1552, this language and the practice vanished (it was somewhat restored in the early twentieth century). Anglicans also discarded the Catholic celebration of All Souls (2 November) but re-imagined the Feast of All Saints (1 November) by redefining 'saints' as 'all believers', and used the occasion to commemorate deceased family and friends.
17 Annemarie Schimmel, *The Mystery of Numbers* (Oxford: Oxford University Press 1993), 156–64.
18 *Ibid.*, 179.
19 Robert Pont, *A Newe Treatise of the Right Reckoning of Yeares and Ages of the World, and Mens Liues, and of the Estate of the last decaying age thereof, this 1600 year of Christ (erroneously called a Yeare of Iubilee), which is from the Creation the 5548 yeare; containing sundrie singularities worthie of observation, concerning courses of times and revolutions of the Heaven, and reformation of Kalendars and Prognostications, with a Discourse of Prophecies and Signs, preceding the last daye, which by manie arguments appeareth now to approach* (Edinburgh: Robert Walde-grave, 1599).
20 Marjorie Garber, *Shakespeare After All* (New York: Pantheon Books, 2004), 451–2.
21 *Ibid.*, 452.
22 Harold C. Goddard, *The Meaning of Shakespeare*, 2 vols (Chicago: University of Chicago Press, 1960), I.266. For a précis of scholarly opinion regarding Touchstone's 'a great reckoning in a little roome' as a glance at Marlowe's homicide and the coroner's conclusion that he was killed in a brawl over the bill see Richard Knowles, ed., *As You Like It*, A New Variorum Edition of Shakespeare (New York: MLA, 1977), 188–90.

23 For example: 'Marlow's lyric, "The Passionate Shepherd to his Love", was well known and drew a number of verse replies including versions by Raleigh and Donne.' Hattaway, *As You Like It*, 174n.
24 'The terms of the debate [between romantic and realistic views of country life] are reproduced ... in Shakespeare's *As You Like It*, which clearly refers to Marlowe's death and speaks of Marlowe himself as a "dead shepherd" before quoting from *Hero and Leander*, and in *The Merry Wives of Windsor* ... in which Parson Evans quotes from "The Passionate Shepherd". Lastly, Marlowe himself recurs to "The Passionate Shepherd" when he has Ithamore quote from it in *The Jew of Malta* (IV, ii, 110–11).' Hopkins, *Christopher Marlowe*, 47–8.
25 Marlowe's pastoral poem was still popular and eliciting response forty years after his death, e.g. John Donne's 'The Bait' (pub. 1633).
26 Edward Burns, ed., *King Henry VI, Part 1*, The Arden Shakespeare, Series 3 (London: Bloomsbury, 2000), 75.
27 Logan sees likenesses of Marlowe's Duke of Guise in Shakespeare's Aaron and Richard III. Robert A. Logan, *Shakespeare's Marlowe: The Influence of Christopher Marlowe on Shakespeare's Artistry* (Aldershot: Ashgate Publishing, 2007), 31.
28 Gary Taylor, 'Shakespeare and Others: The Authorship of *Henry the Sixth Part One*', *Medieval and Renaissance Drama in England* 7 (1995), 145–205.
29 Marlowe's *Tamburlaine* and Kyd's *Spanish Tragedy* inspired any number of bloody sequents, e.g. Robert Greene's *Alphonsus King of Aragon* (ca. 1588); Thomas Lodge's *Wounds of the Civil War* (ca. 1589); George Peele's *The Battle of Alcazar* (ca. 1590).
30 Logan believes that '*The Massacre at Paris* had to have been written after the death of Henry III on August 2, 1589.' Logan, *Shakespeare's Marlowe*, 31.
31 'Prettie wit' could mean young William was clever with words. Or it could be that he was pretty as well as witty.
32 Anne Righter, *Shakespeare and the Idea of the Play*, Penguin Shakespeare Library (London: Penguin, 1967), 139.
33 What might Shakespeare have learned at Marlowe's knee? Speculatively: the power of blank verse; the art of mining history for theatrical high drama; that the Aristotelian unities were not sacred; suspense and tragedy could be heightened by a sudden infusion of comedy; the greatest drama is not physical action but the psychological struggle within a character's mind; and that a playwright could safely comment on the foibles of contemporary Londoners by writing about long-dead historical figures and/or foreign locales. Marlowe's plays 'examine some of the central cultural and religious issues of his day, and each of these plays

has its finger firmly on the pulse of a crucial aspect of its historical moment.' Hopkins, *Christopher Marlowe*, 166.
34 The pronunciation of 'Jaques' has been much debated, whether the monosyllabic 'Jakes' or the bi-syllabic 'Ja-kwees' as required by the metre at 2.1.26 and 5.4.192. The only other appearance is in *All's Well that Ends Well*, when Helena writes that 'i am saint jaques' pilgrim' and has gone towards his shrine at Campostella, Spain. It would seem Shakespeare preferred a spelling without the 'c', and heard the monosyllabic 'Zhok' or 'Jakes'.
35 Shapiro, *A Year*, 46.
36 *Ibid.*
37 For example: Riggs notes that *'Tamburlaine the Great*, Marlowe's upwardly mobile poet-hero, serenades his future queen with hyperbolic epithets ... "lovelier than the love of Jove, / Brighter than is the silver Rhodope, / Fairer than whitest snow on Scythian hills ...' (1.2.879). Riggs, *The World*, 56.
38 Privy Council, Letter to the Fellows of Cambridge University, 29 June 1587, The National Archives, Kew, Privy Council Registers PC2/14/381.
39 Park Honan imagines that Marlowe 'sailed through the Paris embassy ... there are signs that he delivered and picked up letters there ... [H]e depicts Paris with easy confidence' in *The Massacre at Paris*. Park Honan, *Christopher Marlowe, Poet and Spy* (Oxford: Oxford University Press, 2005), 150.
40 Dusinberre, *As You Like It*, 211n.
41 Rosalind's 'Gundello' would better fit with the travels of the author and playwright Robert Greene (1558–92), whose 'autobiographical pamphlets reveal that he fell in with "wags as lewd as myself, with whom I consumed the flower of my youth, who drew me to travel to Italy"'. Riggs, *The World*, 100.
42 R. B. McKerrow, ed., *The Works of Thomas Nashe*, 5 vols (London: Sidgwick & Jackson, 1904–10, repr. Oxford: Basil Blackwell, 1958), III.76.
43 Knowles, *As You Like It*, 106.
44 *Ibid.*, 106–7.
45 See for example: C. Frederick Barbee and Paul F. M Zahl, eds, *The Collects of Thomas Cranmer* (Cambridge: W. B. Eerdmans, 1999), xi ff.
46 'The archbishop [Parker] endowed these awards for boys "who were likely to proceed in the Arts and afterwards make Divinity their study".' Riggs, *The World*, 70.
47 The following are two typical Collects from the Book of Common Prayer. For Christmas: 'God, whiche makest us glad with the yerely remembraunce of the birth of thy onely sonne Jesus Christ; graunt that

as we joyfully receiue him for our redemer, ...' For Easter: 'Almightie God, whiche through thy onely begotten sonne Jesus Christ hast overcome death, and opened unto us the gate of everlasting life ...'.

48 George Puttenham, *The Arte of English Poesie* (London, 1589), 90.
49 Hopkins, *Christopher Marlowe*, 4. On 18 May 1593 the Privy Council had ordered Marlowe's arrest, and on 20 May commanded him 'to give his daily attendance to their lordships, until he shall be licensed to the contrary.' Riggs, *The World*, 325.
50 In Thomas Beard's *The Theatre of God's Judgments* (London, 1597), I.25, 'Of Epicures and Atheists': 'Not inferior to any of the former in atheism and impiety, and equal to all in manner of punishment was one of our own nation, of fresh and late memory, called Marlin [sic] ... [who] denied God and his son Christ, and not only in word blasphemed the Trinity ... The manner of his death being so terrible (for he even cursed and blasphemed to his last gasp, and together with his breath an oath flew out of his mouth) that it was not only a manifest sign of God's judgment, but also an horrible and fearful terror to all that beheld him.' Beard's judgement was echoed by Frances Meres: 'As Iodelle, a French tragical poet, beeing an epicure and an atheist, made a pitifull end: so our tragicall poet Marlowe for his Epicurisme and Atheisme had a tragical death ... stabd to death by a bawdy Servingman, a riual of his in his lewde loue.' *Palladis Tamia: Wit's Treasury* (London, 1598), 89.
51 Dusinberre, *As You Like It*, 230n.
52 A clue to the locale of Marlowe's death might be hinted at in 'the waters warpe'. Water 'warps' when it freezes in a contained space, and its expansion forces the edges outwards and upwards. The word 'bite' suggests a cove or 'bight' – a body of water enclosed on three sides by land, as in the Seine Bight at the mouth of that river. But a bight is also a sharp bend in a river – such as the great bend in the Thames which separates the Isle of Dogs from Deptford Strand, where Marlowe met his death. The words 'bite', 'sting', and 'sharpe' are all suggestive of a knife as a weapon.
53 Riggs notes, 'The question of whether or not Marlowe was a homosexual is misleading. Marlowe's contemporaries regarded sodomy as an aspect of seditious behaviour rather than a species [sic] of person. The crime of sodomy became visible in connection with other offences – blasphemy, treason, counterfeiting, sorcery – that activated the heavy hand of the law. Marlowe avoided this predicament until the final weeks of his life, when he was accused of atheism, coining and crypto-Catholicism.' Riggs, *The World*, 76. It is also true that during his lifetime, Marlowe's 'name was never coupled with that of a woman ... both *Hero and Leander* and *Edward II* show a clear and open interest in homosexuality'. Hopkins, *Christopher Marlowe*, 21.

54 The notorious 'Baines Note' quotes Marlowe as saying, 'all they that loue not Tabacco & Boies were fooles'. Richard Baines, 'A note containing the opinion of on[e] Christopher Marly concerning his damnable Judgment of Religion, and scorn of Godes word', British Library, London, Harley MS 6848, fols. 307–8. Orlando and Rosalind-Ganymede are both boyish, and the actor peaking Phebe's lines was a boy.

55 Among many examples: Honan, *Poet and Spy*, 106 ff, 241 ff, and Riggs, *The World*, 319 ff.

56 Ethel Seaton, 'Marlowe, Robert Poley, and the Tippings', *Review of English Studies* 5 (1929), 273.

57 Agnes Latham, ed., *As You Like It*, The Arden Shakespeare, Series 2 (London: Methuen, 1975), 79n.

58 Jonathan Bate, *Shakespeare and Ovid* (Oxford: Oxford University Press, 1993), 159; Brissenden, *As You Like It*, 174n; Dusinberre, *As You Like It*, 266n.

59 *As You Like It* contains a number of well-documented nods to Ovid; Knowles' Variorum edition cites those to Ovid himself (7) and to his *Ex Ponto* (1), *Metamorphoses* (14), and *Tristia* (4). Hopkins believes 'Marlowe deliberately constructed his poetic career in opposition to the accepted model, patterning himself on the subversive and licentious Roman poet Ovid rather than Ovid's more pious and civic-minded contemporary, Virgil.' Hopkins, *Christopher Marlowe*, 46.

60 Among other winks at Marlowe in 4.1, Hopkins sees Rosalind's 'The poor world is almost six thousand years old' (85–6) as an echo of the 'Baines Note': 'That the Indians, and many authors of antiquity, have assuredly written of above 16 thousand years agone, whereas Adam is proved [by the Bible] to have lived within six thousand years.' Hopkins, *Christopher Marlowe*, 17.

61 Righter, *Idea*, 139.

62 Affected melancholy had recently been skewered in Ben Jonson's *Every Man in His Humor*, perhaps performed at the Curtain in 1598 by the Lord Chamberlain's Men with Shakespeare in the part of Kno'well.

63 'Note containing the opinion of one Christopher Marly [sic] concerning his damnable judgment of religion, and scorn of God's word.' Baines, 'A note', fols. 185–6. Among Marlowe's 'monstrous opinions' attributed by Baines: 'religion was only to keep men in awe'; 'Christ was a bastard and his mother dishonest', etc.

64 'The Scythians ... take some of this hemp-seed, and, creeping under the felt coverings, throw it upon the red-hot stones; immediately it smokes, and gives out such a vapour as no Grecian vapour-bath can exceed; the Scyths, delighted, shout for joy.' George Rawlinson, ed. and trans., *The History of Herodotus*, 9 vols (New York: D. Appleton, 1885), V.74–5.

65 The terms of the scholarship required 'at first sight to solf and sing plainsong' and 'if it may be, such as can make a verse'. Riggs, *The World*, 36.
66 Shapiro, *A Year*, 46–7.
67 Baldwin believes Burbage played Orlando while Shakespeare took the role of Old Adam, John Heminges that of Duke Senior, and Thomas Pope that of Jaques. T. W. Baldwin, *The Organization and Personnel of the Shakespeare Company* (Princeton: Princeton University Press, 1927), 43.
68 Steve Sohmer, *Shakespeare for the Wiser Sort* (Manchester: Manchester University Press, 2008), 81.
69 Again, I'm indebted to Ms Medawar for calling to my attention this and other appearances of seven.
70 Margie Burns, 'Odd and Even in *As You Like It*', *Allegorica* 5.1 (1980), 119–40. And again in Maurice Hunt, 'Christian Numerology and Shakespeare's *The Tragedy of King Richard the Second*', *Christianity and Literature* 60.2 (Winter 2011), 247–75.
71 Commentators debate whether Shakespeare imagined his play set in Warwickshire or in the Ardennes forest on the French–Belgian border. Hattaway reasoned that 'Arden is a name that not only signifies a "real" habitation in Shakespeare's Warwickshire but also alludes to the topos of the "greenwood" that was venevated in idylls and in ballads.' Hattaway, *As You Like It*, 9.
72 Gary Taylor, 'The Canon and Chronology of Shakespeare's Plays', in Stanley Wells, Gary Taylor, John Jowett, et al., eds, *William Shakespeare: A Textual Companion*, 2nd edition (New York and London: W. W. Norton, 1987), 69–144.
73 Some commentators have inferred that the part of the Clown was performed by Robert Armin, and that the name Touchstone is a glance at 'his training as a goldsmith: a "touchstone" (made of quartz or jasper) was used to register the quality of gold and silver alloys'. Hattaway, *As You Like It*, 87. That Touchstone carries a timepiece may also be a wink at Armin's calling.
74 'From *Julius Caesar* we look backward at *Titus*. *The Taming of the Shrew*, *Two Gentlemen of Verona*, *The Comedy of Errors*, *Richard II* and *III*, and the *Henry IV–V–VI* plays – work which is largely developmental, historiographical or pure entertainment. Looking forward in the playwright's career, one finds the ruthless middle comedies, profound tragedies and, at a breathing distance, the romances. Before creating Caesar, Shakespeare created Falstaff; afterwards, he created Lear. Before creating Brutus, Shakespeare created Bolingbroke; afterwards, he created Hamlet. Before creating Cassius, Shakespeare created Beaufort; afterwards, he created Ulysses.

And before creating Antony, Shakespeare created Juliet; afterwards, he created Cleopatra.' Having done with his histories and comedies (and *Titus*), the thirty-five year-old Shakespeare turned to creating socially relevant and/or metaphysical plays, some of them highly if discreetly seditious.' Steve Sohmer, *Shakespeare's Mystery Play and the Opening of the Globe Theatre 1599* (Manchester: Manchester University Press, 1999), 17–18.

75 Ibid., 28 ff.
76 'Marlowe's resolve to put the first book of Lucan's Civil War into English complemented his decision to translate Ovid's *Amores*. Lucan was Ovid's successor in the ancient line of anti-imperial poets. Where Ovid stood for the cause of personal and erotic liberty, Lucan made the case for armed resistance to Caesar's monarchial yoke. Within the Roman tradition, Ovid's *Amores* and Lucan's Civil War were definitive testaments to erotic and political freedom.' Riggs, *The World*, 187.
77 Hattaway, *As You Like It*, 1.
78 In *Henry V* the Continental 'Salic law' was the subject of the obscurantist disquisition on the title to the French crown by the Archbishop of Canterbury (1.2.178–240). The Succession of the Crown Act (royal assent 25 April 2013) allows the elder child to succeed to the throne regardless of gender.
79 Hattaway cites Leicester's Commonwealth (1584): '[the Earl of Leicester] hath taken from the tenants round about their lands, woods, pastures, and commons, to make himself parks, chases and other commodities therewith, to the subversion of many a good family, which was maintained there, before this devourer set foot in that country.' [T. Morgan?], *The Copy of a Letter, Written by a Master of Art of Cambridge. Leycesters Common-wealth: Conceived, Spoken and Published with Most Earnest Protestation of All Dutifull Good Will ... Towards this Realm, Etc. Sometimes Wrongly Attributed to Robert Persons* (Paris, 1584), 83.
80 The shepherds awaiting the birth of Christ in *The Second Shepherds' Play* (*ca.* 1500) pass the time grousing about the Enclosures Controversy.
81 Readers who remain skeptical of a Shakespeare–Marlowe connection should consider the Oxford editors' decision to credit Marlowe as co-author of *Henry VI*, parts 1, 2, and 3 (*New York Times*, 24 October 2016).

N.B. In 1994 the late Dennis Kaye put the riddle of '*ducdame*' to me during a tutorial. It has taken me twenty years to find a solution and now, regrettably, I am unable to share it with him.

3

The dark lady of
The Merchant of Venice

'The Sonnets of Shakespeare offer us the greatest puzzle in the history of English literature.' So began the voyage of Alfred Leslie Rowse (1903–97) through the murky waters cloaking the identities of four persons associated with the publication in 1609 of Shakespeare's 'sugared sonnets': the enigmatic 'Mr. W.H.' cited in the forepages as 'onlie begetter' of the poems; the unnamed 'fair youth' addressed in sonnets 1–126; the 'rival poet' who surfaces and submerges in sonnets 78–86; and the mysterious 'dark lady' celebrated and castigated in sonnets 127–52.[1] Doubtless, even as Thomas Thorpe's edition was passing through George Eld's press, London's mice-eyed must have begun their search for the shadowy four; it has not slacked since.

As to those nominated as 'Mr. W.H.', the list ranges from William Herbert to Henry Wroithesley (with initials reversed) to William Harvey (Wroithesley's stepfather). In 1964 Leslie Hotson proposed one William Hatcliffe of Lincolnshire [!], while Thomas Tyrwitt, Edmond Malone, and Oscar Wilde all favoured a (fictional) boy actor, Willie Hughes. Among candidates for the 'fair youth', Henry Wroithesley, Earl of Southampton (1573–1624), appears to have outlasted all comers.

Those proposed as the rival poet include Christopher Marlowe (more interested in boys than ladies dark or light); Samuel Daniel (Herbert's sometime tutor);[2] Michael Drayton, drinking partner of Jonson and Shakespeare; George Chapman, whose *Seaven Bookes of the Iliades* (1598) were a source for *Troilus and Cressida*; and Barnabe Barnes, lampooned by Nashe as 'Barnaby Bright' in *Have with you to Saffron-Walden*. Among the less well known pretenders are Richard Barnfield, who published the earliest praise of Shakespeare's work,[3] and Gervase Markham, translator of Ariosto.[4]

Candidates for the dark lady have included Mary Fitton, mistress of William Herbert;[5] the Oxford innkeeper Jane Davenant;[6] and most recently 'Black Luce' (a.k.a. Lucy Negro), a Bankside prostitute nominated by G. B. Harrison.[7] Surveying the arguments for each of these women, in 2004 Paul Edmondson and Stanley Wells concluded,

> these theories assume any such dark lady has naturally left good documentary evidence as to her existence and identity; Shakespeare's lovers have probably left not a wrack behind them, apart from the Sonnets, and then only if the poems represent some kind of autobiography. The case will always remain open.[8]

But perhaps not.

Rowse's dark lady and the furore she caused

In a mere thirty-seven pages – hardly more than a preface to his edition of the sonnets – Rowse presented his 'discovery' that Shakespeare's dark lady was Emilia Bassano Lanier (1569–1645),[9] illegitimate daughter of the Venetian *converso* court musician Baptiste Bassano, and sometime mistress of Henry Carey, Lord Hunsdon, cousin to Queen Elizabeth, Lord Chamberlain, and patron of the company of actors to which Shakespeare belonged.[10] Though Rowse presented his finding as a 'certainty', subsequent investigators have not received it as such. Katherine Duncan-Jones responded: 'Romantic critics have liked to view Shakespeare surprised into sonneteering by some real-life experience. Ever since the edition of Sonnets in 1837 by James Boaden ... scholars have pursued possible personal illusions.'[11] Professor Duncan-Jones seems to infer that Shakespeare's 'fair youth' and dark lady are literary creations which leapt full-formed from poet's imagination. But, really, can this be so?

Ilona Aiello recognizes that 'the sonnets are imbricated in Shakespeare's life, embodied in particular lived circumstances that are known to the addressee but concealed from us'.[12] Garry O'Connor believes Shakespeare's cunning description of the dark lady was intentionally designed to throw his contemporaries off the scent: 'Lanier was a bit too dark to be the real thing. Moreover, Shakespeare would surely never have rendered her so literally ... especially as he was supposed to have inherited her from his patron, the Lord Chamberlain Hunsdon, one of Elizabeth's most formidable warriors and protectors. The aristocracy were touchy about family scandal.'[13] On the contrary, Ms Aiello shrewdly argues that only *some* concealment of the players' identities is intentional. Some is due to the author's confusion: 'Much of what happens in the dark lady sonnets ... is so intimate, so sexual, so fraught with desire and potential scandal that Shakespeare would rather not say – exactly. To make matters even more baffling, there is a great deal he does not know and cannot understand about the man and the lady, and their relationship to each other.'[14] She offers a libidinous and persuasive explanation of why the faces behind the masks are obscured:

> The dark lady sonnets draw us into a world where passion distorts judgment, where duplicity and role-playing are a mark of sophistication, and where it is difficult to distinguish truth from lies. Shakespeare's attempts to see and present her accurately are foiled by his recognition that nothing she says to him and nothing he says about her can be trusted; the more he tries to report what is ... the more desire befuddles judgment.[15]

Despite such caveats, the depth and murkiness of passages through the sonnets have not deterred literary spelunkers.

Emilia and her rivals

Emilia Lanier is only one of the women 'discovered' as the inspiration for Shakespeare's dark lady. Stephen Booth scoffed:

> Sonnets 127–152 include several that refer to or address a woman (or, improbably, some women) of dark complexion and whore-like habits. She, like the male friend ['fair youth'], may be a literary creation; if Shakespeare was talking about real people and events, we have no clue whatsoever as to the woman's identity. Speculation on her identity has ranged from wanton to ludicrous and need not be illustrated.[16]

Yet in our present context it won't be entirely ludicrous to interrogate a few of the candidates nominated as the dark lady.

Arthur Acheson believed she was Mistress Jane Davenant (d. 1622), keeper of the St George inn near Oxford, ardently visited by Shakespeare during his trudges between Stratford and London. Acheson also saw reflections of Jane in the Courtesan of *The Comedy of Errors* and in Cleopatra – and he wasn't the only one.[17] 'Agatha Christie wrote a letter to *The Times* wherein she attributes the character of Cleopatra, written a dozen or more years ... [after the dark lady] affair, to Shakespeare's memory of Emilia Lanier.'[18] Biddy Darlow [sic] settled on Elizabeth Vernon, wife of Southampton,[19] and Hugh Calvert wrote that Leslie Hotson credited G. B. Harrison with

> first identifying (though very tentatively) Lucy Negro [a.k.a.] Abbess de Clerkenwell as the dark lady, also the discredit of believing the lady a blackamoor. Black Luce was of course no more an Ethiope than the Black Prince. Lucy was by 1594 (some five or six years after the sonnets according Hotson's dating) set up as the 'madam' of a house [brothel] in Clerkenwell. The period of Shakespeare's wretched infatuation is fixed by Leslie Hotson with the rest of the sonnets in 1588 or '89.[20]

Just as notions about 'Black Luce' have been discarded, Hotson's dates for the sonnets have been superseded; the scholarly consensus now dates them to 1592–94, or perhaps as late as 1596. The date *ad quem* is thought to be set by Frances Meres' reference in 1598 to the circulation of Shakespeare's 'sugared sonnets among his private friends'.[21]

Another dark lady seeker, F. E. Halliday, began his sortie by admitting the obvious: 'There have been many guesses, but nobody really knows who she was. It seems reasonable to identify her with a mistress stolen from Shakespeare by his friend.' He then volunteered further candidates: 'Ivor Brown thinks she was Anne Whateley; perhaps "Rosalind" is a clue: the Rosalinds of *Romeo and Juliet* and of *Love's Labour's Lost* are both black beauties.'[22] All such finger-pointing culminated in Rowse's announcement in 1963 that Emilia Lanier was the dark lady. Since which date criticism of and hostility towards Rowse's conclusion have never flagged.

Rowse vs. his critics

In the latter years of the twentieth century the trend among contemporary critics was ruthlessly to weed the author out of his work. Roger Prior observed that 'Modern literary criticism is dedicated to removing the author from the text ... The author's thoughts and intentions can never be known, it is claimed, and are in any case quite irrelevant to our understanding of his work' – an

The dark lady of The Merchant of Venice

extraordinary statement for a serious critic of literature.[23] Susanne Woods believes that 'It is this doctrine that is threatened by Rowse's discovery and fuels much of the hostility to it.' For her part, Woods not only denies Rowse's 'discovery' but asserts that what inspired Shakespeare was not an individual woman but *a type* – another remarkable notion:

> To those of us steeped in the sonnet tradition much of this language seems a witty response to the conventional virtuous beauty of courtly love ... The whole point of sonnet writing was to weave variations on common themes and to overgo predecessors; whether or not a real dark lady inspired Shakespeare's sonnets, they're an immediately recognizable (often delightful, sometimes provocative) response to a popular and well understood set of conventions.[24]

But even if Shakespeare's sonnets were merely an exercise in the form (which they are not), that hardly precludes them being inspired by real and familiar persons.

Katherine M. Wilson went one better, characterizing the dark lady and her sonnets as 'pure parody': 'Indeed nothing is easier to show than that they are parodies. [T]here can be no mistake about Sonnet 130. This could be nothing other than parody.'[25] Wilson contends that some of the sonnets which Shakespeare parodied are readily identifiable. Sonnet 127 'is a direct and incontrovertible comment on Sydney's seventh in *Astrophil and Stella*. Black eyes were not the correct sort in sonnet convention, but the real Stella had this so Sydney poetizes them in sonnet VII.'[26] But commenting on a pre-existing sonnet does not necessarily make 127 a parody. Taking her argument a bridge too far, Wilson believes that Shakespeare's sonnets parody the genre itself: 'Like 130, sonnet 141 parodies not one particular sonnet, but the convention as a whole.'[27] The difficulty with Wilson's argument is two-fold: firstly, parody does not preclude a real female being Shakespeare's inspiration; secondly, where else in the canon has the poet written a parody which is merely a parody and nothing but? Nowhere.

Some of Rowse's sternest critics acknowledge that Lanier may have been a dark lady even if not *the* dark lady. Woods concedes: 'It is certainly possible. David Lasocki has found a report from 1584 that describes two of her cousins as a little black man who was booted (probably Arthur Bassano) and a tall black man ... [which] must refer to their dark complexion and black hair, typical of Italians but rare in England at the time.'[28] Woods is sufficiently intrigued to wonder whether Lanier had contact with Shakespeare and/or his works, and whether the experience might have encouraged her own volume of poetry, Salve Deus Rex Judaeorum (London, 1611).

It would be interesting to know whether Lanier and Shakespeare ever met. Whether they did or not, Lanier was likely to have read his narrative poems, since Salve Deus shows her to have been interested in the genre (sometimes called epillyon, a nineteenth-century coinage meaning 'little epic'), and to have been reading others in the same general type. She may also have attended or read his published plays, but I leave that debate to others.[29]

While there is no evidence that Lanier knew Shakespeare or his work, she could hardly have been unaware of him. Jacobean London was little more than a large town with a population of some 200,000 – equivalent to modern Yonkers, New York, or the London Borough of Harrow – that is, small enough that anybody who was anybody knew everybody who was anybody. Public entertainments were limited to theatrer, bear-baiting, pubs, whorehouses, and sermons; plays in quarto were cheap and relatively plentiful; thanks to the roles Shakespeare wrote for him, Richard Burbage was the Elizabethan equivalent of a rock star. Shakespeare was also a celebrated performer. Is it conceivable that a woman of Emilia's means and education would have been deaf and blind to Shakespeare's works and the man himself?

The dark lady's promiscuity

Another issue which has provoked cries of 'Foul!' from the defenders of Emilia's honour is the dark lady's apparent liberality in bestowing sexual favours. Woods insists there is 'no convincing evidence she [Lanier] was promiscuous'.[30] Duncan-Jones is equally indignant: 'The monstrously sexist assumption that a woman who was sufficiently attracted to one man to consummate her love without marriage would have been prepared to have sex with anyone ... crucially underpins Rowse's support for Emilia Lanier, which seems to depend on the belief that a woman who was Lord Hunsdon's mistress would be willing to have sex with anyone including, therefore, Shakespeare.'[31] On the contrary, the mistress of a rich and powerful grandee would have multiple reasons for being

The dark lady of The Merchant of Venice 59

choosy about her partners. And having sex with a celebrated poet, playwright, and actor is hardly having sex with 'anyone'.

By contrast, Garry O'Connor is less judgemental and more realistic. He notes that Simon Forman, who claimed to have 'supped with her [Lanier] and stayed all night' describes her as a harlot who "useth sodomy". [W]hile he felt all the parts of her body "willingly" and often kissed her, she would not "halek" [have sex] with him (a halek is a little fish used for making pickle; to be in a pickle is to be in a hole).' O'Connor believes this 'a convincing picture of the Elizabethan coquette, especially of how such a creature's sexual dalliance never felt the need to go the whole way in terms of intercourse. Elizabethan men were great fumblers and feelers of women.'[32]

On the other hand, David Bevington considers the issue of the dark lady's coquetry from a purely practical perspective. Hunsdon was a powerful and influential man as well as a proven warrior and companion of 'sword and buckler' men. He was also in a position to influence Shakespeare's career as dramatist and actor. 'One might wonder if Southampton and Shakespeare would have … thought it prudent to pursue a lady who, in 1592–94 (Rowse's years for the sonnet narrative), was for the most if not all this period the mistress of the Lord Chamberlain?'[33] From what we know about Shakespeare, who seems to have been a man of considerable discretion,[34] would he have jeopardized his career by risking the jealous ire of a magnate like Hunsdon? One hardly thinks so.

Indeed, René Weis infers that Shakespeare was sufficiently prudent to embark on his affair with Emilia *after* her marriage in October 1592 to the court musician and her cousin once-removed Alfonso Lanier (d. 1613). If the affair began after the birth of Henry Lanier (1593–1633), this would push its dates to 1593–94 or 1595. Though Shakespeare indulged enthusiastically in their adulterous affair, Weis notes that *both partners* were married and that the poet expressed feelings of guilt in Sonnet 152: 'In loving thee thou know'st I am forsworn, But thou art twice forsworn, to me love swearing, In act thy bed-vow broke and new faith torn, In vowing new hate after new love bearing.' 'The poet's confession … must refer to his marriage vows.'[35] Can we not see how the poet's sense of being both betrayer and betrayed would constrain *and* inflame his appetite for his dark lady?

Reviewing such politely couched opinions on the allure of Shakespeare's dark lady and their furious, exalting relationship, one is drawn to the conclusion that many of his commentators have led lives of quiet deprivation, never having enjoyed a love affair with a truly bad woman or frivolous man. They evince no feeling for that all-consuming, frantic passion that consists of equal parts love and rage, orgasmic joy, and searing pain. Anyone privileged to have suffered such an affair can understand the turbulent mood-swings in Shakespeare's sonnets. Had his dark lady not been promiscuous – as well as a liar, cheat, seductress, casual fornicator, and, thereby, beyond the sole possession of any one man – she wouldn't have been nearly so desirable. To make a good-bad thing better (worse), Shakespeare was married, the father of three, and perhaps bisexual.

In sum: Shakespeare's dark lady was everything he wanted and couldn't-shouldn't have. His sonnets should be recognized for what they are: the poetry of obsession.

Emilia Lanier, poet

Whether or not she was the dark lady, Emilia's career was extraordinary almost from beginning to end. Born illegitimate, the penniless orphan was swept into manorial luxury, educated better than virtually all her female contemporaries, seduced by one of the greatest men in the realm. Perhaps the lover and inspiration of the greatest poet ever to write in English, she outlived them all and died in 1645, aged seventy-six, having witnessed the beginning of the civil war that would topple the monarchy. She also published in 1611 the first significant book of poetry by an Englishwoman, *Salve Deus Rex Judaeorum*, and could lay claim to the title of first professional female English poet. Her book begins with a series of poetical dedications to a number of the leading ladies of the realm which preface a lengthy meditation on Christ's Passion from a decidedly feminist perspective.

Lanier offers a passionate defence against prevailing misogynist views of women's weakness. Although she admits that a 'Woman writing of divinest things' is 'seldome seene',[36] she boldly offers a polemical counternarrative to biased accounts of women in biblical history: 'I have written this small volume, or little booke, for the generall use of all virtuous Ladies and Gentlewomen of this kingdome ... And this have I done, to make knowne to the world, that all women deserve not to be blamed.'[37] Lanier portrays biblical women as instruments sent by God to counter sinful men. Pontius

The dark lady of The Merchant of Venice

Pilate's wife serves as one of the text's central emblems of spiritual virtue for her efforts to prevent the Crucifixion. Pilate's wife delivers a diatribe that rates the sin of Eve (foremother of female weakness) less egregious than the evil deeds of Christ's male crucifiers.[38]

The modern reader can perceive the magnitude of Emilia's task in defending women only by placing it in apposition to the remarkable fourteen-hundred-year misogynist tradition of the Church. In the third century AD Tertullian addressed women at large:

> And do you not know that you are Eve? God's sentence hangs still over all your sex and His punishment weighs down upon you. You are the devil's gateway; you are she who first violated the forbidden tree and broke the law of God. It was you who coaxed your way around him [Adam] whom the devil had not the force to attack. With what ease you shattered that image of God: Man! Because of the death you merited, even the Son of God had to die. ... Woman, you are the gate to Hell.[39]

In the fourth century Augustine of Hippo demanded: 'What is the difference whether it is in a wife or a mother? It is still Eve the temptress we must beware in any woman.'[40] The notion that Eve and, therefore, all women were responsible for the Fall of Man was still commonplace in the sixteenth century; in 1558 John Knox railed against their sex: 'your free will [sexual appetite] has brought yourself and mankind into the bondage of Satan'.[41]

So when Emilia took up the cudgels in the name of womanhood, she was tangling with a millennial tradition of Christian misogyny. In her 'To the Virtuous Reader' she rises to a strident defence of women against calumnies 'practised by euell disposed men, who forgetting they were borne of women, nourished of women, and that if it were not by the means of women, they would be quite extinguished out of the world ... doe like Vipers deface the wombes wherein they were bred'.[42] Extraordinary rhetoric for the Elizabethan age.

In what would be a thrilling – if proven – hypothesis, Kate Emery Pogue suggests that the publication of *Salve Deus* in 1611 was Emilia's rejoinder to the lurid portrait of her which appeared in Shakespeare's sonnets two years earlier: 'Emilia's poems, published in 1611 and strongly defending women, can be read as a riposte to the slanderous characterization.'[43] If London's mice-eyed decipherers had recognized Emilia as the dark lady, perhaps such a response was warranted. Pogue's is an appealing notion even if unsupported (so far).

In a certain sense, Rowse was enemy to his own thesis; he misread Simon Forman's description of a 'very brave' woman as 'very brown', and mistook her husband's name as Will when it was Alfonso. More generally, Rowse's close reading of the sonnets is so persnickety as to imply we can recover whether the toast was burned at breakfast. We may never know if there is any validity to Rowse's inference. But there are broader, tantalizing clues which suggest that Shakespeare and the lady enjoyed the lusty if tempestuous relationship described in the poems. To those already known this chapter proposes to add one more: that Emilia Bassano Lanier provided the model for Shakespeare's Jessica in *The Merchant of Venice*.

A dark Venetian Jew

When Baptiste Bassano, Venetian *converso* Jew and court musician, died in 1576, he left his daughter Emilia penniless; she would receive a legacy of £100 only on attaining the age of twenty-one. For reasons unknown Emilia was taken into the household of Susan Bertie, Countess of Kent (b. 1554); whether as a servant or a ward is still debated. A proto-feminist, Bertie believed that girls should be as well educated as boys. Emilia learned Latin and read the classics, surely along with continuous lessons in poise, grooming, courtly manners, witty conversation, and other ladylike skills – perhaps including mastery of the virginals, a suitable pastime for a musician's daughter.

With her dark skin, raven hair, fine education, and courtly manner Emilia must have been a most desirable young woman. Within months of her mother's death in 1587, eighteen year-old Emilia became the mistress of one of the greatest men in England: Henry Carey, aged sixty-one and old enough to be her grandfather.[44] In the dedication of *Salve* she remembered her patroness as 'the Mistris of my youth, The noble guide of my ungovern'd days'.[45]

According to the diary of Simon Forman (1552–1611), Carey delighted in his young lover and lavished her as well as ravished her. On 3 June 1597 Forman noted, 'She was maintained in great pomp [and] hath 40£ a yere', a substantial stipend.[46] When in 1592 Emilia became pregnant, Carey married her off to her slightly distant cousin Alfonso Lanier, also a court musician. Forman recorded on 17 May 1597, 'yt seams that being with child she was for colour married to a minstrel'.[47] When she bore a son in 1593, plucky Emilia named him Henry, as either a tribute to his natural father or a prod.

As noted, it seems unlikely that Shakespeare would have presumed to share the favours of the mistress of his patron Carey, an old lion inclined to 'sword and buckler men'.[48] That could have been a dangerous game. However, the actor-playwright may well have met Emilia during her liaison with the Queen's cousin, and then offered his services once she was committed to an unwelcome marriage to a poor player and delivered of her child. If Emilia was, in fact, Shakespeare's dark lady, she may have become his mistress *circa* 1594–95, which accords with the putative dates of the writing of the sonnets.

Her marriage proved a sorry one for Emilia, but a brilliant coup for Alfonso; according to Forman, his bride was 'was welthy to him that married her in monie & Jewells'.[49] But a subsequent entry recorded that her dowry had been quickly spent and her marriage a disappointment: 'a nobleman that is ded [Carey] hath Loved her well & kept her and did maintain her longe but her husband hath delte hardly with her and spent and consumed her goods and she is nowe ... in debt'.[50]

Somehow, resilient Emilia not only survived Alfonso and her marriage, but flourished intellectually if not financially. In 1611 she published *Salve Deus Rex Judaeorum*, still considered a work of distinction. Though her dowry had been squandered, her education in the household of Susan Bertie had not; after her husband's death in 1613 Emilia started a school for children of the nobility at St-Giles-in-the-Fields (the venture failed).[51]

Shakespeare's Venetian-Jewish play

That Shakespeare had a passion for Italy seems beyond doubt. From his earliest comedy, *Two Gentlemen of Verona*, to his last solo creation, *The Tempest*, Shakespeare's plays are dotted with Italian locations and characters. Many scholars believe Shakespeare read (and may have spoken) Italian;[52] I've suggested elsewhere that the playwright knew Bandello's *Giulietta e Romeo* in its Italian original.[53] It also seems likely that Shakespeare knew one or more sources of

Twelfth Night – *Gl'ingannati* (1537) and/or *Nicuola and Lattantio* (1554) – in either Italian or French translation. Did Shakespeare acquire his Italian from or because of Emilia? And how did she come by her skill at poetry? Was it at the knee of the Countess or through her own later reading? Or was she perhaps inspired and tutored by the greatest poet of the age? Alluring as those speculations are, one must remember that even the pair's mutual acquaintance is unsubstantiated. As David Bevington asked, 'why doesn't Shakespeare hint at a husband who abuses his wife and spends all the money she brings in from the aging great lord that keeps her, as evidently was the case with Lanier and his wife?'[54]

I suggest that Shakespeare did exactly that – but not in the sonnets. Instead, the playwright wrote into his *The Merchant of Venice* a portrait of wilful Emilia and her failed marriage which, if merely coincidental, is uncannily true to life.

Shakespeare's Jessica is a Venetian Jew kept in the household of a wealthy elderly man. Emilia was twice kept; once by Carey, once by the Countess. In 2.3 we meet Jessica colluding with the servant Lancelet to effect her elopement.[55] That done, in her next breath she announces her intention to forsake her birthright: 'Alack, what heinous sin is it in me To be ashamed to be my father's child! But, though I am a daughter to his blood, I am not to his manners' (16–18). The received (and deeply unsatisfying) interpretation of these lines is that Jessica deplores being a Jew and daughter to a money-lender. But Jessica nowhere shows disdain for Judaism *per se*, nor does she exhibit any hint of Christian religiosity. Besides, money-lending was one of the few legitimate occupations open to the Jews of early modern Venice, and Shylock appears to be a respected member of the Jewish community.[56]

However, if one puts Jessica's words into the mouth of young Emilia Bassano, strong resonances become audible. Emilia was a bastard, and a bastard bore the sin of her conception to the tenth generation according to Deuteronomy 23:2, a book which came in for a good deal of close reading under Queen Elizabeth's father.[57] So a bastard had the best possible reason to declare she was 'ashamed to be my father's child'. Furthermore, though Emilia was 'daughter to the blood' of Baptiste, she had been raised and educated in the household of a countess; surely, she no longer shared his 'manners'. By naming the spendthrift lover of *Merchant* 'Bassanio', was Shakespeare preparing us to receive his portrait of

Emilia née Bassano as Jessica? The names 'Emilia', 'Bassano', and their cognates have long careers in the canon, and Shakespeare created another Emilia in his other Venetian play, *Othello*. Circa 1592 – at the very moment when Emilia's liaison with Carey was ending and she was being shopped to Alfonso – both an Aemilius and a Bassianus appear in *Titus Andronicus*.[58] In *The Taming of the Shrew*, arguably written in 1593, a year after Emilia's troubled marriage to Alfonso, the names of her husband (Alfonso), her father (Baptista), herself (Emilia) appear. Did Emilia's nuptials provide Shakespeare's inspiration for the alliance of his shrewish Katherine with Petruchio? In the final act of *Merchant* her new husband calls Jessica 'little shrew' (5.1.21).

In *Merchant* 2.6 Jessica elopes with Lorenzo. But first she lowers down to him a casket of money and jewels, then pauses to 'gild myself With some more ducats' (50–1). Exactly as Emilia did, Jessica left her old man's household laden with riches to be married to a 'Venetian' boy (though probably born in Rouen, Alfonso was Emilia's cousin). After she has made her escape, we learn of Jessica by hearsay. And what we hear is a study in profligacy. Salanio reports that Jessica made off with 'two sealed bags of ... double ducats' and 'two rich and precious stones' (2.18–20). Shylock learns worse from Nathan: 'Your daughter spent in Genoa, as I heard, one night fourscore ducats' (3.1.98–9). Worse even than that, one of Antonio's creditors 'showed me a ring that he had of your daughter for a monkey' (107–8) which sends Shylock into a paroxysm of grief: 'Thou torturest me, Tubal. It was my turquoise: I had it of Leah when I was a bachelor. I would not have given it for a wilderness of monkeys' (109–11).

Intriguingly, in each report it is 'your daughter', Jessica – not her new lord and husband Lorenzo, and not 'they' together – who squanders Shylock's ducats and trades away his intended's precious gift. If Jessica is the spendthrift of the pair – if she herself wasted her self-bestowed dowry – is that a glance at the fortune which pursued Emilia and her poorish husband Alfonso? Was Forman mistaken (or misled), and was it Emilia herself, accustomed to living on £40 a year plus gifts of jewellery and other emoluments – and not Alfonso – who squandered the endowment Carey made when he passed her off to her cousin? In 3.2 Jessica and Lorenzo are ensconced in the palatial manor at Belmont while Portia and Nerissa ride to the rescue of Antonio. Whether the newlyweds chose to go there – or had to go there because Jessica's stolen dowry was exhausted – is a nice question.

Jessica is now as well set up as, say, Emilia in the household of the Countess of Kent. But her reception in Belmont is not without incident. Greeting her, Gratiano jokes, 'But who comes here? Lorenzo and his infidel?' (217), implying that the stain of Jessica's former religion – exactly like the stain of Emilia's bastardy – wasn't entirely washed away by the baptism she would have had to undergo before she could marry Lorenzo. Despite this momentary flash of prejudice it seems that once settled in Belmont, Jessica has landed on Easy Street. But no.

In 5.1 we discover Jessica and Lorenzo together before the Belmont mansion as a rancorous dialogue ensues. It's night. Lorenzo begins:

> The moon shines bright. In such a night as this,
> When the sweet wind did gently kiss the trees
> And they did make no noise, in such a night
> Troilus, methinks, mounted the Trojan walls
> And sighed his soul toward the Grecian tents,
> Where Cressid lay that night. (1–6)

Readers of Chaucer's *Troilus and Criseyde* or Shakespeare's rewrite would know that while Troilus was mooning over her, Cressida lay with the unappetizing Greek, Diomede. Lorenzo's sweet-sounding words don't conjure an image of love but of a deflowered young woman seizing on the protection of an older man, as Emilia did with Carey.

To Lorenzo, Jessica replies: 'In such a night Did Thisbe fearfully o'ertrip the dew, And saw the lion's shadow ere himself; And ran dismayed away' (6–9). Those who knew the legend or had seen Shakespeare's *A Midsummer Night's Dream* would know that Thisbe's flight led directly to the deaths of Pyramus and herself.

The young Venetian couple's conversation wanders on to Dido (who killed herself because of the inconstancy of Aeneas) and Medea (betrayed by Jason, she murdered him, his new love, the girl's father and everyone else within reach before banishing herself to exile or death).

Then things turn personal.

Lorenzo calls his wife a thief and profligate: 'In such a night Did Jessica steal from the wealthy Jew, And with an unthrift love did run from Venice As far as Belmont' (14–17). Is this a wink at Alfonso's part in the squandering of Emilia's dowry? Jessica returns the compliment, accusing Lorenzo of lying 'with many vows of faith, And ne'er a true one' (17–20) to win her. Lorenzo denies her allegation, saying, 'In such a night Did pretty Jessica, like a little shrew, Slander her love, and he forgave it her' (20–2). Jessica isn't done yet; she declares, 'I would out-night you did nobody come' (23) – I'd go you one better but here comes an intruder.

This is not a happy couple. Indeed, we're given to understand that though Lorenzo still lusts for her, he's lost his luster for her. Jessica has made a bad marriage.

In case we have missed the point, a few moments later Lorenzo waxes rhapsodical:

> Look how the floor of heaven
> Is thick inlaid with patines of bright gold.
> There's not the smallest orb which thou behold'st
> But in his motion like an angel sings,
> Still quiring to the young-eyed cherubins.
> Such harmony is in immortal souls … (58–63)

This is the cue for musicians to enter – just as Emilia's father Baptiste and his colleagues must have been summoned from below stairs to serenade a gaggle of courtiers. Lorenzo cries to them, 'Come, ho! and wake Diana with a hymn, With sweetest touches pierce your mistress' ear, And draw her home with music' (66–8). But when they begin to play, Jessica declares, 'I am never merry when I hear sweet music' (69). It's the dull sound of the other shoe dropping. Like Emilia Bassano, palmed off on a poor court musician, Shakespeare's Jessica has recognized her marriage as a bitter mistake. And if Emilia became Shakespeare's mistress during her unsatisfying marriage with Lanier, he would have heard an earful of disappointment in her pillow-talk.

The Jewish lady of the sonnets

If Shakespeare's portrait of a wilful and bitterly disappointed Jessica was inspired by Emilia and her marriage, this insight resonates with several clues to the identity of the dark lady in his sonnets. In Sonnet 127:

> In the old age black was not counted fair,
> Or if it were, it bore not beauty's name;
> But now is black beauty's successive heir,
> And beauty *slandered with a bastard shame.*
> (1–4, my emphasis)

Shakespeare's Cleopatra will lament that she is 'black', meaning oldish and unhandsome. But in this sonnet the very personification of beauty is both dark-skinned and raven-haired – and also 'slandered with a bastard shame', the stigma Emilia Bassano bore.[59]

In Sonnet 130, the focus is sharpened to bring out the details of the dark lady's presence:

> My mistress' eyes are nothing like the sun;
> Coral is far more red, than her lips red:
> If snow be white, why then her breasts are dun;
> If hairs be wires, black wires grow on her head.
> I have seen roses damasked, red and white,
> But no such roses see I in her cheeks;
> And in some perfumes is there more delight
> Than in the breath that from my mistress reeks. (1–8)

The first and second couplets could describe any dark-complected woman. But the latter's allusion to black, wiry hair seems to glance at a Mediterranean type, particularly in the presence of 'damasked', a word signifying the complex woven fabrics which originated in eleventh-century Damascus, Syria, a city ruled in biblical times by Jewish Israelites before being annexed to the Assyrian Empire in 732 BC. The final couplet which alludes to the 'breath that from my mistress reeks' may be a wink at the *foetor Judaicus*, that distinctive odour attributed to Jews since the Middle Ages, which perhaps derived from the garlic in their diet. Garlic was unknown in England before the mid-sixteenth century. 'Reek' as a noun is a synonym for *foetor*, a Latin word that retains its original form in English. In her *Blood Relations* Janet Adelman wrote that Jews 'are generally depicted throughout the Middle Ages as physically unmistakable, with red or black curly hair, large noses, dark skin, and the infamous *foetor Judaicus*, the bad smell that identified them as Jews.'[60] Garlic was a staple of the diet of Jews dating back to the Egyptian enslavement.[61] 'In Talmud Yerushalmi Tractate Megillah 75a, Ezra [the Scribe] urged men to eat garlic on *Shabbat* as it was an aphrodisiac and would hence help re-populate Israel after the partial return

The dark lady of The Merchant of Venice

from the Babylonia exile.'⁶² In his *Shakespeare and the Jews*, James Shapiro noted that the belief that Jews emitted an unpleasant odour was 'unusually persistent' among Elizabethans.⁶³ Martin Luther, who would in later life turn against the Jews and lay down eight rules for their expulsion from Germany (all of which were adopted during the Third Reich in 1933–45), wrote in his more conciliatory early work *That Jesus Christ was Born a Jew* (1523): 'deal gently with them [the Jews] and instruct them from Scripture; then some of them may come along [be converted]. Instead of this we are trying only to drive them by force, slandering them, accusing them of having Christian blood if they don't stink, and I know not what other foolishness.'⁶⁴ The lady of Sonnet 130 with dark sin, black wiry hairy, and halitosis need not be a Jew. But if she were, the description is remarkably apt. If Emilia's patrimony and misfortune inspired Jessica and her poor choice of Lorenzo in Shakespeare's *The Merchant of Venice*, the vocabulary of Sonnet 134 assumes a new and vibrant hue:

> So now I have confessed that he is thine,
> And I myself am *mortgaged* to thy will,
> Myself I'll *forfeit*, so that other mine
> Thou wilt restore to be my comfort still:
> But thou wilt not, nor he will not be free,
> For thou art *covetous*, and he is kind;
> He learned but *surety-like* to write for me,
> Under that *bond* that him as fast doth bind.
> The *statute* of thy beauty thou wilt take,
> Thou *usurer*, that put'st forth all to use,
> And *sue* a friend came *debtor* for my sake;
> So him I lose through my unkind abuse.
> Him have I lost; thou hast both him and me:
> He pays the whole, and yet am I not free.
>   (1–14, my emphasis)

So much of the drama of *Merchant* is pre-figured in the language of this poem that it seems to demand a connection between his dark lady and the loansharking world of the play Shakespeare wrote in 1596, perhaps within months of writing Sonnet 134.⁶⁵ And finally we come to Sonnet 128:

> How oft when thou, my music, music play'st,
> Upon that blessed wood whose motion sounds
> With thy sweet fingers when thou gently sway'st

> The wiry concord that mine ear confounds,
> Do I envy those jacks that nimble leap,
> To kiss the tender inward of thy hand,
> Whilst my poor lips which should that harvest reap,
> At the wood's boldness by thee blushing stand!
> To be so tickled, they would change their state
> And situation with those dancing chips,
> O'er whom thy fingers walk with gentle gait,
> Making dead wood more bless'd than living lips.
> Since saucy jacks so happy are in this,
> Give them thy fingers, me thy lips to kiss. (1–14)

If we could confirm that Emilia Bassano Lanier had mastered the virginals while in the household of the Countess of Kent – as privileged young women were likely to do, particularly a musician's daughter – I imagine some would consider Emilia's identity as the Dark Lady settled.[66] I already do.

Recognizing that characters and passages in Shakespeare's plays were inspired by people he knew and loved opens a window into the emotional life and mind of the playwright. As we reconsider his *Twelfth Night, or What You Will*, we'll not only marvel at the intellect he marshalled to amuse his Queen and her courtiers. We'll feel the warmth he lavished on friends, his disdain for enemies, and the pangs of Shakespeare's personal losses and the drama of his hopes for heaven.

Notes

1. A. L. Rowse, *Shakespeare's Sonnets* (New York: Harper & Row, 1963), vii.
2. Among Pembroke's advocates: Rowse, *ibid.*, 138–64; John Dover Wilson, *An Introduction to the Sonnets of Shakespeare* (Cambridge: Cambridge University Press, 1964), 72–90; Katherine Duncan-Jones, *Shakespeare's Sonnets*, The Arden Shakespeare, Series 3 (London: Bloomsbury, 2010), 54–7.
3. Leo Daugherty, *William Shakespeare, Richard Barnfield, and the Sixth Earl of Derby* (London: Cambria Press, 2010), 167. Barnfield admired *Venus and Adonis* in 1598 before Shakespeare was known to be its author.
4. F. E. Halliday, *A Shakespeare Companion 1564–1964* (Baltimore: Penguin, 1964), 141–2.

5 First proposed in Thomas Tyler's edition of the *Sonnets* (London: Thomas Nutt, 1890), and later championed by Frank Harris in his play *Shakespeare and his Love* (London: Frank Palmer, 1904) and his book *The Women of Shakespeare* (New York: Mitchell Kennerley, 1911).
6 Shakespeare was variously claimed as natural father or godfather to Jane's son, William, born in 1606. See Arthur Acheson, *Mistress Davenant* (London: Bernard Quaritch, 1913). And he was recently championed by Duncan Salkeld, *Shakespeare among the Courtesans* (Farnham: Ashgate, 2012).
7 G. B. Harrison, *Shakespeare at Work* (London: Routledge, 1933), 310.
8 Paul Edmondson and Stanley Wells, eds, *Shakespeare's Sonnets* (Oxford: Oxford University Press, 2004), 26.
9 A. L. Rowse, *Shakespeare, the Man* (New York: Harper Collins, 1973); A. L. Rowse, ed., *The Poems of Shakespeare's Dark Lady* (New York: Clarkson N. Potter, 1979). For a boisterous and helpful affirmation of Rowse and Emilia, see Martin Green, 'Emilia Lanier IS the Dark Lady'. *English Studie*s 87.5 (October 2006), 544–76. For the dark lady as figment of Protestant imagination see Hugh Richmond, 'The Dark Lady as Reformation Mistress', *The Kenyon Review* 8.2 (1986), 91–105. G. B. Shaw's play *The Dark Lady of Shakespeare's Sonnets* (1910) is a pastiche appeal for the building of a National Theatre on the Bankside (twenty-eight years later he got his wish).
10 The spelling of Lanier's name in sources is given as Aemilia or Emilia, and Lanier or Lanyer. On the basis of spelling in Lorna Hutson, 'Lanier [*née* Bassano], Emilia (*bap.* 1569, *d.* 1645)', *Oxford Dictionary of National Biography*, rev. first published 2004; online edition, January 2012, http://dx.doi.org/10.1093/ref:odnb/37653 (accessed 16 March 2013). I have standardized these throughout as Emilia and Lanier.
11 Katherine Duncan-Jones, ed., *Shakespeare's Sonnets*, The Arden Shakespeare (London: Bloomsbury, 2010), 49.
12 Ilona Aiello, 'Rethinking Shakespeare's Dark Lady', in Michael Schoenfeldt, ed., *A Companion to Shakespeare's Sonnets* (Oxford: Blackwell Publishing, 2007), 294.
13 Garry O'Connor, *William Shakespeare: A Life* (London: Houghton & Stoddard, 1991), 144.
14 Aiello, 'Rethinking', 295.
15 *Ibid.*, 299.
16 Stephen Booth, *Shakespeare's Sonnets* (New Haven: Yale University Press, 1978), 549.
17 Acheson, *Mistress Davenant*, 187, 194.
18 Rowse, *Dark Lady*, 29.
19 Biddy Darlow, *Shakespeare's Lady of the Sonnets* (London: Palantype Organization, 1974).

20 Hugh Calvert, *Shakespeare's Sonnets and Problems of Autobiography*. (London: Merlin Books, 1996), 205.
21 Frances Meres, *Palladis Tamia: Wit's Treasury* (London, 1598).
22 F. E. Halliday, *A Shakespeare Companion 1550–1950* (New York: Funk and Wagnalls, 1952), 610.
23 Roger Prior and David Lasocki, *The Bassanos: Venetian Musicians and Instrument Makers in England, 1531–1665* (Menston: Scolar Press, 1995), 115–16.
24 Susanne Woods, *Lanier: A Renaissance Woman Poet* (Oxford: Oxford University Press, 1999), 92.
25 Katherine M. Wilson, *Shakespeare's Sugared Sonnets* (London: Allen and Unwin, 1974), 83.
26 *Ibid.*, 88.
27 *Ibid.*
28 Woods, *Lanier*, 98.
29 *Ibid.* Also see Susanne Woods, ed., *The Poems of Aemilia Lanier: Salve Deus Rex Judaeorum* (New York: Oxford University Press, 1993).
30 Woods, *Lanier*, 98.
31 Duncan-Jones, *Sonnets*, 53.
32 O'Connor, *Shakespeare*, 143. O'Connor cites a number of reasons why a coquette (or any fastidious Elizabethan) would abstain from intercourse: 'Deficiencies in personal hygiene and widespread gynecological disorders made intercourse often disagreeable or uncomfortable; rotting teeth, bad breath, nauseating skin conditions and constant stomach complaints cannot have helped – and these are apart from the ever-present pox. The man rarely washed anything but his face, neck, hands, and teeth, while a woman neglected her "concealed parts" – witness the Earl of Rochester's later plea: "Fair nasty nymph, be clean and kind And all my joys restore By using paper still behind And sponges for before."' *Ibid.*, 144.
33 David Bevington, 'A. L. Rowse's Dark Lady', in Marshall Grossman, ed., *Aemelia Lanier: Gender, Genre, and the Canon* (Lexington, KY: University Press of Kentucky, 1998), 21.
34 Henry Chettle, *Kind-Hart's Dreame* (London, 1592).
35 René Weis, *Shakespeare Unbound: Decoding a Hidden Life* (New York: Henry Holt and Company, 2007), 169.
36 Aemilia Lanier, *Salve Deus Rex Judaeorum* (London, 1611), 41.
37 *Ibid.*, 77.
38 Jean R. Brink, 'Domesticating the Dark Lady', in Jean R. Brink, ed., *Privileging Gender in Early Modern England*, Sixteenth Century Essays & Studies 23 (1993), 96 ff.
39 Tertullian, *On the Apparel of Women*, I.1, www.newadvent.org/fathers/0402.htm (accessed 5 May 2013).

40 Felecia McDuffie, 'Augustine's Rhetoric of the Feminine in the Confessions: Women as Mother, Woman as Other', in Judith Stark, ed., *Feminist Interpretations of Augustine* (New York: Pennsylvania State University Press 2007), 106. Even the great Thomas Aquinas (1225–74) held bizarre ideas about sex and reproduction: 'woman is defective and misbegotten, for the active force in the male seed tends to the production of a perfect likeness in the masculine sex; while production of woman comes from a defect in the active force or from some material indisposition.' *Summa Theologica*, Ia q.92, a.1, www.newadvent.org/summa/ (accessed 11 August 2011).
41 John Knox, *The First Blast of the Trumpet against the Monstrous Regiment of Women* (Geneva, 1558).
42 Lanier, *Salve Deus*, 19–25.
43 Kate Emery Pogue, *Shakespeare's Friends* (Westport, CT: Praeger, 2006), 63–5.
44 Some believe the liaison began in 1582 when Emilia was thirteen.
45 Woods, *The Poems of Aemilia Lanier*, 18.
46 Simon Forman, Diaries, Bodleian Library, Oxford, MS Ashmole 200, fol. 100*v*.
47 *Ibid.*
48 Wallace T. MacCaffrey, 'Carey, Henry, first Baron Hunsdon (1526–1596)', *Oxford Dictionary of National Biography*, first published 2004; online edition, www.oxforddnb.com/view/article/4649?docPos=15 (accessed 21 June 2012), cites R. Naunton (1649), 102.
49 Forman, Diaries, fol. 100*v*.
50 *Ibid.*, fol. 201.
51 Hutson, 'Lanier [*née* Bassano], Emilia'.
52 A survey by the author of Michele Marripodi's panel on 'Shakespeare and Italy' at the International Shakespeare Conference (Prague, 19 July 2009) revealed that all ten panellists believed Shakespeare read Italian.
53 Steve Sohmer, *Shakespeare for the Wiser Sort* (Manchester: Manchester University Press, 1999), 55 ff.
54 Bevington, 'Dark Lady', 22.
55 Text and lineation from Stanley Wells, Gary Taylor, John Jowett and William Montgomery, eds, *William Shakespeare: The Complete Works*, 2nd edition (Oxford: Oxford University Press, 2005).
56 A more cogent and simpler explanation for Jessica's flight is that she, like Portia, has heated blood, and bridles at being curbed by a father's will.
57 The Geneva text reads: 'A bastard shall not enter into the Congregation of the Lord: euen to his tenth generation shall he not enter into the Congregation of the Lord.'

58 There is also an Aemilia in *The Comedy of Errors*, which is variously dated 1589–95, and an Amelia in *The Winter's Tale* (1611); the female lead of *Two Noble Kinsmen* (1613–14) is named Emilia.
59 In Sonnet 131 it is not only the lady who is 'black', i.e. dark-complexioned, but her deeds. In Sonnet 132 her blackness becomes the paradigm of beauty. But by Sonnet 147 she takes on an even darker coloration: 'For I have sworn thee fair and thought thee bright. Who art as black as hell as dark as night' (13–14).
60 Janet Adelman, *Blood Relations: Christian and Jew in* The Merchant of Venice (Chicago: University of Chicago Press, 2008), 79.
61 Numbers 11:5.
62 Rabbi Arthur Segal, http://rabbiarthursegal.blogspot.com (accessed 6 June 2013).
63 James Shapiro, *Shakespeare and the Jews* (New York: Columbia University Press, 1997), 36.
64 Martin Luther, *That Jesus Christ was Born a Jew* (Wittenberg: Cranach & Doring, 1523).
65 See Sohmer, *Wiser Sort*, 38. Some scholars believe the sonnets were written during the closings of the theatres in 1592–94. But it is possible that the dark lady sequence was written later, perhaps as late as 1596, the year in which Shakespeare wrote and set the action of *Merchant*.
66 The name 'virginals' likely derives from the Latin *virga* signifying the rods which were driven by the keys. More wistfully, the name may be a reflection on the instrument's delicate sound, which is likened to the voices of young girls.

PART II
Queen Elizabeth's *Twelfth Night*

4

Twelfth Night on Twelfth Night

Suppose I could convince you that William Shakespeare wrote *Twelfth Night* for a performance before Queen Elizabeth I on Twelfth Night, 6 January 1601/02? Suppose I demonstrated that Shakespeare laced his play with anagrams because the Queen loved word-games, and anagrams were all the rage at Court? What if I persuaded you that Thomas Nashe (masquerading as the court fool Will Sommers) was his inspiration for Feste? And I deciphered the name of the mysterious Quinapalus as an anagram of two saints – and Pigrogromitus as the anagram of a Pope? To ice this improbable cake, what if I could prove beyond a reasonable doubt that, *by royal fiat*, the 'twelfe day of December' was Christmas in Elizabeth's England – and Sir Toby's mock-carol is only one of the play's calendrical pranks? Finally, suppose I could persuade you that Shakespeare's comedy about fraternal twins (with the boy believed lost at sea and drowned) is the playwright's attempt to reconcile himself to the death of his only son?

If I could do all that, it would change the way you (and the rest of us) think about *Twelfth Night* – wouldn't it?

That's precisely what I intend to do – and I'll begin by proving that during the Christmas revels of 1601/02, Shakespeare and Company played before Queen Elizabeth on Twelfth Night.

The royal performance on Twelfth Night

John Manningham's diary tells us that on the night of 2 February 1601/02 a crowd of privileged young Englishmen and their mistresses and wives attended a play believed to be Shakespeare's *Twelfth Night* in the hall of the Middle Temple, one of London's four legal-social men's foundations collectively known as the Inns of Court.¹ The occasion was Candlemas, officially the Feast of the Presentation of Our Lord in the Temple (Anglican), the Purification of the Blessed Virgin Mary (Catholic), and the Blessing of the Candles (both). It was also a traditional night for playing, being the closing night of Elizabethans' hyper-extended wintertime revels which began at Christmas.²

In 2000, Anthony Arlidge QC, defender of the White House Farm murderer Jeremy Bamber and Master of Entertainments at the Middle Temple, proposed that *Twelfth Night* had its premiere at that venue on Candlemas 1601/02.³ Arlidge's brief received cool reception; there was a sense that we had been down this road (to disappointment) before with Leslie Hotson.⁴ What most severely taxed Arlidge's argument is that the play is named for Twelfth Night, not *Candlemas, or What You Will*. That it might have been written for or received a first performance on 2 February struck a loud discordant note.

I propose to put the question of *Twelfth Night's* royal (and perhaps first) performance to rest.⁵

Although scholars have carefully scrutinized the records of year-end royal revels for 1601/02, they have failed to notice an important detail. I will demonstrate that Shakespeare's company performed before the Queen on a previously unrecognized date: Twelfth Night, 6 January 1601/02. Allow me to make that good.

During the Christmas revels of 1601/02 seven court performances are recorded. The dates are 26 and 27 December; 1, 3, 6, and 10 January; plus one more on 14 February, St Valentine's Day.⁶ So there was a performance of a play before the Queen on Twelfth Night, 6 January. But records show that the company which performed that night wasn't the Lord Chamberlain's Men but the Children of the Chapel. For their part, we know that the Chamberlain's Men (likely including Shakespeare) performed before the Queen on four dates: 26 and 27 December, 1 January, and 14 February.

What scholars have failed to recognize is that Sunday 27 December 1601 in the antiquated English Julian calendar was, according to the reformed Gregorian calendar, Sunday 6 January 1602, Twelfth Night.

Figure 1 shows the rival calendars with the eight last days of Julian 1601 matched to the corresponding dates in the Gregorian

Twelfth Night *on Twelfth Night* 79

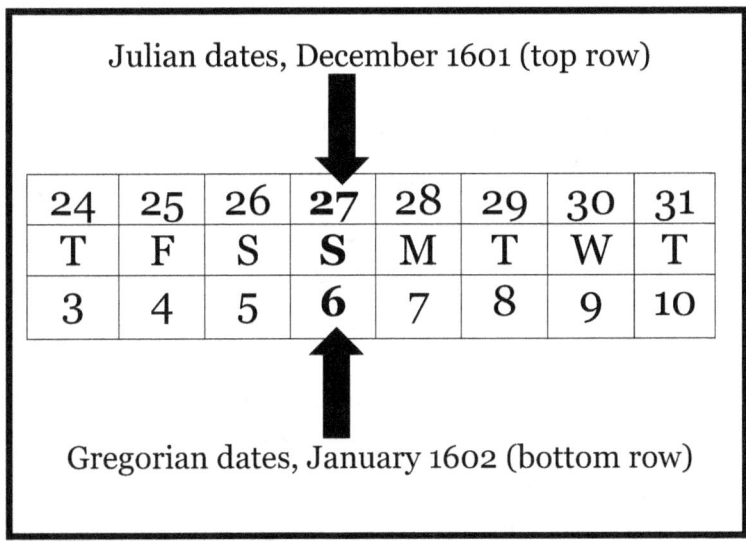

1 Julian and Gregorian calendars, 1601–02

calendar for January 1602. As one can see, the date on which Shakespeare's company performed at Court – Sunday 27 December Julian – was Sunday 6 January Gregorian, Twelfth Night.[7] But would Elizabethans who were living by the scientifically discredited Julian calendar be aware of the 'correct' date in the Gregorian reformed calendar?

After the Bible, almanacs were the most widely circulated printed documents in Shakespeare's England. Almanac-makers – who counted many recusant Catholics among their subscribers – routinely printed the rival calendars side by side in so-called 'dual almanackes' as an 'aide to travellers', or so they claimed. Figure 2 shows a typical example, December in *Farmer's Almanacke*: the Julian dates are in the first left column, the Gregorian in the fifth. Looking closely at the entry for 27 December Julian, one can see that the left column lists the Julian 27 December beside the entry 'John Evang.', signifying the Feast of St John Evangelist. The corresponding Gregorian date is 6 January, which is followed by the entry 'Epiphanie', that is, Twelfth Night.

It was common knowledge among lettered Elizabethans that while they were observing the Feast of St John the Catholic world

Julian date				Gregorian date		
24	a	< ffast	Capri. 1.	3	d	
25	b	Christmas day	Capri. 14	4	e	New Moone.
26	c	Steben martyr	Capri. 25	5	f	the.xxb.day
27	d	John Ebangelist	Aqua. 9	6	g	Epiphany
28	E	Innocents	Aqua. 20	7	A	

2 *Farmer's Almanacke*, December 1601

was celebrating Twelfth Night. And that included many families in those parts of England where the Old Religion haunted the shadows. As Richard Wilson exhibited so persuasively in *Secret Shakespeare*, the playwright's home town of Stratford and the county of Warwickshire were thick with recusants and riddled with priest-holes. Shakespeare, we can be sure, knew 27 December was Twelfth Night. [8]

We now recognize that Shakespeare and company performed before the Queen on Twelfth Night. But was their play *Twelfth Night*? While we have no certain knowledge, we may be able to draw an appealing inference.

In December 1601 the company's repertory included a number of luminous alternatives. Setting aside Shakespeare's histories as long in the tooth and inappropriate for a festive evening, the company might have played *Julius Caesar* or an early *Hamlet* (neither a dainty dish to set before a Queen) or *As You Like It*, which I believe they had played before Elizabeth on Twelfth Night one year earlier during the visit of Duke Orsini (see the discussion below). Among other candidates, *Much Ado* had been assigned to the printers, as had *Merchant*, *A Midsummer Night's Dream*, and *Romeo and Juliet*, which suggests that those plays were past their prime.

Yes, the company could have played any number of old plays by Shakespeare or new plays by other authors. But, thumbing the company's repertory of Shakespeare plays on hand, *Twelfth Night* becomes an attractive choice for a royal audience, a royal venue, and, above all, the occasion. I will show that on the basis of internal evidence, that Shakespeare wrote *Twelfth Night* with an eye towards two performances: one before Elizabeth on 6 January 1602 Gregorian, and a second at the Inns of Court on 2 February 1601/02 Julian.

Twelfth Night, Twelfth Night, and Candlemas

The holy day known as Twelfth Night is also known as the Feast of the Epiphany of Our Lord (Anglican and Catholic),[9] which remembers the discovery by the Magi of the infant Jesus in the manger.[10] In Shakespeare's *Twelfth Night* the action climaxes when – for the first time in three months and one day – Viola and her brother Sebastian discover each other alive. Seeing the identical (though fraternal) twins side by side before her, Olivia cries, 'Most wonderful!' (5.1.219). In Shakespeare's time 'wonderful' had not lost its sense of the miraculous. In *Henry V*, when the King reads out a report of the scale of the English victory at Agincourt, Exeter exclaims, ''Tis wonderful!', that is, miraculous (4.8.114). Henry immediately declares, 'Come, go we in procession to the village: And be it death proclaimed through our host To boast of this or take that praise from God Which is his only' (115–18).

Candlemas celebrates two acts of recognition described in the Gospel of St Luke, chapter 2. On the fortieth day after the birth of Jesus, Mary and Joseph went to the Temple in Jerusalem to complete the rites of *post-partum* purification required of Jewish mothers. She brought with her the infant Jesus, a first-born son. In the Temple the family first encountered Simeon, to whom it had been revealed 'by the Holy Ghost, that he should not see death before he had seen the Lord's Christ'. Luke describes Simeon taking the baby Jesus in his arms and declaring, 'mine eyes have seen thy salvation ... A light to lighten the Gentiles, and the glory of thy people Israel' (Luke 2:22–32). This is overheard by the elderly widow and prophetess Anna, who 'gave thanks likewise unto the Lord, and spake of him [Jesus] to all them that looked for redemption in Jerusalem' (Luke 2:38).

On Candlemas, 2 February, the audience at the Inns of Court was offered a play which climaxes in two acts of recognition, Viola-Sebastian and Sebastian-Viola, presented on a holy day commemorating two acts of recognition. Perhaps this association stuck; twenty years later Shakespeare's company, then the King's

Men, would perform *Twelfth Night* before James at Whitehall on Candlemas, 2 February 1622.[11]

But *Twelfth Night* is equally appropriate as an entertainment for Twelfth Night, 6 January, the Feast of Epiphany and commemoration of the recognition of the infant Jesus by the Magi. The fifth act of Shakespeare's play is packed with epiphanies large and small – including Olivia's discovery Malvolio is not mad, his discovery that Maria wrote the letter that gulled him, everyone's discovery that Toby and Maria have married. The centrepiece of these epiphanies is the twins' discovery that they're both alive – coupled with Orsino discovering that Cesario is the eligible female Viola – and Olivia's discovery that her new husband Sebastian is a complete and utter stranger (which, remarkably, doesn't alarm her in the slightest).

Clearly, the play is appropriate to both occasions. But wherefore came its strange title, *Twelfth Night, or What You Will*?

What who will?

For centuries, the phrase *or What You Will* has been a bafflement to Shakespeare's commentators and directors alike. Much of this difficulty derives from mistaking 2 February as the date of the play's first performance, or for which it was purpose-written. True, time out of mind, religious plays and pageants had been performed in English churches at Candlemas; many portrayed the visit of Mary and Joseph to the Temple and the recognition of infant Jesus. And *Twelfth Night* does climax with a powerful scene of mutual recognition. But, as noted, Shakespeare named his play for Twelfth Night, not Candlemas.

As to speculation about the first night of *Twelfth Night*, Leslie Hotson simply got it wrong when he argued Shakespeare wrote the play as the entertainment at Whitehall on Twelfth Night 1600/01 for Elizabeth and Duke Orsini. Shakespeare's play features a young woman nicknamed 'Madonna' – a name associated with the Virgin Queen of Heaven – who is courted by a duke named Orsino. And Elizabeth did style herself the 'Virgin Queen'. But had Virginio Orsini really travelled to London with flirtation in mind? Virginio was married, and a play implying a liaison with Elizabeth would have given offence to both parties, not to mention Orsini's wife, Flavia. In fact, after the play Orsini wrote to her, describing the evening's entertainment as *una comedia mèscolata, con musiche e balli*, a comedy mixed with music and dancing.[12]

Regarding the choice of entertainment, we know that Lord Chamberlain George Carey earlier had made a note to remind himself

> to confer with my Lord Admirall and the Master of the Revells for taking order generally with the players to make choyse of play that shalbe best furnished with rich apparel, have great variety and change of Musicke and daunces, and of a Subject that may be most pleasing to her Majestie.[13]

Twelfth Night fulfils all the conditions of Orsini's and Carey's descriptions save one: there are no dances intrinsic to the play except for the capering of Toby and Andrew in 1.3, though the players may have performed their traditional jig at its conclusion. On the other hand, both Orsini's and Carey's descriptions neatly fit *As You Like It*; as noted, I believe this play joined the repertory of the Chamberlain's Men by May 1600, and it was this play that was performed before Orsini, Queen, and Court on Twelfth Night 1600/01. *As You Like It* includes music, singing, and dancing as well as Rosalind's gentle jibe at Italian influence on the tastes and manners of English tourists returning from the Continent – certain to elicit a round laugh from its English auditors and a knowing smile from their noble guest (4.1.30–4). As I have suggested above, Shakespeare had completed *As You Like It* in early 1600 to commemorate the seven years' anniversary of the death on 30 May 1593 of his friend and mentor, Christopher Marlowe.[14] The play was in hand, and was a letter-perfect response to Carey's requirements for a royal performance on Twelfth Night 1600/01.

As for *Twelfth Night*, in 1958 L. G. Salingar noted that the play embodies the sense of revelry and misrule that were traditional in Elizabethan celebrations of the Twelve Nights of Christmas.[15] Though certain modern directors have attributed an 'autumnal' atmosphere to the play,[16] its links with Twelfth Night are certainly beyond dispute, and its title is more than appropriate – at least the *Twelfth Night* part. But what about that dependent phrase? What did Shakespeare intend to convey when he wrote '*or What You Will*'? And, not incidentally, who is *You*? Is *You* us, the audience? Or just some general *You*? Or can *You* be a certain someone who had the power to will today's date?

Scholarly attempts to crack the *or What You Will* crux have a long, inglorious, and often humorous history. Lewis Theobald (1688–1744), no mean Shakespearean – he produced in 1726 the Variorum and *Shakespeare Restored*, followed by his own edition of the plays in 1733 – wrote to William Warburton: 'There is no circumstance that I can observe in the Play to give occasion to this name; nothing either to fix it down particularly to Twelfth Night, or to leave it so loose and general a description as What You Will.'[17] A hundred years later, Joseph Hunter (1783–1861) found the play's title 'has no kind of propriety or congruity when looked at in connection with this play; and this must have been evident to Shakespeare himself, since he added to it *or What You Will*. It might be called *Twelfth Night* or by whatever other name.'[18] In July 1887, Hermann Conrad writing in the *Preussische Jahrbücher* inferred that Shakespeare, after puzzling over a title for his play, threw up his hands, crying, 'What to call it, I know not.' Modern editors have done no better.[19] But the keen-eyed Barbara Everett recognized that 'the "sub-title" [*or What You Will*] is really no sub-title, but a generic, perhaps primary, and certainly important part of the title.'[20] In fact, the answer to this riddle is surprisingly simple and as calendrical as play's title.

The Equinoctial Rule of Eusebius

It had been known for a millennium that the calendar which *Julius Caesar* imposed on the Roman world in 45 BC was faulty. It depended on an estimate of the length of the solar year which was a trifle too long. As a result, the Sun ran ahead of the Julian calendar by one day every 128 years, and the solstices and equinoxes arrived one day earlier each year.[21] By AD 325 the Vernal Equinox which Caesar had set on 23–4 March had precessed to 21 March. This presented a significant problem for the Church: Roman and Alexandrine mathematicians could not agree on the date of Easter, the most important date in the Church calendar. To deal with this and other schismatic issues Emperor Constantine convened the Council of Nicaea, whose leading light was Bishop Eusebius of Caesarea (265–340?). When the Council discovered that their hard-pressed mathematicians still could not agree a solution, they decided to hack the Gordian knot. They published and promulgated an Equinoctial Rule for uniformly dating Easter throughout the Church: henceforth, the first new Moon after 21 March would be recognized as the Paschal Moon, and Easter would be celebrated on the Sunday following. The Equinoctial Rule associated with Eusebius remained in force for 1,257 years.

In 1582, after his own mathematicians had struggled with the problem for more than a decade, Pope Gregory XIII imposed on Catholic Europe the reformed calendar which bears his name and is now the standard for most of the world. By then, the equinoxes and solstices were observed thirteen days before their nominal dates in Caesar's original calendar; for example, the Vernal Equinox expected on 23–4 March was observed on 10–11 March. To excise the extra days accumulated by the faulty Julian calendar, Gregory removed ten days from October 1582; the day after 4 October became 15 October. Curiously, Gregory did not fully correct the calendar to the year when Caesar imposed it – nor to the year of the birth of Christ – either of which would have obliged him to excise thirteen days from the present year. Instead, Gregory and his advisors chose to align their reformed calendar to AD 325 – when the Equinox had been observed on 21 March – perhaps to commemorate the Council of Nicaea and the Equinoctial Rule of Eusebius, perhaps because ten was an easier (safer?) number to accommodate than thirteen.[22] Gregory's alteration left England, which reckoned by the old Julian calendar, ten days behind. To keep Sun and calendar in synch in future, Gregory decreed that only centennial years divisible by 400 would be leap years – which meant England would fall another day behind in 1700, 1800, and so on.

Not one to be left ten days behind the whole world, Elizabeth consulted mathematicians John Dee, Thomas Herriot, and Thomas Digges, who satisfied her that the Gregorian reform – though Catholic and based on the Nicaean formulation rather than Caesar's original – was substantially correct.[23] But when Elizabeth moved to adopt the new calendar Archbishop Grindal declared he would support a reformed calendar (and martyrology) only 'after consultation with our brethren [co-religionists] overseas'.[24] To allow Grindal to do so would have effectively repealed the Act of Appeals (1533); it was a price Elizabeth could not and would not pay. Despite calls in Parliament for calendar reform, Elizabeth stood firm. As a consequence England continued to live by its outdated, discredited Julian calendar until Lord Chesterfield's reform took effect in 1752.

So it was Elizabeth's royal will – though not her fault – that fixed the English Twelfth Night on 27 December for the next 168 years.

And it is Elizabeth who is the You of Shakespeare's title, *Twelfth Night, or What You Will*.

That is the solution to one of Shakespeare's most long-debated and vexatious riddles. Below, I'll suggest solutions to a number of *Twelfth Night*'s other nagging cruces: Who is Quinapalus? Pigrogromitus? Who inspired Malvolio and Feste? And what's the meaning of those exasperating letters *M.O.A.I.*?

Notes

1. Manningham wrote: 'Feb. 2. At our feast wee had a play called "Twelue Night, or What You Will," much like the Commedy of Errores, or *Menechmi* in Plautus, but most like and neere to that in Italian called *Inganni*. A good practise in it to make the Steward beleeve his Lady widdowe was in love with him, by counterfeyting a letter as from his Lady in generall termes, telling him what shee liked best in him, and pre-scribing his gesture in smiling, his apparaile, &c., and then when he came to practise making him beleeue they tooke him to be mad.' John Bruce, ed., *Diary of John Manningham, of the Middle Temple, and of Bradbourne, Kent, Barrister-at-Law, 1602–1603* (Westminster: J. B. Nichols and Sons, 1868). Manningham took Olivia to be a widow, perhaps because of her black apparel of mourning for her brother.
2. On Candlemas Eve, families across England took down the ivy, holly, mistletoe, and assorted greens that had decked their halls and cottages since Advent, and began looking forward to the start of a New Year – 25 March according to the English Julian calendar – the withering of winter and first whispers of spring.
3. His most intriguing argument relies on Feste's description of Malvolio's dungeon, 'Why it hath bay windows transparent as barricadoes, and the clearstores toward the south north are as lustrous as ebony' (4.2.36–8), which hardly describes a dungeon but could make a fair description of the hall of the Middle Temple. Anthony Arlidge, *Shakespeare and the Prince of Love: The Feast of Misrule in the Middle Temple* (London: Giles de la Mare Publishers, 2000).
4. Hotson argued that *Twelfth Night* premiered before Elizabeth and an Italian visitor, Don Virginio Orsini, Duke of Bracciano (1572–1615), on Twelfth Night 1600/01. Leslie Hotson, *The First Night of Twelfth Night* (London: Macmillan, 1954).
5. Hotson did scholarship a serious disservice by titling his book *The First Night*. ... It hardly seems likely that Shakespeare's company would have performed a new play for the very first time before the monarch.

Court performances were lucrative and prestigious for players, playwright, and patron; they were not to be taken lightly. If my inference is correct and *Twelfth Night* was purpose-written for two performances on 6 January 1602 Gregorian and 2 February Julian 1601/02 ... and if the former date was the Elizabethan equivalent of the modern English 'press night' or premiere ... when and where might the players have 'previewed' their new play so as to work out the staging and the kinks before a live audience? I'd be glad to hear from anyone who can offer insight at drsohmer@aol.com.

6 Arlidge, *Shakespeare*, 237.
7 Which Elizabethans often referred to as 'Twelfth Day at night' in order to clearly signify not the eve but the evening of 6 January.
8 Richard Wilson, *Secret Shakespeare: Studies in Theatre, Religion and Resistance* (Manchester: Manchester University Press, 2004), 82.
9 During the medieval period, when a day was reckoned to begin at sunset, the eve rather than the night of 5–6 January constituted Twelfth Night.
10 Some scholars believe this visit, if it took place at all, came at a time when Jesus was two years of age. See Bonnie Blackburn and Leofranc Holford-Strevens, eds, *The Oxford Companion to the Year* (Oxford: Oxford University Press, 1999), 21.
11 John H. Astington, *English Court Theatre 1558–1642* (Cambridge: Cambridge University Press, 1999), 255.
12 Hotson, *Twelfth Night*, 15.
13 David Cook, ed., *Dramatic Records in the Declared Accounts of the Treasurer of the Chamber, 1558–1642*, Malone Society Collections 6 (Oxford: Malone Society, 1962), 31.
14 *As You Like It* was entered in the Stationers' Register on 4 August 1600, but remained unpublished until the First Folio of 1623.
15 'The sub-plot shows a prolonged season of misrule, or "uncivil rule", in Olivia's household, with Sir Toby turning night into day; there are drinking, dancing and singing, scenes of mock wooing, a mock sword fight, and the gulling of an unpopular member of the household, with Feste mumming it as a priest and attempting a mock exorcism in the manner of the Feast of Fools.' L. G. Salingar, 'The Design of Twelfth Night', *Shakespeare Quarterly* 9 (1958), 118.
16 Roger Warren and Stanley Wells cite productions by John Barton and Peter Hall in their edition *Twelfth Night, or What You Will*, The Oxford Shakespeare (Oxford: Oxford University Press, 1994), 6.
17 Quoted in John Nichols, *Illustrations of the literary history of the eighteenth century: Consisting of authentic memoirs and original letters of eminent persons; and intended as a sequel to the Literary anecdotes* (London, 1817), II.354.

18 Joseph Hunter, *New Illustrations of the life, studies, and writings of Shakespeare* (London, 1845), I.396.
19 Hermann Conrad, 'Was ihr wollt', *Preussische Jahrbücher*, July–December 1887 (Berlin: George Reimer, 1887), 1–33.
20 Barbara Everett, 'Or What You Will', *Essays in Criticism* 35 (1985), 304.
21 Caesar's Egyptian mathematician, Sosigenes, calculated the solar tropical year at 365.25 days. To account for the quarter-day, Caesar added a leap day in February every four years so as to keep the date aligned with the cycle of the Sun. But the solar year was only 365.224 days long; Sosigenes' tiny error – 11 minutes, 42 seconds – accumulated to a full day every 128 years. That is: every 128 years the Sun, solstices, and equinoxes precessed (moved earlier) by one day in the calendar.
22 Or perhaps because Caesar was a pagan and it was more fitting to refer to a 'Christian' decree than an idolater's.
23 Lord Burleigh has left us a charming aide-memoire in which he recalls perusing a treatise by John Dee and consulting him. Dee proposes an alteration of eleven days, and Burleigh admits, 'I am not skillfull in the theoreeks to discern the pointes and minutes, but yet I am inclined to thinke him in the right line.' Burleigh proposes a conference of mathematicians from the universities to assess Dee's proposal. The note closes with a mysterious reference: 'There appeareth great cawse to have this conference accelerated, for that it [the calendar] is requisite, for a secrett matter, to be reformed by November.' William Cecil, 1st Baron Burleigh, 'Memorial Concerning Dr. John Dee's Opinion on the Reformation of the Calendar', British Library, London, MS Lansd. No. 39, Art 14, Orig.
24 Edmund Grindal, Archbishop of Canterbury, Letter to Queen Elizabeth, 6 March 1583, British Library, London, Add. MS 32092.

5
Shakespeare's *Twelfth Night* wordplay

This chapter examines two aspects of *Twelfth Night* which support my suggestion that Shakespeare wrote the play for performance before the Queen. One is his repeated intrusion of anagrams; the word-game was popular at Court, and the Queen herself known to play at it. The second is the previously unrecognized subject of Feste's 'gracious fooling' to which Andrew refers on the night of their confrontation with Malvolio (2.3). Both would have been of particular amusement and interest to Elizabeth.

Before deconstructing the anagrams in *Twelfth Night* the modern reader should understand the rubrics of the game – the 'posie transposed' – as it was played by Elizabethans. For that purpose we have a rulebook formulated by the author, literary critic, and serial rapist George Puttenham (1529–90). In *The Arte of English Poesie* (1589), he laid down the rules of the game based on transposing the letters of a word (or phrase) to form another:

> One other pretie conceit we will impart vnto you and then trouble you with no more ... the posie transposed or in one word a transpose, a thing if it be done for pastime and exercise of the wit without superstition commendable inough and a meete study for Ladies.[1]

The 'pretie conceit' to which Puttenham refers as a 'pastime and exercise of the wit' was the game with words and their letters that we call anagrams. The fact that Puttenham chose to devote two pages of his treatise to the anagram speaks to the game's popularity in Elizabethan England. Here he explains how the game is played:

> They that vse it for pleasure is to breed one word out of another not altering any letter nor the number of them, but onely transposing of

the same, wherupon many times is produced some grateful newes or matter to them for whose pleasure and seruice it was intended: and bicause there is much difficultie in it, and altogether standeth vpon hap hazard, it is compted for a courtly conceit.[2]

By definition, an anagram is a word, name, or phrase – or complete sentence – formed from another by rearranging its letters, neither adding nor omitting any letter. Among the superstitious, an anagram created from someone's personal name or title was thought capable of providing an insight into the true character of that person, or even rendering a prediction of her or his future fortune. Contriving and interpreting anagrams was a game for the well-educated with the leisure to play it, a 'courtly conceit'.

Puttenham did not invent the game. The anagram had a long history; some think it as old as Moses. Puttenham traced the sport to the Greek Lycophron (third century BC), poet and curator of plays at the library of Alexandria. In the Middle Ages anagrams were an accepted means of interpreting Scripture. Two of the best-known survivals are, first, the opening words of the 'Hail, Mary':

> *Ave Maria, gratia plena, Dominus tecum.*
> Hail, Mary, full of grace, the Lord is with thee.

As an anagram, the Latin becomes:

> *Virgo serena, pia, munda et immaculata.*
> Serene virgin, holy, pure and immaculate.

The other, perhaps more famous model is based on Pilate's question to Jesus, '*Quid est veritas?*' – 'What is truth?' – which becomes the anagram '*Est qui vir adest*' – 'It is the man before you.'

The game was also popular in Italy and France. Catherine de Medici (1519–89) was a fan. Louis XIII (1601–43) employed a Royal Anagrammatist, Thomas Billon, who created from the names and titles of courtiers anagrams which were both entertaining and (believed to be) revelatory.[3] French writers sometimes created *noms de plume* by anagramming their own names. John Calvin (1509–64) turned 'Calvinus' into *Alcuinus* (V and U were considered interchangeable) after the early English theologian (AD 740?–804). François Rabelais (1494–1553) fashioned himself *Alcofribas Nasier*. In fact, Calvin and Rabelais exchanged bitter

Shakespeare's Twelfth Night *wordplay* 91

anagrams of each other's names. Calvin referred to Rabelaesius as *Rabei laesus*, the 'mad man'. Rabelais dubbed J. Calvinus a '*Jan Cul*', that is 'Jackass' (hardly an anagram, but effective).

Puttenham recorded that Queen Elizabeth herself took pleasure in turning courtiers' names into anagrams (note the absent H and the doubled S replacing Z in the Queen's name):

> being informed that her Maiestie [Elizabeth] tooke pleasure sometimes in desciphring of names, and hearing how diuers Gentlemen of her Court had essayed but with no great felicitie to make some delectable transpose of her Maiesties name ...
>
> I tooke me these three words ...
>
> *Elissabet Anglorum Regina.*
>
> Which orthographie (because ye shall not be abused) is true & not mistaken, for the letter zeta, of the Hebrewes & Greeke and of all other toungs is in truth but a double ss hardly vttered, and H. is but a note of aspiration onely and no letter, which therefore is by the Greeks omitted. Vpon the transposition I found this to redound.
>
> *Multa regnabis ense gloria.*
> By thy sword shalt thou raigne in great renowne.

Then transposing the word [*ense*] it came to be

> *Multa regnabis sene gloria.*
> Aged and in much glorie shall ye raigne.
>
> Both which resultes falling out vpon the very first marshalling of the letters, without any darknesse or difficultie, and so sensibly and well appropriat to her Maiesties person and estate, and finally so effectually to mine own wish (which is a matter of much moment in such cases) I tooke them both for a good boding, and very fatalitie to her Maiestie appointed by Gods prouidence for all our comfortes.[4]

Puttenham is quite pleased with his creations, particularly with the ease with which they came to hand, and interpreted that as a good omen for Queen and people. He speaks of these being his first two solutions among *five hundred tries*.[5] Clearly, anagrams was a game for the leisure class.

Another indicator of the popularity of anagrams can be found in *The Works of William Drummond of Hawthornden* (1711). A Scots poet and essayist, Drummond (1585–1649) is best remembered for his conversations with his visitor Ben Jonson in 1613, who himself glanced at the popularity of anagrams among the leisure class in *Epicoene, or the Silent Woman:*

> Cent. 'Tis true, Mavis: and who will wait on us to coach then? or write, or tell us the news then? make anagrams of our names, and invite us to the Cock-pit, and kiss our hands all the play-time, and draw their weapons for our honours? (4.3.45–6)[6]

In Drummond's essay 'On the Character of a Perfect Anagram', he laid down rules for anagramming personal names.[7] One is of immediate interest: 'It was said that no Letter should be taken away; yet, if there be any great Reason ... a Letter may be doubled, as when two Letters appear in a Name one may be abolished, so one of Necessity may be doubled.'[8] *That is, any letter which is present may be repeated more than once, and a letter appearing more than once can be reduced to one appearance.*

Certain letters – S and Z, U and V – were considered identical and therefore interchangeable. I will show that in creating his anagrams for *Twelfth Night* Shakespeare followed these rules. I will also show that some of his anagrams burlesque the conflict between the rival Julian and Gregorian calendars.

How Olivia got a brand new name

Shakespeare's most unmistakable signal of his anagrammatical intent in *Twelfth Night* are the names of his leading ladies. According to Elizabethan rubrics, OLIVIA and VIOLA are anagrams of each other. Both employ all and only the letters A, I, L, O, and V – with Olivia utilizing the letter I twice (as Drummond allowed and as Puttenham did when he anagrammed Elizabeth's name).[9]

Not incidentally, Viola = violet, a flower associated with resurrection since antiquity. Cybele was said to have created violets from the blood of her beloved Attis, who was killed while hunting a wild boar – events replayed in Shakespeare's *Venus and Adonis*. In Christian legend violets sprang spontaneously from the graves of saints and virgins. So Shakespeare built his fraternal twins' link with resurrection into the daughter's very name.

Though their names are anagrams, the two women are of very different stations. Viola's condition is merely 'gentle', while Olivia is a countess and virgin ruler of a household and estate.

Shakespeare gives us several reasons to receive Olivia as an *imaguncula* of Queen Elizabeth, the most conspicuous being Feste's nickname for his mistress, 'Madonna'. The word is Italian, and means 'lady' or 'my lady'. But to the ears of Elizabethans (and us) it recalls the Madonna, Blessed Virgin Mary, mother of Jesus and Virgin Queen of Heaven. As noted, Elizabeth was styled 'the Virgin Queen'. Though Shakespeare could have set Olivia mourning for the death of her brother only, instead she has both a father and brother lost, as had Elizabeth in Henry VIII (d. 1547) and Edward VI (d. 1553).

How Feste got his name

'Feste' is a Shakespearean nonce-word in which commentators have long recognized a hint of 'festive', 'feast', or 'festival', an appropriate connotation for a licensed fool. But Feste would have been recognizable to Elizabeth and her courtiers as the shade of a once-familiar figure at the Queen's court: the jester 'her father took much delight in', Will Sommers (d. 1560); if Olivia is an effigy of Elizabeth, her father was Henry VIII.

Shakespeare could not have known Sommers personally, but he certainly knew his ghost had been dragooned by Thom Nashe as interlocutor of his pageant *Summer's Last Will and Testament*. Nicholl believes that the play was performed – perhaps with Nashe in the title role – in October 1592 at Croydon Palace during the bishopric of John Whitgift, perhaps with Shakespeare in attendance.[10] Nashe's masque begins with the stage direction 'Enter WILL SUMMER, in his fool's coat but half on, coming out.' He declares, 'Will Summer's ghost I should be, come to present you with "Summer's Last Will and Testament.'[11] The play first appeared in print in late 1600, shortly before Shakespeare began work on *Twelfth Night*. As we'll see, Nashe, Sommers, and 'Summer' were intimately bound up in Shakespeare's mind.

The playwright created the name FESTE by rearranging the four letters of the French word for 'summers' – ÉTÉS – as E S T E, then prefixed the letter F signifying 'Foole', as we might use M. for Mister or *Monsieur*, or S. for Saint.

F(oole) ÉTÉS = FESTE.

And likewise: Feste = F(oole) Summers = Sommers.

Whether Elizabeth, who spoke six languages including French, could have deciphered this anagram by ear is doubtful; Feste's name is mentioned only once. So Shakespeare's Valentine drops a heavy hint to the inspiration for Feste when he describes him as 'the jester ... the lady Olivia's father took much delight in' (2.4.11–13). The Queen and her courtiers could hardly disremember the fool who delighted her father for more than two decades. Sommers had served as court fool to Henry VIII from 1525 until the king's death, then under Edward and Mary; he attended Elizabeth's coronation on 15 January 1559 before retiring. Sommers died in 1560 and was buried at St Leonard's, Shoreditch, the parish church of two theatres, the Curtain and the Theatre, which the sometime local resident Shakespeare knew as actor, playwright, and parishioner. James Burbage, Richard Tarlton, and other luminaries of the Elizabethan stage were buried there, as was the infant son of Shakespeare's brother, Edmund – all perhaps with Shakespeare in attendance. I will show that he remembers St Leonard in *Twelfth Night* 3.1.

Shakespeare's saintly anagram

There is another anagram early in the play and, like OLIVIA-VIOLA, it was easily solved by players who knew the rules. It appears when Feste prays,

> Wit, an't be thy will, put me into good fooling! Those wits, that think they have thee, do very oft prove fools; and I, that am sure I lack thee, may pass for a wise man: for what says Quinapalus? 'Better a witty fool, than a foolish wit.' (1.5.29–33)

As to the identity of the mysterious *Quinapalus*, the Oxford footnote speculates that 'Feste invents an authority (Quinapalus). Hotson thinks that the name may be pseudo-Italian, meaning "there on the stick" and referring to the figure of a jester ... Terry Hands thinks it may be French.'[12] But once we recognize that Feste and Shakespeare are playing at anagrams by then-prevailing Elizabethan rules, the solution to this crux is easily within reach.

QUINAPALUS = AQUINAS + PAUL.

Following the rules, the two A's in *Quinapalus* can be increased to three to reveal 'Aquinas' and 'Paul'. As an Elizabethan audience

Shakespeare's Twelfth Night *wordplay* 95

would be well aware, both saints had a good deal to say about fools, fooling, and foolishness.

The scene between Feste and Olivia is rife with theological overtones; a few lines later, Feste offers a parody of the Gospel of St Mark: 'bid the dishonest man mend himself: if he mend, he is no longer dishonest; if he cannot, let the botcher mend him. Anything that's mended is but patched' (1.5.41–3). Mark had quoted Jesus about patching: 'No man sews a piece of new cloth on an old garment: else the new piece take away from the old, and the rent be made worse' (Mark 2:21). This connection would have rung clear during the play's performance at the Inns of Court on Candlemas; Mark 2:21 is the prescribed Gospel reading for the morning service on 2 February. Shakespeare's Inn auditors would have heard or read these words that very morning. This is another indicator that Shakespeare had this performance date in mind when he wrote *Twelfth Night*.[13]

Feste's 'gracious fooling'

Now that we have recognized Nashe-Summer-Sommers behind the mask of Feste, we can turn to the matter of his 'gracious fooling'. On the night of their drinking bout and confrontation with Malvolio, Andrew recalls that Feste

> wast in very gracious fooling last night, when thou spokest of *Pigrogromitus*, of the *Vapians* passing the equinoctial of *Queubus*:'twas very good, i' faith. (2.3.20–3)

What were Feste, Andrew, and Toby talking about last night? The first item that jumps out at us is 'the equinoctial of *Queubus*', which by now should not be difficult to recognize as Andrew's drunken slurring of 'the Equinoctial Rule of Eusebius', the decree issued by the Nicaean Council.[14] But how did Eusebius get mixed up with *Pigrogromitus* and the *Vapians*?

To parse *Pigrogromitus* we must first correct a typesetter's error. Typographical mistakes were common with letters which employ the *minim* or short vertical stroke, as does 'm'; here the typositor set an 'm' where Shakespeare wrote 'n'. Once we have corrected the text to Shakespeare's original '*Pigrogronitus*', it's a simple matter to discover the name concealed in this anagram:

PIGROGONITUS = PONT. GRIGORIUS.

'Pont.' is an abbreviation of *Pontifex*. *Pigrogronitus* is an anagram of the Latin name of Pope Gregory, *Pontifex Grigorius,* who issued the reformed calendar.

What of the '*Vapians*'? This appears to be an obvious anagram for 'Pavians', the mathematicians at the University of Pavia, who included Girolamo Cardano (1501–76), the compulsive gambler who first formulated rudimentary laws of probability. If this inference is correct, we could decipher and paraphrase Andrew's statement as 'Pope Gregory and the Pavians ratifying the Equinoctial Rule of Eusebius'[15] – that is, the Pope's decision to remove ten days from October 1582 to conform his new calendar with the radix at the time of the Council of Nicaea.

During his travels Feste has learned about the Gregorian reform and has tried to explain it to Toby and Andrew. That Toby sings 'O, the twelfe day of December' suggests that he, at least, got the point (see the discussion below). But Andrew drunkenly slurs the words he heard on the previous night – and hasn't a clue what they meant; that is probably a fair reflection of the way calendar reform was misunderstood by many of Elizabeth's courtiers. For those with little training in history or maths, calendar reform must have appeared an abstruse, problematical subject. After speaking before Parliament on the subject of the need for calendar reform in 1751, Lord Chesterfield wrote to his son:

> I have of late been a sort of an *astronome malgre moi*, by bringing last Monday, into the House of Lords, a bill for reforming our present [Julian] Calendar, and taking the [Gregorian] New Style. Upon which occasion I was obliged to talk some astronomical jargon, of which I did not understand one word, but got it by heart, and spoke it by rote from a master [crib].[16]

Like Andrew and Lord Chesterfield, many of Elizabeth's courtiers were entirely flummoxed by calendar reform. But not the Queen.

The proper date of Christmas

This brings us to Toby's song, 'O[h], the twelfe day of December' (2.3.83). Commentators' guesses at the significance of Toby's verse run the gamut from improbable to absurd. But the solution to this crux is quite simple and must have been instantly apparent to

Elizabeth and at least some of her courtiers while attending a play called *Twelfth Night* on the Julian 27 December.

Gregory had excised only ten days from the calendar – whereas the Sun had run thirteen days ahead of the Julian calendar since Caesar imposed his reform in 45 BC.[17] Consequently, in Julian England the true anniversary of the birth of Christ – Christmas – was 12 December, that is, 12 + 13 = 25. Clearly, calendar maths and disconnects among the Julian, Gregorian, and Caesar's original calendars were in the air that evening in Illyria when Toby, Andrew, and Feste woke up the house and provoked the ire of Malvolio.

As has become apparent, *once the context of the Julian-Gregorian calendar controversy is recognized*, solving Shakespeare's anagrams in *Twelfth Night* becomes child's play. Scholars who have been reluctant to accept Shakespeare's intense interest in calendar lore and chronometry may wish to reconsider their views.

But here's a good question – how could Elizabeth and her courtiers guess that the comedy that evening concerned calendar reform? Well, if someone took to you to the theatre on the Julian 27 December, the Feast of St John – which your almanac told you was 6 January, Twelfth Night – and you discovered that the name of the play was *Twelfth Night* – and a major domo announced the play by proclaiming 'Your Majesty, *Twelfth Night, or What You Will*' – well, I suspect some of us would instantly be in on the joke. Surely, Elizabeth was.

Notes

1. George Puttenham, *The Arte of English Poesie* (London, 1589), 91.
2. *Ibid.*
3. See for example Billon's pamphlet *Les presages d'bon-heur du Roy, et de la France* (Paris: A. Savgrain, 1617), which offers forty-five anagrams on the phrase 'Louis Treisiesme de Bourbon Roy de France et de Navarre', each one a prediction of the future.
4. Puttenham, *Arte*, 92–3.
5. 'The same letters being by me tossed & tranlaced fiue hundreth times, I could neuer make any other, at least of some sence & conformitie to her Maiesties estate and the case.' *Ibid.*, 93.
6. *The Works of Beniamin Ionson* (London: William Stansby, 1616).
7. John Sage and Thomas Ruddiman, eds, *The Works of William Drummond of Hawthornden* (Edinburgh: James Watson, 1711), 230–1.

8 *Ibid.*
9 Patrick Hanks, Kate Hardcastle, and Flavia Hodges, *A Dictionary of First Names*, 2nd edition Oxford Paperback Reference (Oxford: Oxford University Press, 2006), 210. I'm indebted to Paul Budra for pointing out that 'Olivia' appears as a given name as early as the early thirteenth century.
10 Charles Nicholl, *A Cup of News: The Life of Thomas Nashe* (London: Routledge & Kegan Paul, 1984), 136.
11 Ronald B. McKerrow, ed., *The Workes of Thomas Nashe*, 5 vols (London: Sidgwick and Jackson, 1904–10, repr. Oxford: Basil Blackwell, 1958), III.227 ff.
12 Roger Warren and Stanley Wells, eds, *Twelfth Night, or What You Will*, The Oxford Shakespeare (Oxford: Oxford University Press, 1994), 104n.
13 Not incidentally, in Act 5 Shakespeare jokes about the rigid linking of scriptural readings to specific dates. Feste declares that 'a madman's epistles are no gospels, so it skills not much when they are delivered' (5.1.270–1), a wink at the rubrics of the Book of Common Prayer which required that passages of Scripture be delivered on particular days.
14 Andrew's drunken slurring of 'Eusebius' into 'Queubus' may have been inspired by Shakespeare's recollection of a passage in Nashe's *The Unfortunate Traveler, or the Life of Jack Wilton*. Jack persuades a hapless Captain to embark on a fool's mission to enter the enemy camp and assassinate the French King. The King wisely insists that his officers search the Captain: 'In was Captain Gog's Wounds brought, after he was throughly searched; not a louse in his doublet was let pass but was asked *Queuela* and charged to stand in the King's name ....' (McKerrow, *Nashe*, II.223.12). *Queuela* is a curious construction, perhaps a Nashean wordplay. McKerrow thinks it derived from *Qui va là?* – meaning 'Who goes there?' – the familiar challenge. From Nashe's neologism Shakespeare fashioned Andrew's *Queubus* – that is, '*Queu–bus*'. Andrew, who has never heard the name but once and cannot remember it, is saying 'whatshisname-bus'.
15 Though the solution seems simple enough, Shakespeare's reference to 'the Pavians' is something of a conundrum. The principal work on calendar reform was not done by Cardano and the Pavians; rather, it was led by the Veronese mathematicians Aloysius Lilius (1510–76) and Pietro Pitati (fl. *ca.* 1550) and the German Christopher Clavius (1538–1612). By 1603–04 Shakespeare seems to have become aware of the link between mathematicians and Verona; his 'great arithematician' in *Othello*, Michael Cassio, is Veronese, not Florentine as the liar Iago suggests. See my essay '"Mention my name in Verona": Is Cassio

Florentine?', in Frank Occhiogrosso, ed., *Shakespeare Closely Read* (Lanham, MD: Rowman & Littlefield, 2011), 69–80.
16 Charles Sayle, ed., *Letters Written by Lord Chesterfield to his Son* (New York: Walter Scott, 1900), 199.
17 Between Caesar's reform in 45 BC and Gregory's in 1582, the Sun had run ahead of the Julian calendar $12.71 = 13$ days. The math is: $(45 + 1582) \div 128 = 12.71$.

6

Shakespeare and Paul in Illyria

In his lectures on *Twelfth Night* Emrys Jones insisted that 'the whole play drives toward the moment of the twins' reunion'. Indeed, reunion – better yet, *resurrection* – is (to use Molly Mahood's choice words) the principal 'governing idea' of the play. I will show that there is a link between reunion-resurrection, Candlemas, and William Shakespeare's own real-life drama that has been overlooked by his commentators and is key to appreciating his play.

Twelfth Night begins with Viola convinced that her brother, Sebastian, is dead; with practically her first breath she tells us 'My brother he is in Elysium' (1.1.4). So what we will be confronted with in 5.1 is not merely a family reunion but something of a resurrection. We must bear this in mind when we consider the personal significance for William Shakespeare of his play's performance on Candlemas.

Though *we* know Sebastian is alive, to Viola he is so convincingly dead that she has turned herself into his image. When she looks into her mirror she sees not herself but Sebastian.

> I my brother know
> Yet living in my glass; even such and so
> In favour was my brother, and he went
> Still in this fashion, colour, ornament,
> For him I imitate. (3.4.376–80, my emphasis)

This echoes Constance's (and Shakespeare's) lament for a lost son in *King John*: 'Grief fills the room up of my absent child … Puts on his *pretty looks* … Stuffs out his *vacant garments*' (3.4.93–8, my emphasis). Arthur had been kidnapped; Shakespeare's own son Hamnet has died. The grieving mother, sister, and playwright-father remember their boys' *favour* = pretty looks and *fashion* = vacant garments. This is not just poetry; it's personal.

The date of Candlemas, 2 February, had a deeper significance for Shakespeare than has been recognized. His own fraternal twins, Judith and the deceased Hamnet, had been baptized in Holy Trinity Church at Stratford-upon-Avon on Candlemas, 2 February 1585. The date of *Twelfth Night*'s performance at the Inns, 2 February 1602 – a date which can be expressed as 2.2.2 – was the seventeenth anniversary of the twins' baptism. By age eleven Hamnet was dead. Whether the cause of the boy's death was accident or illness – or did he perhaps drown in the River Avon? – is unknown. The parallels between the real and fictional fraternal twins are simply too pointed and poignant to ignore. Did Shakespeare recognize in his Judith flashes of his lost Hamnet? In Sebastian has Shakespeare, on a wish, resurrected his Hamnet and fashioned him as dashing, loyal, brave, handsome, witty – and then married him to a countess?

Curiously, from the dialogue between the twins at their reunion, neither seems prepared to take their good fortune at face value. Just as Viola believes her brother drowned, Sebastian believes Viola dead. There is wariness and scepticism in their words:

> *Seb.* Do I stand there? I never had a brother;
> Nor can there be that deity in my nature,
> Of here and every where. I had a sister,
> Whom the blind waves and surges have devour'd.
> Of charity, what kin are you to me?
> What countryman? what name? what parentage?
> *Vio.* Of Messaline: Sebastian was my father;
> Such a Sebastian was my brother too,
> So went he suited to his watery tomb:
> If spirits can assume both form and suit
> You come to fright us.
> *Seb.* A spirit I am indeed,
> But am in that dimension grossly clad
> Which from the womb I did participate.
> Were you a woman, as the rest goes even,
> I should my tears let fall upon your cheek,
> And say 'Thrice-welcome, drowned Viola!' (5.1.222–37)

Even now, Viola still doubts. She tries him with two more details.

> Vio. My father had a mole upon his brow.
> Seb. And so had mine.
> Vio. And died that day when Viola
> from her birth had number'd thirteen years.
> Seb. O, that record is lively in my soul!
> He finished indeed his mortal act
> That day that made my sister thirteen years. (5.1.238–44)

This is a reunion – and epiphany – very different from the sudden 'O, she's warm!' of Leontes in *The Winter's Tale* or Claudio's 'Another Hero!' at his bride's unmasking in *Much Ado*. In the climax of *Twelfth Night*, the parties to the mutual act of recognition approach each other with that precursor to and enemy of faith, *doubt*, before they embrace their resurrection and each other. It is their mutual doubt that lifts the moment above what might otherwise have passed as coincidence.

I suggest that on 2 February 1601/02 Shakespeare put before the auditors at the Inns of Court a play that was a mimetic response to his own misfortune, the tragedy of his own twins. And what he set on stage before the Queen on the true date of Epiphany was his own hope of heaven. The twins' reunion scene is steeped in pathos. To write it, Shakespeare must have paid a high price. He may have been a fervent Protestant or a recusant Catholic; we just don't know. But he couldn't have written this scene – this play – unless he was, at heart, a believer and a grieving father.

Shakespeare's Paul

To judging from his frequent citings, the Psalms and the Epistles of St Paul were among Shakespeare's favourite passages of Scripture. He wrote two plays set in locales Paul knew well: *The Comedy of Errors* in Ephesus and *Twelfth Night* in Illyria. Paul preached the Gospel in both places, and both plays were written for and/or performed before elite auditors at the Inns of Court and Whitehall. As Shakespeare developed each of these scripts he drew his plots from previously published plays and novels: Plautus' *Menaechmi* for *Errors*, Barnaby Riche's *Apolonius and Silla* for *Twelfth Night*. Then Shakespeare extensively engaged two of the Epistles of Paul: for *The Comedy of Errors* the Epistle to the Ephesians; for *Twelfth Night* the Epistles to the Corinthians. Shakespeare also relocated the action: Plautus' Epidamnum became Paul's Ephesus; Riche's Constantinople became Paul's Illyricum. By examining the secular and sacred sources of *Twelfth Night* in tandem, I propose to interrogate Shakespeare's method of composition and discover why he relocated the action in his source.

Corinthians and Illyrians

Shakespeare's principal source for *Twelfth Night* was the tale of *Apolonius and Silla*, which stood second in a collection by Barnaby Riche (*ca.* 1540–1617), *Riche's Farewell to the Militarie Profession* (1581). Some scholars are inclined to believe that Shakespeare also knew, in either its Italian original or French translation, *Gl'ingannati* ('The Deceived'), composed by the members of the Academy of the *Intronati* (The Bewildered) of Siena, performed in 1532 and published in 1537. I intend to briefly revisit each of these putative sources to consider elements Shakespeare may have drawn from them, and to illustrate material alterations he made as he merged the sources with Paul's letters to the Corinthians.

Gl'ingannati is a stagey but funny, bawdy play; by comparison Shakespeare's version is stuffy. The Italian comedy is set in contemporary Siena and, as it begins, young heroine Leila is already disguised in boy's clothing, has taken the name Fabio, and is employed as a page by her beloved Flamminio, who is lovesick for Isabella, who scorns him but lusts for Leila-Fabio. A similar love triangle appears in *Twelfth Night* with Viola-Cesario as the hypotenuse. The Italian play also includes wily servants, silly old men, and the timely return of Leila's twin brother, Fabrizio, kidnapped during the siege of Rome in 1527. When the latter is locked in Isabella's bedroom, she mistakes him for Leila-Fabio and beds him on sight, after which all conturbations sort themselves out (sort of). The idea to craft this story into a play purpose-written for performance on Twelfth Night may have occurred to Shakespeare while reading the prologue of *Gl'ingannati*. Its authors declare: 'The story is new and taken from nowhere but their own industrious pates whence also are taken your lots on Twelfth Night.'[1] A reference to Twelfth Night also occurs in 1.2 of the Italian play.

Riche's tale – itself based on Luigi Bandello's story *Nicuola and Lattantio* – is less sexual but far more sensational; the two iterations contrast the differing mores of (liberal) Italian and (repressed) English society. Riche provides only a half-hearted attempt at rape and a threatened but never-acted suicide. There is a shipwreck of which Silla is the sole survivor, an identical brother and sister, and the familiar tactic of a woman disguised as a man. In Riche's version, the missing brother, Silvio, is merely away from home. In Shakespeare's he becomes Sebastian, the fraternal twin believed drowned and dead. Both these alterations elevate the pathos of loss and thrill of reunion in *Twelfth Night* and demonstrate Shakespeare's skill at raising the stakes.

Shakespeare's most significant alteration to Riche's tale is the relocation of the action from the exotic venues of Constantinople and Cyprus to little-known Illyria. This raises an intriguing question: why was it necessary to remove the two stories to venues associated with Paul's letters? Couldn't the *sententiae* of Ephesians or Corinthians have been equally relevant in, say, Vienna or Venice? Of course they could. But Shakespeare relocated the stories to venues associated with his New Testament sources because *in these places God enabled Paul to perform conspicuous miracles*. Shakespeare moved the setting for *Errors* to Ephesus because it was there, St Luke tells us, that 'God wrought no small miracles by the handes of Paul' (Acts 19:11). In 2 Corinthians Paul declares, 'The signes of an Apostle were wrought among you with all patience, with signes, and wonders [miracles], and great workes' (12:12). Shakespeare's Olivia will declare the appearance or reunion of the twins before her 'Most wonderful' (5.1.235), that is, miraculous.

Shakespeare would make miracles happen in his Ephesus and Illyria as they did in Paul, and he wished his audience to be inclined to accept them as something more than coincidences. *The Comedy of Errors* includes what seems a minor miracle but is actually colossal; a clock that twice strikes the hour of one (4.2.52–62), which suggests that time went backwards to spare the life of Egeon until his family recognized him and each other. Such a miracle is recorded only once in the Old Testament; no commentator seems to have traced it to the prophets Hezekiah and Isaiah in 2 Kings 20 (see 'No small miracle: the twice-striking clock in *The Comedy of Errors*' in 'Longer notes' below). The miracle in *Twelfth Night* is visual rather than aural, and far more sensational: Shakespeare resurrects a 'dead' brother and reunites him with the twin sister whom he believed drowned and dead.

The Elizabethans' Illyria

What did 'Illyria' signify for Shakespeare's Elizabethan auditors? And what impression of Illyria did his auditors carry with them into the playhouse? For one thing, Elizabethans knew Paul brought the Gospel to Illyria. He says so in Romans: 'Through mighty signs and wonders [miracles], by the power of the Spirit of God; so that from Jerusalem, and round about unto Illyricum, I have fully preached the gospel of Christ' (15:19).[2] The region lies along the eastern Adriatic and now includes parts of the Balkan countries.

Between 229 and 169 BC, Romans crossed the Adriatic in successive waves of bandits, legions, merchants, and administrators who established the province of Illyris Romana, known as Barbara for its unruly tribes. By the time Paul arrived in Illyricum (*ca.* AD 54–8) Nero reigned as Emperor at Rome and there were thriving ports along its Dalmatian coast. Paul preached there while shuttling to and fro from Corinth. Figure 3 shows a portion of the calendar of daily readings for January in the Book of Common Prayer (1599).

Against the date 20 January (left arrow) is noted the Feast of Fabian (and Sebastian). A feast day began with its vigil, that is, at sunset of the prior day. The reading of 1 Corinthians began with evening prayer on the night of 19 January (right arrow), the vigil of the Feast of Fabian and Sebastian. So perhaps it's no coincidence that Shakespeare endowed two characters in *Twelfth Night* with the names of these minor saints.[3] I will show that many of the themes Shakespeare explores in *Twelfth Night* were drawn directly from Paul's complaints about the behaviour of the Corinthians.

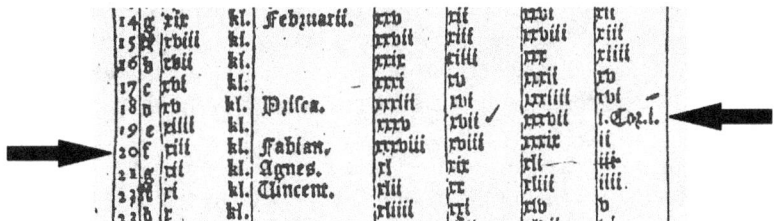

3 Book of Common Prayer calendar, January

Paul harangues the Corinthians

Paul wrote two lengthy letters to the Corinthians and visited them three times.[4] He lavished attention because the idolatrous crew were having a hard time adapting to Paul's ascetic, egalitarian brand of Christianity. Let me enumerate some of their foibles which Paul castigated in 1 Corinthians; Shakespeare visited every one of these misbehaviours on his Illyrians.

Paul complains of divisions and factionalism between and within households: 'For it hath bene declared vnto me, my brethren of you by them that are of the house of Cloe, that there are contentions among you' (1 Corinthians 1:11). Certainly, there are contentions in the household of Olivia.

Paul deplores reports that stewards (like Malvolio) were in danger of becoming unfaithful: 'let a man so thinke of us, as of ... the disposers [King James Version: stewards] of the secrets of God. And as for the rest it is required of the disposers [stewards] that euery man be found faithful' (1 Corinthians 4:1–2).

Servants (Malvolio) were seized with ambition; Paul warned, 'Let euery man abide in the same vocation wherein he was called' (1 Corinthians 7:20). To those bridling at their low station he wrote, 'Art thou called [galled at] being a seruant? care not for it' (7:21). The marginal gloss in the Geneva Bible reads: 'Althogh God hathe called thee to serue in this life, yet thinke not thy condition vnworthie for a Christian ... For he that is called in the Lord, being a seruant, is the Lords freeman.'

Paul complains, 'It is heard certainly that there is fornication among you' (1 Corinthians 5:1). Paul orders Corinthians (Toby and Maria?) to 'Flee fornication: euery sinne that a man doeth, is without the bodie: but hee that committeth fornication, sinneth against his owne bodie' (6:28). Paul's sequence of ideas fornication → body apparently stuck in Shakespeare's mind: in 1.3 Toby urges Andrew to 'Accost [Maria] ... front her, boord her' (54–5); when she rebuffs him, the pair fall to talking about the quality of their bodies: hair, legs, throats, and dancing skills (92–100, 110–37).

Paul protests the Corinthians' bouts of raillery and drunkenness much like the revels in Olivia's household: 'When ye come together therefore into one place, this is not to eate the Lords Supper. For euery man when they should eate, taketh [eats] his owne supper afore, and one is hungry, and another is drunken.' (1 Corinthians 11:20–1). Indeed, for Shakespeare and Elizabethans Corinth was synonymous with dissipation and licentiousness; in *1 Henry IV* the tavern-boys salute the layabout, carousing Hal as 'a Corinthian' (2.4.11).

Another problem: Corinthian men are becoming haughty. To use Paul's phrase, 'puffed up': 'Some are puffed vp as though I woulde not come vnto you.' (1 Corinthians 4:18). That's Malvolio's condition, as Fabian observes, 'see how imagination [ambition] blows him [up]' (2.5.40–1).

Paul also complained that some Corinthians were speaking in strange and undecipherable tongues, as will Andrew and Feste:

> if I come vnto you speaking diuers tongues, what shall I profite you, except I speake to you, either by reuelation, or by knowledge, or by prophecying, or by doctrine? So likewise you, by the tongue, except yee vtter wordes that haue signification, howe shall it be vnderstand what is spoken? (1 Corinthians 14:1–9).

In 2.3, Andrew muddles, 'thou spok'st of *Pigrogronitus,* of the *Vapians* passing the equinoctial of *Queubus*', and Feste replies with a muddle of his own: 'I did impeticos thy gratillity: for Maluolios nose is no Whip-stocke. My Lady has a white hand, and the *Mermidons* are no bottle-ale houses' (2.3.21–27).[5]

A problem which Paul particularly deplored was that *caritas* was in decline among the Corinthians, and the collecting of alms had lapsed. Paul commanded them: 'Concerning the gathering [of alms] for the Saintes ... Euery first day of the weeke, let euery one of you put aside by himselfe, and lay vp as God hath prospered him, that then there [need] be no gatherings when I come' (1 Corinthians 16:1–3). Paul was a great beggar (as is Feste), who brought a substantial sum to support the Apostles and brethren in Jerusalem after fourteen years; I will show that Shakespeare remembers Paul's tale of this donation in Galatians 1:1 during Feste's exchange with Sebastian in 4.1.

Elizabethans who were regular readers of the Bible could not have failed to recognize a multitude of parallels between the problems Paul confronted in Corinth and those which Shakespeare contrived for his Illyria. Paul also reprimanded Christians for bringing lawsuits against each other in pagan courts: 'Dare any of you, hauing businesse against an other, be iudged vnder the vniust [pagans], and not vnder the Saintes? ... I speake it to your shame ... a brother goeth to law with a brother, and that vnder the infidels' (1 Corinthians 6:1–6). Doesn't this finally explain Shakespeare's sudden and otherwise inexplicable allusion to Malvolio's lawsuit against Viola's loyal Captain, 'The Captain that did bring me first on shore ... upon some action is now in durance at Malvolio's suit' (5.1.258–60)?

Most significant, Paul chastised the Corinthians for losing faith in the resurrection of the dead: 'Now if it be preached, that Christ is risen from the dead, how say some among you, that there is no resurrection of the dead?' (1 Corinthians 15:12–18). Isn't this the issue when Feste chastises Olivia for the protracted mourning of her brother?

> *Clo.* Good madonna, why mournest thou?
> *Ol.* Good fool, for my brother's death.
> *Clo.* I think his soul is in hell, madonna.
> *Ol.* I know his soul is in heaven, fool.
> *Clo.* The more fool, madonna, to mourn for your Brother's soul
>   being in heaven? (1.5.62–7)

Twelfth Night is, first and foremost, a play about resurrection and reunion, the central, overarching and defining promise of Christianity: that faith in Christ can bring believers eternal life. Believing that Jesus was raised from the dead is the acid test for every Christian; the question for the faithful is not whether Jesus lived and died, but whether he died and lived. Faith in a resurrection and reunion with lost loved ones in another, better world is the preeminent governing idea of Shakespeare's play. It is present at Viola's first appearance: 'What should I do in Illyria? My brother he is in Elysium' (1.2.2–3). The wordplay on Illyria-Elysium immediately conjures a connection. Below I will have more to say about why I believe this was the opening scene of the play.

As Shakespeare did when he relocated *The Comedy of Errors* to Ephesus, he shifted the action of *Twelfth Night* from Constantinople to Illyria in order to bring into play an Epistle of St Paul. Paul's letter to the Corinthians not only inspired many themes of Shakespeare's comedy; it wraps the climactic reunion in Paul's promise of the miraculous resurrection of the dead. It's not difficult to see how, in the mind of a playwright mourning his only son, this scene was a dream come true.

Notes

1 Geoffrey Bullough, *Narrative and Dramatic Sources of Shakespeare*, 7 vols (New York: Columbia University Press, 1975), II.287.
2 Modern commentators are divided as to whether Paul preached the Gospel in Illyria itself or merely 'as far as' Illyria, meaning he reached only the district's southern borders north of Greece.
3 Keir Elam, ed., *Twelfth Night*, The Arden Shakespeare, Series 3 (London: Bloomsbury, 2009), 23.
4 A third letter to the Corinthians is believed to have existed but is now lost.
5 The exact meaning of Feste's reposte still eludes Shakespeare's commentators. What seems plain is that Feste either pocketed the coin or slipped it to his leman = lady friend. 'Mermidons' is perhaps a glance at the Mermaid Inn, where Shakespeare and Jonson are said to have taken liquid refreshment of proper kegs, not bottled ale.

7

Nashe and Harvey in Illyria

I've suggested that in *As You Like It* Shakespeare etched into Touchstone an effigy of Thomas Nashe. I will show that in *Twelfth Night* Shakespeare produced another, more highly developed portrait of Nashe as Feste – and thrust him back into conflict with his real-life nemesis Gabriel Harvey, whom Shakespeare cast as Malvolio – 'He who wishes evil' – the pretentious, over-ambitious steward. We will find that Shakespeare has drawn a Pauline Feste-Nashe with an adroitness and sophistication which leaves one quite awestruck, and that he derived his caricature of Malvolio-Harvey (and the letter-plot that precipitates his downfall) from accounts of Harvey's follies published by Nashe. By so doing, Shakespeare enabled the departed Nashe to continue to persecute and torment his *bête noire*. I will also show that Shakespeare blended Nashe and Paul to create an extraordinary fool whose humour, *gravitas*, and ultimate pathos surpass anything in Touchstone – and did so by exploiting the Epistles to the Corinthians.

A Pauline Feste

Circa AD 5, the theologian we know as St Paul was born Saul, a Jew and Roman citizen, in Tarsus, south-central Turkey, a dozen miles from the sea; in *Antony and Cleopatra* Shakespeare remembers that illustrious couple's fateful meeting on Tarsus's River Cydnus. Saul was a compulsive wanderer who was to scour Asia Minor preaching the faith of Jesus. But he began his travels in his youth and was raised a Pharisee in Jerusalem, where he studied with Rabbi Gamaliel, so he was predisposed to believe in the resurrection of the dead.[1] Young Saul deplored Christians and became an enthusiastic persecutor of the sect. He is thought to have been the man who guarded the clothes of the mob who stoned Saint Stephen *circa* AD 35 (Acts 7:58).

On his way to Damascus Saul-Paul's wanderings took an unexpected turn. In Acts 9:1–2, Luke writes that 'Saul yet breathing out threatnings and slaughter against the disciples of ye Lord, went vnto the hie Priest, And desired of him letters to Damascus to the Synagogues, that if he found any that were of that way [Christians] (either men or women) hee might bring them bound vnto Hierusalem.' But en route a miracle occurred: 'Now as he iourneyed, it came to passe that as he was come neere to Damascus, suddenly there shined rounde about him a light from heauen. And hee fell to the earth, and heard a voyce, saying to him, Saul, Saul, why persecutest thou me?' (9:3–4). Blinded and taken to Damascus to heal, Saul was converted to Christianity, renamed himself Paul, and, after bitter disagreements with Peter, appointed himself 'Apostle to the Gentiles' and embarked on a career as a peripatetic missionary. He brought the good news to places as distant as Illyricum and Rome.[2]

Paul was an inveterate nomad, a professional wanderer. The first thing we learn about Feste is that he's a wanderer. Maria chides him, 'Nay, either tell me where thou hast been, or I will not open my lips so wide as a bristle may enter in way of thy excuse: my lady will hang thee for thy absence' (1.5.1–3). Feste won't say where he's been, nor does he cease wandering; throughout the play he is back and forth between the houses of Olivia and Orsino. We cannot be sure whether Nashe was himself a traveller; his most distant destination seems to have been Yarmouth, 140 miles north of London. But in *The Unfortunate Traveler, or the Life of Jack Wilton* (1594), Nashe – writing in the first person – fantasized wide-ranging travels in both space and time.[3] Perhaps Jack Wilton was the link in Shakespeare's mind connecting Nashe to the peripatetic life.

Paul was also the New Testament authority on things foolish. 'Fool' and its variants appear forty-one times in the New Testament – thirty-one of those in the writings of Paul, and most of these in his 'Call me fool' letters to the Corinthians. *Twelfth Night* is Shakespeare's great play about fools, foolishness, and foolery; the word 'fool' and its variants appear in this play more than seventy times, far more than in any other play in the canon. And the fool in charge of fooling (and perhaps the wisest character) is Feste. I will show that Shakespeare conceived Feste as a Pauline 'Fool' – a wise man in motley – and that he is not merely quick of wit and glib of tongue, but also the bringer of good news to Illyria.

Moth as rehearsal for Feste

Shakespeare rehearsed his portrayal of Nashe in *Love's Labour's Lost*; he wrote a warm, light-hearted miniature of his friend into the character of Moth (an anagram of Thom). Like Thom, Moth is small of stature, sharp of mind and tongue, and a masterful debunker of ignorance as personified by his master, the original bloviating ignoramus, Don Adriano de Armado. The play was written in 1595–96; Shakespeare's likeness of Nashe may have been sufficiently transparent for many of his first auditors to recognize. Those who conned Nashe as Moth likely detected Nashe's persistent literary opponent, Gabriel Harvey, behind the mask of Armado. Since 1592 Nashe and Harvey had achieved estimable notoriety through their no-holds-barred exchange of vitriolic pamphlets. And Nashe was very much a man-about-London; he hadn't yet written his share of *The Isle of Dogges* – perhaps a sortie into class warfare which dispatched him into self-imposed internal exile. Furthermore – and this is the heart of the matter – Nashe was a friend of Shakespeare and Harvey not. Scholars now generally accept Thom as the model for Moth, and should recognize Harvey lampooned in Armado.[4] But what has gone unnoticed is that Shakespeare once again pitted Nashe against Harvey in *Twelfth Night*.

Portraits of Nashe, pre- and post-mortem

When Shakespeare wrote *Twelfth Night* – most likely in the latter half of 1601 – both Nashe and Harvey had been silenced two years and Nashe was dead. We do not know the date of his death; we lose sight of him after the publication of *Nashes Lenten Stuffe* and the burning of his and Harvey's books in the summer of 1599.[5] The consensus holds that Nashe died in the interval 1599–1601. Though he had been forbidden to publish, somehow Nashe's *Summer's Last Will and Testament*, written in 1592, was registered for publication by Cuthbert Burby on 28 October 1600 and emerged from the press before the end of that year with Nashe named as author. Perhaps because the pageant had been written for and performed at the residence of Archbishop Whitgift it was considered immune to sanction – or, more likely, because Nashe had recently died. The registration date of *Summer's Last Will* may set a date *ad quem* for Nashe's death, and would narrow it to between June 1599 and October 1600. If my inference that a still-living Nashe mocks the world from behind the mask of Touchstone, that further narrows the date of his death to between spring 1600 and October of that year. This may explain the stark difference between Shakespeare's portrait of Nashe as Touchstone in *As You Like It* – a man entirely without spiritual bent – and Shakespeare's Feste-Nashe, the Pauline clown whose borrowings from the Gospels run from Mark to Galatians.[6] It is also possible that the publication of *Summer's Last Will* called to mind the link between Sommers and Nashe which Shakespeare deftly exploited.

In 1996 Katherine Duncan-Jones discovered among papers at Berkeley Castle a previously unknown elegy for Nashe entitled 'To the dear memory of Th. Nashe from his dearest friend Ben Jonson'. It is not very well known and merits quoting in full:

> Mortals that yet respire with plenteous breath
> View here a trophee of that tyrant deathe
> And let the obiect strike your melting eyes
> blind as the night, when you but read, Here lies
> Conquerd by destiny & turned to earthe
> The man whose want hathe causd a generall dearthe
> Of witte; throughout this land: none left behind
> to equall hym in his ingenious kynd
> I vrge not this as being his parasite
> who lou'd him least will doe him greater right
> Noe well deserving muse but will impart
> her flowers to crown his Industrie & art
> when any wrongd him lyuing they did feele
> his spirite quicke as powder sharp as stele
> But to his freindes her faculties were faire
> pleasant and milde as the most temp'rate ayre
> O pardon me deare freind yf fear controule
> the zealous purpose of my wounded sowle
> feare to be censured glorious in thie praise
> (A maime[d] sone taken in these hum'rous dayes
> where every dudgeon iudgement stabs at witt
> yette (for thie loue) this truth Ile not omitte
> Which most may make thie merites to appeare
> & ioye thie glad suruiuing freindes to heare),
> *thou diedst a Christian faithfull penitent*

> Inspir'd with happie thoughtes & confident
> This though thie latest grace was not the least
> Which still shall lyue when all else are deceast
> farewell greate spirite my pen attird in blacke
> shall whilst I am still weepe & mourn thie lacke [my emphasis].[7]

If we may take Jonson at his word, Nashe found religion, he died 'a Christian faithfull penitent', and his 'grace' will live after him. Nashe's redemption explains and justifies Shakespeare's portrait of his friend as a Pauline fool.

The evolution of Shakespeare's Nashe from the jocular juvenile of *Love's Labour's Lost* to the cynical seducer of shepherdess Audrey in *As You Like It* to the Scripture-spouting wanderer of *Twelfth Night* may depict Nashe's personal (spiritual) journey. If so, the triptych constitutes a unique literary document, and one that deserves more thoughtful consideration than I can give it here. That Shakespeare created three portraits of Nashe suggests a close and influential bond between the men; so far as we know Shakespeare fashioned nothing of the kind for anyone else.[8] It may be that Shakespeare felt as great a literary debt to Nashe as to Marlowe.

The wisest fool

I will surely find agreement when I suggest that Feste is the most intelligent, perceptive, and thoughtful character in the play. In every conversation from his first encounter with Maria to his final thrust at Malvolio, 'thus the whirlegigge of time, brings in his reuenges' (5.1.370) Feste comes out on top. In 3.1 he may see through Viola's disguise and recognize 'Cesario' is female. He perceives Viola's affection for Orsino and scents the Toby–Maria tryst. Feste is a bright mind and a 'corrupter of words'; Nashe was both. He tells Viola, 'wordes are growne so false, I am loath to proue reason with them' (3.1.23–4). Shakespeare dots Feste's dialogues with clues to the man behind the mask.[9] Some are faint, as when Feste encounters Viola-Cesario:

> *Vio.* Save thee, friend, and thy music: dost thou live by thy tabour?
> *Clo.* No, sir, I live by the church.
> *Vio.* Art thou a churchman?
> *Clo.* No such matter, sir: I do live by the church; For I do live at my house, and my house doth stand by the church. (3.1.1–7)

Nashe being redeemed, dead, and buried, his house (grave) would stand in a churchyard. The Grave-digger in *Hamlet* boasts: 'the houses that he makes last 'til doomsday' (5.1.55). But Feste's dialogue is also painted with the colours of St Paul:

> *Vio.* I warrant thou art a merry fellow and carest for nothing.
> *Clo.* Not so, sir, I do care for something; but in my conscience, sir, I do not care for you. (3.1.25–8)

The Christian conscience was a Pauline conception. It was Paul in 1 Corinthians who commanded a Christian taking Holy Communion to first clear his conscience: 'Let euery man therefore examine himselfe, and so let him eate of this bread, and drinke of this cup. For he that eateth and drinketh vnworthily, eateth and drinketh his owne damnation' (11:28–9).

Later in their scene Viola demands of Feste, 'Art not thou the Lady Olivia's fool?' and receives a Nashean reply:

> *Clo.* No, indeed, sir; the Lady Olivia has no folly: she will keep no fool, sir, till she be married; and fools are as like husbands as pilchards are to herrings; the husband's the bigger: I am indeed not her fool, but her corrupter of words. (3.1.31–5)

The comparison of herrings with pilchards is a wink at *Nashes Lenten Stuffe*, in which he apotheosized the red herring at the expense of pilchards: 'if Cornish pilchards, otherwise called fumados … be so saleable as they are in France, Spain and Italy (which are but counterfeits to the red herring, as copper to gold, or occamy to silver), much more their elbows itch for joy when they meet with the true gold, the true red herring itself' (3.1.7–13).[10] Then Shakespeare swings Feste's pendulum back towards Paul and the ubiquity of fools; he declares, 'Foolery, sir, does walk about the orb like the sun, it shines every where' (37). Viola has had enough. She breaks off, saying, 'Nay, an thou pass upon me, I'll no more with thee. Hold, there's expenses for thee.' But Feste would have more than one coin:

> *Clo.* Would not a pair of these have bred, sir?
> *Vio.* Yes, being kept together and put to use.
> *Clo.* I would play Lord Pandarus of Phrygia, sir, to bring a Cressida to this Troilus.
> *Vio.* I understand you, sir; 'tis well begged.
> *Clo.* The matter, I hope, is not great, sir, begging but a beggar: Cressida was a beggar. (3.1.48–54).

Paul was a beggar, too. As noted, he begged of the Corinthians in 1 Corinthians 16:1–2. A few scenes later, Sebastian will likewise try to buy his way out of a confrontation with Feste:

> *Seb.* I prithee, foolish Greek, depart from me: There's money for thee: if you tarry longer, I shall give worse payment.
> *Clo.* By my troth, thou hast an open hand. These wise men that give fools money get themselves a good report – after fourteen years' purchase. (4.1.17–22)

Sebastian's jibe at Feste as a 'foolish Greek' is as fitting an epithet for the anagrammatizing Feste as for Paul, the peripatetic Fool for Christ. Though born *Sha'ul* – as he describes himself, 'a Hebrew born of Hebrews' (Philippians 3:5) – Paul changed his name to the Greek Παῦλος = *Paulos* (Acts 13:9). Paul's everyday language may have been Greek, the *lingua franca* of the Roman Empire. His Epistles were certainly written in Greek; his translator, St Jerome (AD 347– 420), groaned that Paul's Greek was inelegant and clumsy.[11]

Feste's reference to 'fourteen years' has mystified commentators. But this is another of Shakespeare's winks at Paul. During his missionary journeys Paul begged and gathered alms for Peter, John, and the 'Jerusalem faction' of early Jewish Christians. And, indeed, he returned to Jerusalem with the money – *after fourteen years*: 'Then fourteene yeeres after, I went vp againe to Hierusalem with Barnabas' (Galatians 1:2). After some debate, Paul and his donation received a warm welcome from the Apostles: 'And when Iames, and Cephas [Peter], and Iohn, knew of the grace [alms, money] that was giuen vnto me ... they gaue to me and to Barnabas the right hands of fellowship, that we should preach vnto the Gentiles, and they vnto the Circumcision' (2:9). Paul bought his way into the Apostles' club.

There's an impious play on words in Feste's speech which commentators have overlooked. It appears in his phrase 'these wise men that give fools money'. In Paul's parlance of inversion 'wise men' = fools, and 'fool' = Paul. To be 'a fool for Christ' one must believe in the crucifixion and resurrection. Glib Feste is saying that believers are foolish to donate their money to Paul only to get a 'good report' to the 'Saintes' in Jerusalem after fourteen years.

Feste begs again in 5.1, this time from Orsino. After the Duke refuses him more than two coins, Feste turns the conversation towards sin:

> *Du.* You can foole no more money out of mee at this throw: if you will let your Lady know I am here to speak with her, and bring her along with you, it may awake my bounty further.
> *Clo.* Marry sir, lullaby to your bountie till I come a-gen. I go sir, but I would not haue you to thinke, that my desire of hauing is the sinne of couetousnesse: but as you say sir, let your bounty take a nappe, I will awake it anon. (37–45).

Feste's reference to the 'sinne of couetousnesse' recalls one of Paul's passages that has become proverbial; in Timothy 6:7–10 – which the Geneva glosses as 'Against couetousnes' – Paul wrote: 'For the desire of money is the roote of all euill, which while some lusted after, they erred from the faith, and pearced themselues through with many sorowes.' So Feste is touching the heart of the Pauline notion of sin and evil as he decries covetousness.

When Viola sums up the character of Feste she offers us a thumbnail of Nashe – but her punchline is pure St Paul:

> This fellow is wise enough to play the fool;
> And to do that well craves a kind of wit:
> He must observe their mood on whom he jests,
> The quality of persons, and the time,
> And, like the haggard, cheque at every feather
> That comes before his eye. This is a practise
> As full of labour as a wise man's art
> For folly that he wisely shows is fit;
> But wise men, folly-fall'n, quite taint their wit. (3.1.57–66)

What Viola closes on is a wink at Paul in 1 Corinthians 3:19–20: '[T]he wisdome of this worlde is foolishnesse with God: for it is written, He catcheth the wise in their owne craftinesse.' That Feste is Shakespeare's Pauline fool must have been transparent to his elite first auditors. And, doubtless, some recognized Nashe behind his motley. But Nashe-Feste also wears another disguise.

Sommers as Nashe's red herring.

Feste's name is mentioned only once in *Twelfth Night*: Curio's 'Feste, the jester, my lord; a fool that the lady Olivia's father took much delight in' (2.4.11–12). This is an allusion to fool Will Sommers' long service to Henry VIII. Shakespeare drops other hints at the fool's identity in Feste's first scene with Maria, which includes nods to both Nashe and Sommers. Maria warns the wanderer, 'my lady will hang thee for thy absence' (1.5.3). To Feste's quip 'He that is well hanged in this world needs to fear no colours ... [because] He shall see none to feare' (4–7), Maria replies, 'A good Lenten answer' (8), perhaps recalling *Nashes Lenten Stuffe*. Feste responds, 'Many a good hanging prevents a bad marriage; and, for turning away, *let summer bear it out*' (18–19, my emphasis). That final, awkward phrase has elicited painfully weak interpretations; for example, the pleasant summer weather would make Feste's dismissal bearable. I suggest that its awkwardness is Shakespeare's conspicuous hint – one might even say a sharp elbow – jogging his auditors to identify Feste, jester to the late father of 'Madonna' Olivia, with Sommer(s).

But if Shakespeare based the character of Feste on Thom Nashe, why does he drop these hints to Will Sommers?[12] The answer may be this simple: Nashe had been banned, and it may not have been considered politic to stage a banned man or his writings before the Queen.

Gabriel Harvey in Illyria

Since the publication in 1980 of J. J. M. Tobin's iconic monograph, 'Gabriel Harvey in Illyria', the scholarly consensus accepts that Shakespeare modelled his ambitious steward on that pedant, self-styled poet and critic, and social gadfly.[13] Anyone who doubts that Harvey provided the model for Malvolio should weigh the evidence marshalled by Professor Tobin. He begins by demonstrating that the language of *Twelfth Night* is rife with borrowings from Nashe's pamphlets *contra* Harvey:

> There are words and phrases in *Twelfth Night*, often unique or rare in the Shakespearean canon, which occur in *An Almond for a Parrat* (1590), *Pierce Penilesse* (1592), *Strange Newes* (1592), *Have with you to Saffron-Walden* (1596), and *Nashes Lenten Stuffe* (1599). *An Almond for a Parrat*, an anti-puritan pamphlet, provided Shakespeare in the composition of his play set in Illyria a reference to 'Illirians', the nouns 'sheepbyter', a term of abuse for puritans, 'souter', a similarly puritan-associated epithet, 'Brownist', 'bibble babble', the verb 'fadge(s)' the only other use of which in the canon occurs in *Love's Labour's Lost*, a play replete with Nashean echoes, and the adjectives 'malapert' and 'huperbolical'.[14]

But Tobin also demonstrates that Shakespeare's appropriations go beyond Nashe's diction. Each point in the Maria–Toby plot to humiliate Malvolio can be traced to a single episode in Nashe's satirical 'biographies' of Harvey.

In his *Saffron-Walden*, Nashe recounts that Harvey was jailed for debt in the Fleet. The circumstances were these: in response to Nashe's *Pierce Pennilesse*, Harvey dashed off *Pierses Supererogation* (1593). Nashe writes that Harvey promised to reimburse his printer, John Wolfe (1548?–1601), the cost of publication, £36. When Harvey repeatedly failed to pay up, Wolfe laid a trap to ensnare and arrest him.

The plot included a misleading letter. Nashe describes how Wolfe

> went and feed baylies, and gets one Scarlet (a friend of his) to goe and draw him [Harvey] foorth, & and hold him with a tale whiles they might steale on him & arrest him ... and to the intent he [Harvey] might suspect nothing by Scarlets coming, there was a kind letter fram'd in Wolfes name, with To the right worshipfull of the Lawes, in a great Text hand, for a superscription on the out-side; and underneath at the bottome, Your worships ever to command, and prest to doo you service, John Wolfe.[15]

Wasn't this Shakespeare's inspiration for the forged letter that led to Malvolio's downfall? The reference to 'a great Text hand', the style of the salutation, and the inclusion of both a superscription and a subscription may have suggested to Shakespeare the form of Maria's letter, which begins with the superscription: '*To the unknown beloved*' (2.5.90). Malvolio remarks on the penmanship: 'I think we do know the sweet Roman hand' (3.4.27). The letter also contains a postscript: 'Here is yet a postscript. *Thou cans't not choose but know who I am ...*' (2.5.169).

Nashe writes that while Harvey perused Wolfe's letter, two bailiffs 'stept into the roome boldly (as they were two well bumbasted swaggering fat-bellies, having faces as broad as the backe of a chimney, and as big as a towne bag-pudding) and clapping the Doctor with a lusty blow on the shoulder ... [cried] in Gods name and the Queenes wee doo arrest you'.[16] In *Twelfth Night* 3.4, Toby dispatches Andrew to look for Viola-Cesario, saying, 'scout me for him at the corner the orchard like a bum-baily' (171–2) – the sole appearance of the term in the Shakespeare canon and the first recorded by *OED*. Tobin is certainly correct to see this portmanteau word compounded by Shakespeare from Nashe's 'bum ... bellies' and 'baliffs'.

Carried off to the Fleet prison, Harvey carried on like a madman: 'O you prophane Plebeyans, exclaimed hee, I will massacre, I will crucifie you for presuming to lay hands thus on my reverent person. All this would not service him, no more than Hackets *counterfeit* madness woulde keep him from the Gallowes.'[17] After menacing the terrified wife of the jailer with his dagger, Harvey was finally subdued. Details from Nashe's report abound in Shakespeare's gulling and segregation of Malvolio – from the forged letter and the term 'bum-baily' to Sir Topas-Feste's question, 'but tell me true, are you not mad indeed, or do you but *counterfeit*?' (4.2.114, my emphasis). Among many parallels cited by Tobin, he fails to notice that prisoners Harvey and Malvolio are both visited and freed by a divine. In Malvolio's case it is Feste as Sir Topas; Harvey had been freed by the intervention of 'the Minister then serving at Saint Albanes in Wood-street,' a man apparently surnamed Harvey who 'enterd bond for him to answere it at law, & satisfied [paid] the House for his [Harvey's] lodging and Mangerie'.[18]

Summing up, Tobin characterizes Shakespeare's and Malvolio's debt to Nashe:

> Because Shakespeare had read Nashe's works with interest, and, one suspects, admiration for their verbal pyrotechnics, he may well have recalled unconsciously some of the more striking words and phrases during his own writing. However, the large number of words and phrases present in *Twelfth Night* and unique in the canon and present also in *Have with you to Saffron-Walden*, a number of themes from pedantry to cowardice, insanity and presumption, and the central Malvolio-like character of Gabriel Harvey all suggest that Shakespeare read intentionally this most successful of Nashe's anti-Harvey attacks, looking for materials which he could incorporate into his romantic comedy with its puritan gull.[19]

Once we have in hand Nashe's portrait of Harvey, it's easy to see how it shaped Shakespeare's invention of Malvolio's name. It is an Italian name compounded of *mal*, which signifies bad, evil, or ill, and *voglio*, the first person present of 'to wish' or 'to desire'. Queen Elizabeth had remarked that Harvey 'lookt like an Italian' (see the discussion below), and he certainly wished Nashe ill. Though Riche's *Apolonius and Silla* is accepted as the proximate source of

Twelfth Night, Shakespeare's inspiration for the forged letter plot that gulled and humiliated Malvolio – including the mysterious M.O.A.I. – were drawn whole cloth from events in Harvey's life found in Nashe's *Saffron-Walden*.

Feste's final lament

When the comedy is ended, a stage direction indicates *'Exeunt'* and Feste is left alone on stage. He begins to sing. And his song is an odd admixture of reminiscence, ribaldry, and pathos:

> When that I was and a little tiny boy,
> With hey, ho, the wind and the rain,
> A foolish thing was but a toy,
> For the rain it raineth every day.
> But when I came to man's estate,
> With hey, ho, & c.
> 'Gainst knaves and thieves men shut their gate,
> For the rain, & c.
> But when I came, alas! to wive,
> With hey, ho, & c.
> By swaggering could I never thrive,
> For the rain, & c.
> But when I came unto my beds,
> With hey, ho, & c.
> With toss-pots still had drunken heads,
> For the rain, & c.
> A great while ago the world begun,
> With hey, ho, & c.
> But that's all one, our play is done. (5.1.382–400)

The final line which appears in the Folio – 'And we'll strive to please you every day' – seems inappropriate for performance before a royal audience and, likely, was a later interpolation appropriate to a public playhouse (see the discussion below).

With Feste's lapse into silence the on-stage action concludes. Doubtless, auditors recognized his ditty as a parody of one of the best-loved passages in the New Testament, 1 Corinthians 13:11–13:

> When I was a childe, I spake as a childe, I vnderstoode as a childe, I thought as a childe: but when I became a man, I put away childish thinges. For nowe we see through a glasse darkely: but then shall wee see face to face. Nowe I know in part: but then shall I know euen as I

am knowen. And nowe abideth faith, hope and loue, euen these three: but the chiefest of these is loue.

If there had remained any doubt in the minds of Shakespeare's auditors that an incarnation of Paul stood before them, Feste's final song settled the matter. But what does Feste's song mean? What is it doing at the end of *Twelfth Night*? And why does it introduce an undeniable note of melancholy into an otherwise happy ending? Certainly, it locks the connection between Feste and Paul. But one must not forget Nashe also is present – and that, perhaps, explains its tone and abrupt *caesura*.

Of all the generations of scholarly brains flung at Feste's song, the clearest and most convincing interpretation is Verity's one-liner: 'My foolish deeds were thought little of when I was a boy: not so when I came to manhood; then men's doors were shut against me.'[20] This could pass as a concise biography of Nashe.

Nashe had entered St John's College, Cambridge, *circa* 1581, and five years later earned his bachelor's degree. His colourful history at Cambridge is recapitulated in *The Trimming of Thomas Nashe, Gentleman* (1597), which represents itself as written '*by the high-tituled patron Don Richardo de Medico Campo, Barber-Chirurgion to Trinitie Colledge in Cambridge.*' The polemic was likely written by Harvey, but the attribution is to his crony-barber, Richard Lichfield, whom Nashe had facetiously named as dedicatee of *Saffron-Walden* in the prior year. 'Litchfield' reports that Nashe's departure from Cambridge was precipitated by his contribution to a student play: 'suspecting himself that he should be stared for *egregie dunsus*, and not attain to the next Degree [MA], said he had commest enough, and so forsook Cambridge, being a Batchelor of the third yere'.[21] Nashe's play is thought to have made importunate comments on the royal succession, and the prank to have been sufficiently serious to precipitate the dismissal of a co-author. Though Nashe claims in *Saffron-Walden* that he could have become a fellow of St John's,[22] he departed the college in 1589 – *the year he turned twenty-one, ended his minority and reached 'man's estate'* – and was shown the gate without proceeding MA.

But how do we explain Feste's 'But when I came, alas! to wive ... With swaggering by could I never thrive'? So far as we know, Nashe never married. However, his Jack Wilton, having witnessed a final, grotesque act of violence, most certainly did marry his Diamante – and, yes, renounced his swaggering life: 'To such straight life did it thenceforward incite me that ere I went out of Bologna, I married my courtesan, performed many alms-deeds ... and feasted many days.'²³

Finally, what of the drunken tosspots who persisted in their revelry when he 'came unto my beds' – that is, neared death – particularly as Jonson's recently discovered encomium for Nashe tells us he 'diedst a Christian faithfull penitent'? Could this be Nashe's lament that his fellow writers (tosspots) had profited nothing by his sudden conversion – much like Paul on the Damascus road – and still had drunken heads? Likely, Nashe's abrupt conversion suggested to Shakespeare the linking of Nashe and St Paul in Feste.

We don't know enough (yet) about Nashe's life and death to answer these questions. But we do know that Nashe led a windy, rainswept life. Professor Elam is correct when he deduces that 'At the end of its rapid journey through life, the song seems about to make an important statement about the world, but immediately drops the idea.'²⁴ Breaking off in mid-thought is emblematic for the sudden muzzling of Nashe in 1599. It is affecting, puzzling, poignant. In the silence that follows, Shakespeare's effigy of Nashe departs the stage. It is his third and last appearance. He will never return.

With the battle lines now carefully drawn – pitting Paul-Feste-Nashe against Malvolio-Harvey – we can move on to discovering the solution to one of Shakespeare's most debated, stubborn, and infuriating cruces, the 'fustian riddle' of *M.O A.I.*

Notes

1 Pharisees – 'separate ones' – were also legalists, debaters, students of and rigid upholders of the law, and zealots. They believed in the resurrection of the dead, free will (and predestination, sort of), and prayers three times a day including the *Sh'ma*. One can easily see how Paul, the Pharisee Christian-hater, could flip-flop and become a zealous Christian proselytizer.
2 In his Epistle to the Galatians, Paul says that after his conversion he immediately went to 'Arabia', by which some scholars believe he meant Petra in modern Jordan, then travelled to Damascus to teach.
3 Born in Lowestoft, Suffolk, Nashe attended Cambridge, moved to London, was on the Isle of Wight at Christmas 1593, and exiled himself to Great Yarmouth after the *Isle of Dogges* affray in 1597. Nashe

also made a brief visit to antiquary Robert Cotton at Conington in Huntingdonshire in 1593. But in *The Unfortunate Traveler* his charming con-man protagonist engages in lusty, picaresque time-travel through France and Italy, often at the risk of his life. Though not held in great esteem today, the book is a landmark in English letters. In 1887 Jean Jules Jusserand (1855–1932) declared Nashe had been first to indicate 'the road that was to lead to the true novel ... to relate in prose a long-sustained story, having for its chief concern: the truth ... No one, Ben Jonson excepted, possessed at that epoch, in so great a degree as himself, a love of the honest truth [realism]. With Nash, then, the novel of real life, whose invention in England is generally attributed to Defoe, begins.' Jean Jusserand, *Le roman au temps de Shakespeare* (Paris: Asnières, 1887), 347–8 (my translation). Defoe published his first novel, *Robinson Crusoe*, only in 1719 when Nashe had been dead 119 years.

4 For example: G. R. Hibbard, *Thomas Nashe* (London: Routledge and Kegan Paul, 1962).
5 But McKerrow reports that in a copy of *The Hospital of Incurable Fooles* (London: Edward Blount, 1600), a certain 'P.W.' has left a manuscript note: 'Tho. Nashe had some hand in this translation and it was the last thing he did as I heare.' See William E. Miller, 'The Hospitall of Incurable Fooles', *Studies in Bibliography* 16 (1963), 204–7.
6 R. Chris Hassel, Jr., catalogues a number of Feste's borrowings from the Epistles of Paul but does not detect the presence of Nashe. See *Faith and Folly in Shakespeare's Romantic Comedies* (Athens, GA: University of Georgia Press, 2011), 169–75.
7 Quoted in Katherine Duncan-Jones, '"They say a made a good end"', *The Ben Jonson Journal* 3 (1996), 1–6.
8 J. J.M. Tobin, 'Gabriel Harvey in Illyria', *English Studies* 61 (1980), 321. Maurice Hunt, 'Thomas Nashe, *The Unfortunate Traveller*, and *Love's Labour's Lost*', *Survey of English Literature* 54 (Spring 2014), 297–314.
9 Nicholl detects Nashe behind the mask of Feste: 'If Nashe is [regarded as] a 'minor' author, or at any rate a flawed one, his stylistic influence was none the less major. His richly textured language is discernible in the comedies of Jonson and the journalism of Dekker, and is more subtly present in Shakespeare: in the Falstaff scenes, in the bitter clowning of *Twelfth Night*, and even in *Hamlet*' (108).
10 McKerrow, *Nashe*, III.192.7.
11 St Jerome, *The Vulgate Preface to Paul's Letters*, trans. Kevin P. Edgecombe, www.tertullian.org/fathers/jerome_preface_pauls_letters.htm (accessed 4 August 2011).
12 Sommers was certainly bright in living memory and would remain so for many years; as late as 1605 Samuel Rowley brought Sommers back

to the stage in *When You See Me You Know Me*. And Sommers was the subject of two popular books, *A Nest of Ninnies* by Robert Armin (1608) and the anonymous *A Pleasant History of the Life and Death of Will Summers* (1676).
13 J. J. M. Tobin, 'Gabriel Harvey in Illyria', *English Studies* 61 (1980), 318–28. Professor Tobin was perhaps not the first to detect the Malvolio–Harvey connection. 'In 1962 G. R. Hibbard in his book on Nashe noted the analogy between Harvey and Malvolio without suggesting a satiric identity, and cited Muriel Bradbrook's recognition of a somewhat similar parallelism.' Tobin, in correspondence, 27 August 2012.
14 Tobin, 'Gabriel Harvey in Illyria', 318.
15 Ronald B. McKerrow, ed., *The Works of Thomas Nashe*, 5 vols (London: Sidgwick & Jackson, 1904–19, repr. Oxford: Basil Blackwell, 1958), III.97–8.
16 *Ibid.*, III.98.
17 *Ibid.*, III.99. William Hacket (d. 1591) was a puritan who conspired to stage an ecclesiastical and civil *coup d'état*. Convicted of treason, he was hanged. Hacket believed himself the Messiah, which may account for the reference to crucifixion, an obvious invention of Nashe's.
18 *Ibid.*, III.101.
19 Tobin, 'Gabriel Harvey in Illyria', 325.
20 A. W. Verity, ed., *Twelfth Night, or What You Will*, The Pitt Press Shakespeare for Schools, repr. (Cambridge: Cambridge University Press, 1961), 135.
21 *The Trimming of Thomas Nashe, Gentleman* in Alexander Balloch Grosart, ed., *The Works of Gabriel Harvey* (London: privately printed, 1884–85). Grosart, among others, believed Harvey to be the author.
22 McKerrow, *Nashe*, III.127.32–3.
23 Thomas Nashe, *The Unfortunate Traveler, or the Life of Jack Wilton* (London, 1594), 327.32.
24 Keir Elam, ed., *Twelfth Night*, The Arden Shakespeare, Series 3 (London: Bloomsbury, 2009), 354n

8

M.O.A.I. deciphered at last

In *Twelfth Night* 2.5, the billet-doux which gulls Malvolio proclaims,

> *I may command where I adore,*
> *but silence like a Lucresse knife:*
> *With bloodlesse stroke my heart doth gore,*
> *M.O.A.I. doth sway my life.* (100–3)

For four hundred years the cryptic letters *M.O.A.I.* have remained a stubborn, even notorious crux. In his Arden Series 3 edition, Keir Elam declared, 'This fustian riddle has proved ... as much a trap for critics as for Malvolio.'[1] Indeed, *M.O.A.I.* personifies the definition of a crux: 'A difficulty which it torments or troubles one greatly to interpret or explain' (*OED*). Among notable scholars tormented or troubled, J. O. Halliwell-Phillipps thought *M.O.A.I.* 'purposely meaningless, or intended for, My Own Adored Idol, or some such words ... [or] cypher'.[2] Fredrick Fleay saw a vision of 'IO: MA, [John] Marston's abbreviated signature', then grumbled, 'These anagram conceits are so common in the sixteenth and seventeenth centuries as to need no further notice.'[3] Modern commentators have fared no better. L. S. Cox unearthed 'an anagram of "I am O[livia]".[4] Leslie Hotson felt the play of four elements: '*Mare* – Sea, *Orbis* – Earth, *Aer* – Air, and *Ignis* – Fire'.[5] Lothian and Craik dodged the bullet: 'Attempts to wring further meaning from [*M.O.A.I.*] are misplaced.'[6] Elizabeth Donno gave the crux a wide birth, merely comparing Orlando's 'Thy huntress' name that my full life doth sway' (*As You Like It* 3.2.10).[7] In 1984, Elam perceived 'Malvolio's hermeneutic labours as a parody of the earnest anagrammatic endeavours of Renaissance magi to discover the sacred Tetragrammaton'.[8] In 1991 another quasi-religious epiphany struck Inge Leimberg: 'What Malvolio ought to have seen at a glance ... is his own image mirrored in a very simple anagram reflecting the creed of man fallen off from the love of God and thrown into the outer darkness of self-love: "*Eritis sicut deus*," says the devil, and Adam *homo* promptly replies: I'M A & O!' [Alpha and Omega].[9] By contrast, in 1998 Peter Smith sounded an earthy 'key in the Renaissance conception of meaning' leading to 'Sir John Harrington's Ovidian parody *Metamorphosis of Ajax* [A Jakes = privy]'.[10] A decade later, Elam summed these sorties: 'Despite the unenviable fate of the steward, and despite the unflattering image of interpretation that the episode represents – Shakespeare's twitting of 'mice-eyed decipherers' – the fustian riddle has proved an equally fatal attraction to the comedy's spectators and commentators.'[11] And there the case has stalled until now.

One aspect of Shakespeare's presentation of the M.O.A.I. crux – a tactic which makes its puzzle particularly alluring and vexatious – is its insistent repetition. Most of Shakespeare's foolers occur only once, for example Hamlet's 'dram of eale' (Second Quarto (Q2), throughline 1432) and the playwright's tantalizing allusion to the words Cicero said and Casca dared not repeat (*The Tragedy of Julius Caesar* 1.2.299). By comparison, Shakespeare's presentation of the forged letter and M.O.A.I. crux – the turning-point in the play – is appropriately elaborate.

For centuries, M.O.A.I. has tenaciously resisted solution. And Shakespeare's harping only enhances its magnetism. The four enigmatic letters are repeated five times, at 2.5.102, 106, 115, and 131 plus Malvolio's attempt to decipher them one by one as the conspirators echo him. Figure 4 shows how this appears in the Folio. Clearly, Shakespeare is intentionally goading his auditors to play along; repetition is a playwright snapping his fingers at us, a way of saying 'Listen up!' and challenging auditors to rake for his meaning.

In fact, M.O.A.I. has eluded Shakespeare's commentators for four hundred years because of a small but significant alteration of his source. But the cryptic letters *were* meant to be recognizable to at least some of his first auditors.

Harvey, Malvolio, and M.O.A.I.

Given that Nashe's polemics against Harvey so heavily invested Shakespeare's design for Malvolio – suffusing the steward's

> in me? Softly, *M.O.A.I.*
> *To.* O I, make vp that, he is now at a cold fent.
> *Fab.* Sowter will cry vpon't for all this, though it bee as ranke as a Fox.
> *Mal.* M. *Maluolio, M.* why that begins my name.
> *Fab.* Did not I fay he would worke it out, the Curre is excellent at faults.
> *Mal. M.* But then there is no confonancy in the fequell that fuffers vnder probation : *A.* fhould follow, but *O.* does.
> *Fa.* And *O.* fhall end, I hope.
> *To.* I, or Ile cudgell him, and make him cry *O.*
> *Mal.* And then *I.* comes behinde.
> *Fa.* I, and you had any eye behinde you, you might fee more detraction at your heeles, then Fortunes before you.
> *Mal. M,O,A,I.* This fimulation is not as the former: and yet to crufh this a little, it **would bow** to mee, for euery one of thefe Letters are in my name. Soft, here fol-

4 *Twelfth Night*, act 2, scene 5, from the Bodleian First Folio

character and the incident which brings him to ruin – it seems appropriate to sift Nashe's writings for clues to the meaning of M.O.A.I., the letters which lure Malvolio to destruction. I will show that their meaning and connection with Harvey can be discovered in Nashe's (and Harvey's) accounts of an incident in the career of the latter – one well known to Elizabethans who had followed their pamphlet war.

During 26–31 July 1578, Queen Elizabeth and her retinue were on progress at Audley End, a palatial estate in the immediate vicinity of Saffron-Walden, home town of Gabriel Harvey and some thirteen miles from Cambridge, where he was Fellow of Pembroke College and Reader of Rhetoric. On 27 July at Audley End, members of the university including Harvey held a Latin disputation before Howard, Leicester, Oxford, and other visiting grandees. The events of that afternoon were immortalized in Latin verse by Harvey, and by Nashe in not one but two of his books.

Nashe's first telling appeared in *Strange Newes*, his pamphlet issued in reply to Harvey's deeply offensive *Four Letters and Certain Sonnets* (1592), which had vilified both Nashe and the memory of his recently deceased friend and collaborator, Robert Greene. Nashe prefaced his account of the incident at Audley End with a warning to the nobility: 'Lette all Noblemen take heede how they giue this Thraso the least becke or countenance, for if they bestowe but halfe a glaunce on him, hele straight put it verie solemnly in print, and make it ten times more than it is.'[12] That is, should a grandee show the socially ambitious Harvey even the slightest regard, Harvey is likely to publish a book declaring them fast friends. Then Nashe turns to an occasion involving the Queen, the Earls of Leicester and Oxford, and Harvey:

> Ile tell you a merry ieast. The time was when this Timothie Tiptoes made a Latine Oration to her Maieste.[13] Her Highnes as shee is vntu all her subiects most gratious; so to schollers she is more louing and affable than any Prince vnder heauen. In which respect of her owne vertue and not his desert, it pleased hir so to humble the height of hir judgement, as to grace him a little whiles he was pronouncing, by these or such like tearmes. Tis a good pretie fellow, *a lookes like an Italian*; and after hee had concluded, to call him to *kisse her royall hand* [my emphasis]. Hereuppon hee goes home to his studie, all intraunced, and writes a whole volume of Verses; first, *De Vultu Itali*, of the countenance of the Italian; and then *De Osculo Manus*, of his kissing the Queenes hande. Which two Latin Poems he publisht in a booke of his cald *Ædes Valdinenses*, proclaiming thereby (as it were to England, Fraunce, Italie, and Spaine) what fauour hee was in with her Maieste.[14]

Clearly, Nashe did not have Harvey's text before him. He was writing from memory and mis-remembered Harvey's Latin. Harvey had written: 'de Regiae Manus osculatione' – which Nashe remembered as '*De Osculo Manus*'. And Harvey had written 'deque, eo, quod vultum Itali habere' – which Nashe turned into '*De Vultu Itali*'.

Four years later in *Have with you to Saffron-Walden*, Nashe revisited Harvey's fateful encounter with the Queen. In this telling, Nashe begins by assuring us that, though seeming incredible, the anecdote is wholly true.

> I have a tale at my tongue's end of this hobby-horse [Harvey] revelling & domineering at Audley End when the Queen was there, to which place Gabriel (to do his country more worship & glory) came

ruffling it out, hufty-tufty, in his suit of velvet ... You will imagine it a fable, percase ... but it is 10 times more unfallible than news of the Jews rising up in arms to take in the Land of Promise, or the raining of corn this summer at Wakefield.[15]

Nashe then proceeds to denounce Harvey's soaring ambition: at Audley End 'did this, our *Talatamtana* or Doctor Hum, thrust himself into the thickest ranks of the noblemen and gallants, and whatsoever they were arguing of, he would not miss to catch hold of, or strike in at the one end, and take the theme out of their mouths.'[16]

Having characterized as preposterous Harvey's velvet attire and arrogance, Nashe passes to another of his recurring themes, Harvey-the-sensualist: 'In selfsame order was he at his pretty toys and amorous glances and purposes with the damsels, & putting bawdy riddles unto them, etc.'[17] Nashe now approached his main event.

After Harvey concluded his Latin oration 'by some better friends than he was worthy of [probably the Earl of Leicester] ... he was brought to kiss the Queen's hand, and it pleased her Highness to say (as in my former book I have cited) that he looked something like an Italian'.[18]

The effect on Harvey of Elizabeth's courtesy and (rather faint) praise was electric. Nashe reports that he 'ran headlong violently to his study, as if he had been borne with a whirlwind, and straight knocked me up a poem called his *Ædes [Gratulationes] Valdinenses*, in praise of my Lord of Leicester, of his [Harvey's] kissing the Queen's hand, and of her speech & comparison of him, how he looked like an Italian'.[19]

Harvey's 'poem' comprised four Latin 'letters' to the the Queen, Leicester, Essex, and Sir Philip Sydney and certain other noblemen; it was published in September 1578 by Henry Binneman (London). In his 'letter' to the Queen, Harvey recalled the great encounter: '*Liber Primus: To Queen Elizabeth. Epilogus, de Regiae Manus Osculatione: deque eo quod vultum Itali habere, ab excellentissima Principe diceretur.*'[20] That is, 'Book One: To Queen Elizabeth. The epilogue, of the kissing of the hand of the Queen: and that he was said by this most excellent Princess to have the appearance of an Italian.' Harvey's key phrases – '*Manus Osculatione*' and '*Vultum Itali*' – would provide the basis for Maria's conundrum. But first, another word from Nashe about Harvey's penchant for outlandish attire.

M.O.A.I. *deciphered at last* 131

Some forty lines later in *Saffron-Walden,* Nashe offers a bravura portrait of Harvey's atrocious sartorial taste. 'His father he undid [impoverished] to furnish him to the court once more, where presenting himself in all the colours of the rainbow, and a pair of mustaches like a black horse-tail tied up in a knot, with two tufts sticking out on each side, he was asked by no mean personage, *Unde haec insania*? Whence proceedeth this folly or madness?'[21] This passage may have provided Shakespeare's and Maria's cue for cajoling Malvolio into yellow stockings cross-gartered.

How *M.O.V.I.* became *M.O.A.I.*

The inspiration for Maria's *M.O.A.I.* was Harvey's '*Manus Osculatione … Vultum Itali*', a sequence of words which begin with the letters *M.O.V.I.* But if this is so, how did *M.O.V.I.* become *M.O.A.I.?*

The *V.* became *A.* via a seventeenth-century version of the game that Americans call 'Telephone' and pre-PC Britons call 'Chinese Whispers'.[22] In that parlour pastime a line of people whisper a message one to another. The message, which began as simple and sensible, becomes more garbled with each re-transmission, and emerges at last as laughable gibberish. Here is how Harvey, Nashe, and Shakespeare played the game:

1. In 1578 Harvey had written: '*Manus Osculatione: deque eo quod vultum Itali habere*'.
2. Fourteen years later in *Strange Newes* (1592), Nashe, clearly working from memory and without Harvey's text before him, wrote: '*De Vultu Itali*, of the countenance of the Italian; and then *De Osculo manus*, of his kissing the Queenes hande.' Note that Nashe (a) reversed the order of the phrases; (b) miswrote '*Vultu Itali*' for Harvey's '*vultum Itali*'; and (c) reversed the word-order of the latter phrase while mangling Harvey's '*Manus Osculatione: deque*' into '*De Osculo manus*'. Nashe also translated the former phrase as both 'a looks like an Italian' and 'of the countenance of the Italian'.
3. Four years later in *Saffron-Walden* (1596), Nashe, again writing from memory but without reprising Harvey's Latin, twice expressed the phrase as 'he lookt something like an Italian' and 'he lookt like an Italian'.[23]

If Tobin is correct, *Saffron-Walden* is the text Shakespeare mined for ammunition for *Twelfth Night*.

4. Five years later in 1601, Shakespeare replaced the phrases in their original order. But, relying on *Saffron-Walden* and without access to Harvey's Latin, Jonson's man of 'small Latine and lesse Greeke' translated Nashe's 'lookt like an Italian' as '*Aspectu Itali*' and wrote *M.O.A.I.*[24] Recalling that Harvey wrote in Latin but having only Nashe's Englishing before him, Shakespeare wrote *M.O.A.I.* for '*Manus Osculatione ... Aspectu Itali*'.

That is how the royal *M.O.V.I.* became the fatal *M.O.A.I.* which has cost so many commentators so much face. Shakespeare, unaware of his mistranslation, could have expected his royal auditor and her courtiers who had read Nashe to get his joke. Because the Queen had said that Harvey 'lookt like an Italian' Shakespeare gave his character an Italian name.

One final note: recovering the link between *M.O.A.I.* and Harvey's kiss of Elizabeth's hand throws a fresh and delicious light on the final sentence in Maria's letter (2.5.150–3): '*Go to, thou art made if thou desir'st to be so; if not, let me see thee a steward still, the fellow of servants and not worthy to touch Fortune's fingers*' – or kiss them, for that matter.

Notes

1 Keir Elam, ed., *Twelfth Night*, The Arden Shakespeare, Series 3 (London: Bloomsbury, 2009), 243n.
2 J. O. Halliwell-Phillipps, *Shakespeariana* (London, 1841).
3 F. G. Fleay, *Shakespeariana* (London, 1884), I.136.
4 Lee Sherman Cox, 'The Riddle in *Twelfth Night*', *Shakespeare Quarterly* 13 (1962), 360.
5 Leslie Hotson, *The First Night of Twelfth Night* (London: Macmillan, 1954), 166.
6 J. M. Lothian and T. W. Craik, eds, *Twelfth Night, or What You Will*, The Arden Shakespeare, Series 2 (London: Thomson Learning, 1975), 68n.
7 Elizabeth Story Donno, ed., *Twelfth Night or What You Will*, The New Cambridge Shakespeare (Cambridge: Cambridge University Press, 1985), 91.
8 Keir Elam, *Shakespeare's Universe of Discourse: Language Games in the Comedies* (Cambridge: Cambridge University Press, 1984), 159–64.

9 Inge Leimberg, '"M.O.A.I.": Trying to Share the Joke in *Twelfth Night* 2.5 (a Critical Hypothesis)', *Connotations* 1.1 (1980), 84.
10 Peter Smith, 'M.O.A.I.: "What Should That Alphabetical Position Portend?" An Answer to the Metamorphic Malvolio', *Renaissance Quarterly* 51 (1998), 1199–1224.
11 Elam, *Twelfth Night*, 16.
12 Ronald B. McKerrow, *The Workes of Thomas Nashe*, 5 vols (London: Sidgwick & Jackson 1904–10, repr. Oxford: Basil Blackwell, 1958), I.276.
13 Harvey did not make his oration before the Queen, a detail Nashe corrected in *Saffron-Walden*.
14 McKerrow, *Nashe*, I.276–7.
15 *Ibid.*, III.73–4.
16 *Ibid.*, III.75.
17 *Ibid.*, III.75–6.
18 *Ibid.*, III.76.
19 McKerrow, *Nashe*, III.77.
20 Alexander Bulloch Grosart, ed., *The Works of Gabriel Harvey* (London: privately printed, 1884–85), I.xx xv.
21 McKerrow, *Nashe*, III.79.
22 'In Britain the game is called Chinese Whispers ... In France, the game is sometimes referred to as The Arab Game and ... The Russian Scandal Game.' 'Chinese Whispers.com', www.chinese-whispers.com (accessed 11 May 2013).
23 McKerrow, *Nashe*, III.76.20, III.78.5.
24 *Vultus*, n.m., expression of the face, countenance, look or aspect. *Aspectus*, n.m., appearance, aspect, mein. *Thesaurus Linguae Romanae & Britannicae, tam accurate congestus, ut nihil pene in eo desyderari possit, quod vel Latine complectatur amplifimus Stephani Thesaurus, vel Anglice, totes aucta Eliotae Bibliotheca; opera et industria Thomae Cooperi Magdalenensis* (London: Bertheleti, 1565).

9

Beginning at the beginning

Many Shakespeareans rankled at the final scene of the motion picture *Shakespeare in Love* (1998). Having lost his Viola (Gwyneth Paltrow) to Lord Wessex (Colin Firth), young Shakespeare (Joseph Fiennes) sets quill to paper to capture her spirit in a new play. Here's how Marc Norman and Tom Stoppard wrote the scene[1]:

> INT. WILL'S ROOM. DAY.
> A blank page. A hand is writing: TWELFTH NIGHT. We see WILL sitting at his table.
>   WILL (VO)
> My story starts at sea … a perilous voyage to an unknown land … a shipwreck
>
> EXT. UNDERWATER. DAY.
> Two figures plunge into the water.
>   WILL (VO)
> the wild waters roar and heave … the brave vessel is dashed all to pieces, and all the helpless souls within her drowned.
>
> INT. WILL'S ROOM. DAY.
> WILL at his table writing.
>   WILL (VO)
> all save one … a lady
>
> EXT. UNDERWATER. DAY.
> VIOLA in the water.
>   WILL (VO)
> whose soul is greater than the ocean … and her spirit stronger than the sea's embrace … not for her watery end, but a new life beginning on a stranger shore.

EXT. BEACH. DAY.
VIOLA is walking up a vast and empty beach.
                WILL (VO)
It will be a love story … or she will be my heroine for all time

INT. WILL'S ROOM. DAY.
WILL looks up from the table.
                WILL (VO)
and her name will be … Viola.
He looks down at the paper, and writes: 'Viola'
Then: 'What country friends is this?'

EXT. BEACH. DAY.
DISSOLVE slowly to VIOLA, walking away up the beach towards her brave new world.

                THE END

The sources of scholarly opprobrium were twofold. First, this scene follows shortly after the first performance of Shakespeare's *Romeo and Juliet*, written *circa* 1593 and published in 1597 – whereas *Twelfth Night* must have been written after the visit of Virginio Orsini to London and before its first performance before Elizabeth on 27 December 1601. Secondly, everyone knows *Twelfth Night* begins 'If music be the food of love' not 'What country, friends, is this?'

Stoppard, no slouch as a Shakespearean – remember his devilish deconstruction of *Hamlet* in *Rosencrantz and Guildernstern are Dead* (1966) – should have known better. Then again, Stoppard's Fiennes-Shakespeare was just starting his first draft; on mature consideration, into a subsequent draft he might have inserted the scene in Orsino's court as 1.1. That scene expresses a governing idea of the play – unrequited love – and, by the way, takes advantage of the presence of musicians playing as the audience settle in their seats. On the other hand, in 1.2 – Viola's arrival in Illyria – her Captain expresses an even more pungent governing idea:

>   I saw your brother,
> Most provident in peril, bind himself,
> Courage and hope both teaching him the practise,
> To a strong mast that lived upon the sea;
> Where, like Arion on the dolphin's back,
> I saw him hold acquaintance with the waves
> So long as I could see. (10–16)

Here is the hope of resurrection, complete with a cruciform mast and a glance at Arion, the Greek poet tossed into the sea by pirates but miraculously redeemed by a passing dolphin. Stoppard may have been sufficiently informed to know that from at least the early nineteenth century some performances of *Twelfth Night* began, 'What country (Friends) is this?' In their Arden Series 2 edition (1975), Lothian and Craik didn't think much of this innovation: 'This production of Kemble's [1815] was the first [on record] to reverse the order of the first two scenes, a regrettable change often made since, and occasionally found even today.' The editors cite three reasons why the scenes might have been rudely disordered: 'One is the desire to improve on Shakespeare's dramatic art. A second is the need to get late-comers seated without their or other spectators' missing, or suffering distraction from, the first appearances of the more important characters [!] ... A third is the fact that, in the nineteenth-century theatre, relatively unlocalized scenes were presented before a lowered front curtain, which was afterwards raised to disclose a representational stage-set' such as Orsino's palace.'[2]

But was Kemble's sequencing an innovation? Or was it, perhaps, a throwback?

Though what I am about to suggest may seem near-heresy, my hunch is that Stoppard got it right and Shakespeare's manuscript began with Viola addressing her question not only to her fellow actors but to Queen and Court at Whitehall. I have three reasons – quite apart from any suggested by Lothian and Craik – for embracing this heretical view: one geographical, one structural, one mathematical.

Why 1.2 was 1.1: geography

In Elizabeth's time, prior to the construction of the Victoria Embankment (1865–70), Whitehall stood adjacent to the west bank of the Thames. In the winter of 1598–99 Shakespeare's company had relocated, timbers and all, from The Theatre in Shoreditch to its new Bankside Globe in Southwark, south of city and river.[3] Anyone travelling from Southwark to Whitehall in 1602 would row west across the Thames. The alternative was to go east to the only bridge – London Bridge – and then along the north bank from Eastcheap to Westminster, a journey of four miles. If we consider a map of contemporary London (Figure 5) we can see that travelling

Beginning at the beginning 137

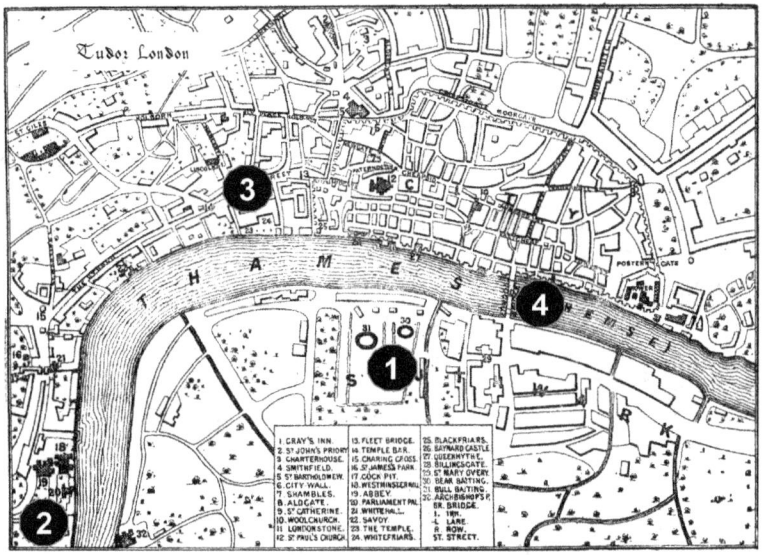

5 Map of Tudor London

from (1) Southwark to (2) Whitehall or (3) the Inns of Court via (4) London Bridge was certainly taking the long way round.

On the Julian 27 December 1601 it seems likely that Shakespeare's playing company crossed from Southwark to Whitehall by boat. And boating accidents on the river were common as crackers. So there's a certain aesthetic elegance and geographical verisimilitude in Viola and her troupe of seafarers stumbling through the doors at Whitehall to greet their audience with her demand, 'What country, friends, is this?' The same opening gambit would have worked equally well for performance at (3) the Inns of Court; the Middle Temple Gatehouse and Inner Temple Gardens sat on the bank of the Thames opposite Southwark.

Why 1.2 was 1.1: structure

Opening *Twelfth Night* with scene 1.2 would also be a great boon to those hearing the play for the first time. When Viola asks 'Who governs here?' her Captain replies:

   A noble duke, in nature as in name.
Vio. What is the name?

> *Cap.* Orsino.
> *Vio.* Orsino! I have heard my father name him:
> He was a bachelor then. (1.2.23–6)

There is absolutely no point in Viola telling the Captain that Orsino is a bachelor if we've aleady watched a scene in which he proclaims his so-far-unrequited love for Olivia. We would have deduced that he must be a bachelor (or a bounder). And it's equally inconceivable that Viola mentions Orsino's bachelorhood because she's aleady thinking of matching herself to a nobleman far above her station. The only function of Viola telling us Orsino is a bachelor is to justify his sighing after Olivia in the scene which begins, 'If music be the food of love ...'.

If we'd already heard Orsino pining for Olivia, the Captain also would be telling us things we already know in 1.2 when he says,

> For but a month ago I went from hence,
> And then 'twas fresh in murmur – as, you know,
> What great ones do the less will prattle of, –
> That he did seek the love of fair Olivia. (28–31)

But if this is 1.1, the mention of Olivia's name serves a useful purpose. When we hear Orsino mention the same name we know that the Captain is a reliable reporter and Orsino is not fickle, as were Romeo or Proteus.

Viola's interest now turns to the identity of Olivia. She asks, 'What's she?' and the Captain replies

> A virtuous maid, the daughter of a count
> That died some twelvemonth since, then leaving her
> In the protection of his son, her brother,
> Who shortly also died: for whose dear love,
> They say, she hath abjured the company
> And sight of men. (33–8)

This sets us up for Curio's 'The element itself, till seven years' heat, Shall not behold her face at ample view' (25–6).

With 1.2 played as the opening scene, in a handful of lines Shakespeare has provided us with two women, Viola and Olivia, both mourning lost brothers. From this springboard he sets his plot afoot. Viola declares, 'O that I served that lady And might not be delivered to the world, Till I had made mine own occasion mellow'

(38–41). But the playwright immediately introduces a complication; his Captain tells Viola, 'That were hard to compass; Because she will admit no kind of suit, No, not the duke's.' Her initial impulse stymied, Viola determines to present herself as a eunuch and offer her services to Orsino. With this scene played, we have been brought to the appropriate moment to meet Orsino, hear his lovesick whine, and learn that he has been sending servants to woo Olivia in his name.

Rereading now the play's traditional opening scene as its second scene will be a useful exercise.

> *Duke.* If music be the food of love, play on;
> Give me excess of it, that, surfeiting,
> The appetite may sicken, and so die.
> That strain again! it had a dying fall:
> O, it came o'er my ear like the sweet sound,
> That breathes upon a bank of violets,
> Stealing and giving odour! Enough; no more:
> 'Tis not so sweet now as it was before ...
> *Cu.* Will you go hunt, my lord?
> *Du.* What, Curio?
> *Cu.* The hart.
> *Du.* Why, so I do, the noblest that I
> O, when mine eyes did see Olivia first,
> Methought she purged the air of pestilence!
> That instant was I turn'd into a hart;
> And my desires, like fell and cruel hounds,
> E'er since pursue me.
> Enter Valentine
> How now! what news from her? (1.1.1–22)

Note that if this scene is played first we have no idea who is the Olivia to whom Orsino refers. But hearing this after the Captain's description of the mourning Countess lends much more colour and depth to Orsino's lament. Valentine now reports the failure of his emissary:

> So please my lord, I might not be admitted;
> But from her handmaid do return this answer:
> The element itself, till seven years' heat,
> Shall not behold her face at ample view;
> But, like a cloistress, she will veiled walk

> And water once a day her chamber round
> With eye-offending brine: all this to season
> A brother's dead love, which she would keep fresh
> And lasting in her sad remembrance. (1.1.23–31)

Having heard the Captain's litany of Olivia's losses we can understand the depth of her mourning.

Now imagine that you are seeing *Twelfth Night* for the first time. You have no inkling of the circumstances in which we meet these characters at rise, not even their names. Which sequence of scenes is more informative, motivating and, therefore, more engrossing? Surely the scene which begins 'What country, friends, is this?' was written to precede 'If music be the food of love'.

Why 1.2 was 1.1: the maths have it

There is a third, and perhaps more important, mathematical reason to believe Shakespeare's manuscript began with Viola's arrival at Illyria. We do not know the date of the shipwreck or Viola's coming ashore. But in 5.1 Shakespeare gives us an unusually precise accounting of the time elapsed during the action of the play. Antonio declares:

> To-day, my lord; and for three months before,
> No interim, not a minute's vacancy,
> Both day and night did we [Sebastian and I] keep company.
> Enter Olivia and Attendants
> *Du.* Here comes the countess: now heaven walks on earth.
> But for thee, fellow; fellow, thy words are madness:
> Three months this youth hath tended upon me.
>   (90–5, my emphasis)

So Antonio rescued Sebastian from the sea *one day* before Viola entered Orsino's employ. We also know that Viola has been employed for *three days* before Orsino sends her to court Olivia in his name. Valentine tells Viola (and us), 'If the duke continue these favours towards you, Cesario, you are like to be much advanced: he hath known you but *three days*, and already you are no stranger' (1.4.1–4). *Whenever Shakespeare is so specific about time he is inviting us – challenging us – to read him very closely.*

If Orsino has already known Viola-Cesario for *three days*, his order that she court Olivia in his name must be given on the *fourth day* of her employment. She visits Olivia and, as their meeting ends, Olivia sends Malvolio after Viola with a ring, saying, 'If that youth will come this way *tomorrow*' (1.5.298, my emphasis). Sure enough, on her *fifth day* in Orsino's employ Viola returns and greets Olivia most memorably: 'Most excellent accomplished lady, the heavens rain odours on you!' (3.1.82–3). Andrew, overhearing, snorts: 'That youth's a rare courtier – "rain odours" – well.' A moment later, he repeats the curious words: 'odours', 'pregnant', 'vouchsafed'. 'I'll get 'em all three ready' (3.1.88–9). The treble repetition of 'odours' suggests that Shakespeare does not want us to overlook Viola's peculiar salutation.

This crux is so obscure that no commentator has attempted it. However, if we bear in mind that Shakespeare frequented Shoreditch as an actor, playwright, and sometime resident – and if we remember that the parish church of Shoreditch was St Leonard's – we can recognize Viola's strange salutation as a calendrical marker for the date on which Shakespeare imagined this scene taking place.

Shakespeare's calendar-play

St Leonard (fl. *ca.* 500) was known as the 'sweet-smelling'. In *The Golden Legend*, that immensely popular gazetteer of saints, Jacobus de Voragine parsed Leonard's name this way: '*Leonardus* means the perfume of the people, from *leos*, people, and *nardus*, which is a sweet-smelling herb; and Leonard drew people to himself by the sweet odor of his good renown.'[4] Sweet-smelling Leonard's feast day was 6 November. Viola greets Olivia with a wink at *Leonardus* on his feast day.

Though obscure to us, Leonard's feast was noted in English calendars of Shakespeare's time. Figure 6 shows a portion of the November table in the Book of Common Prayer (1599). St Leonard's Day, 6 November, is conspicuous between All Saints, 1 November, and the Feast of St Martin, 11 November. Certainly, Leonard's feast day was alive in the minds of many Elizabethans, particularly sometime parishioners of St Leonard's Church, Shoreditch – including William Shakespeare. Traditionally, the church was decked with flowers on the sweet saint's day, 6 November.

Psalmes.			Morning praier.		Evening praier.	
			1. Lesson	2. Lesson	1. Lesson	2. Lesson
1	d	Kalend.	All Saints	Eccl. 3	Heb.12	Eccl. v	Apo.xix
2	e	iiii		Eccl.14	Luk.28	Eccl.	Colo.ii
3	f	iii		xvi	xix	xv	iii
4	g	Pridie.		xviii	xx	xvii	iiii
5	A	Nones.		xx	xxi	xix	iThes.i
6	b	viii	Leonard.	xxiiii	xxii	xxi	ii
7	c	vii		xvii	xxiii	xxiii	iii
8	d	vi		xxix	xxiiii	xxv	iiii
						xxviii	

6 Book of Common Prayer calendar, November

Once we recognize that Shakespeare set Viola's second visit to Olivia on St Leonard's Day – that is, *day five* of her employ is 6 November – we can reconstruct the internal calendar that the playwright imagined for his play. If Viola has been in Orsino's employ three days before her first visit to Olivia on 5 November, she must have begun her employment on 2 November, and was in his service during 2, 3, and 4 November. Small wonder that directors Peter Brook and Trevor Nunn report having felt an 'autumnal' atmosphere in *Twelfth Night*. Shakespeare's internal calendar is quite simple and, doubtless, was transparent to some first auditors. From Antonio's 'three months and one day' we know that the shipwreck, Sebastian's rescue, and Viola's arrival on Illyria took place on 1 November. This sorts remarkably well with her mourning for a brother deemed lost at sea; November was the Elizabethans' month of the dead. 1 November is All Saints' Day, which Elizabethans called All Hallows or Hallowmas, the commemoration of all deceased believers.[5] Figure 7 shows Shakespeare's internal calendar for the first acts of *Twelfth Night*. According to Shakespeare's calendar, Antonio rescued Sebastian on 1 November, the same day Viola arrived in Illyria and one day before she entered Orsino's service on 2 November. Having served Orsino for three days, Viola visits Olivia on 5 November and returns to court her on the 6th, the Feast of St Leonard.

Beginning at the beginning

1 November	Viola comes ashore in Illyria
2 November	Day 1 of Viola's employ
3 November	Day 2 of Viola's employ
4 November	Day 3 of Viola's employ
5 November	Viola's first visit to Olivia
6 November	Viola's second visit to Olivia

7 Internal Twelfth Night calendar

Shakespeare's calendar *demands* that 1.2 must be the opening scene of the play. If 1.1 is played first, any length of time, even a month, might have elapsed between the Duke sighing for Olivia and Viola making landfall, in which case the chronology provided by the Duke and Antonio in 5.1 will make no sense. But, of course, the key question is: *why did Shakespeare settle on three months*? Why not four? Or two or six?

Because if we take Orsino at his word – that he has known Viola for precisely three months – the date of the twins' reunion in 5.1 must be *three months after her entering his employ on 2 November* – that is, *2 February, Candlemas*, the date of the play's performance at the Inns of Court – and the *anniversary of the christening of Shakespeare's twins on 2 February 1585*.

This is further proof that Shakespeare had this performance in mind as he penned his play. We don't know the cause of Hamnet's death, but he was buried on 11 August, the height of summer; did he drown while swimming in the River Avon?

Recovering the link between the reunion of Viola with a brother believed dead and the anniversary of the christening of the playwright's own twins casts a patina of bereavement over the conclusion of Shakespeare's *Twelfth Night* that crystallizes in Feste's song. Shakespeare's airy, seemingly care-free comedy contains a nugget of ineffable pain as it embodies the playwright's hope for another reunion in heaven.

Elizabeth's special day

We can recover one more significant date in the play: the night when Toby, Andrew, and Feste held the conversation that Andrew remembers in 2.3: 'In sooth, thou wast in very gracious fooling last night, when thou spokest of *Pigrogronitus* ...' (20–1). We now recognize that Shakespeare's Feste brought Good News to Illyria as St Paul did. This time it was news of the Gregorian reform. And Feste's attempt to explain it to Toby and Andrew accounts for Andrew's hazy recollection of *Pontifex Grigorius* and the Pavians ratifying the Equinoctial Rule of Eusebius.

Since their drinking bout takes place on the night of Viola's first visit to Olivia (5 November), Andrew's reference to 'last night' suggests that their conversation took place on the night of 4 November, the eve of the Feast of St Elizabeth, mother of John the Baptist, and Queen Elizabeth's name day.

Like Toby and Andrew, the vast majority of Elizabeth's courtiers must have been absolutely baffled by the debate over the new calendar. They had certainly been told that Gregory's calendar was correct. But why that was so surely eluded many courtiers – as it would Lord Chesterfield when he proposed England's eleven-day calendar reform before the House of Lords in 1751. But England's canny Queen who had battled her bishops for calendar reform understood it.

In sum, what Shakespeare has done in framing *Twelfth Night, or What You Will* is to knit together secular and sacred sources (*Gl'ingannati*, Riche, Nashe, St Paul), friends and enemies (Nashe, Harvey), minor saints (Fabian, Sebastian, Leonard), bitter loss (Hamnet), and his own hope for an Elysian reunion – all served up in a text peppered with anagrams, wordplay and snatches of Scripture – and bubbling with topicality. To top this off, Shakespeare gave his play a title which recognized (and celebrated) a decisive Queen and the power of her will. It is a dazzling *coup de théâtre*.

In the final chapter I will examine some of the personal tributes which dot Shakespeare's plays, perhaps less elaborate than his celebration of Marlowe in *As You Like It*, but no less deeply felt.

Notes

1 Marc Norman and Tom Stoppard, *Shakespeare in Love*, undated draft, www.imsdb.com (accessed 21 June 2016).
2 J. M. Lothian and T. W. Craik, eds, *Twelfth Night, or What You Will*, The Arden Shakespeare, Series 2 (London: Thomson Learning, 1975), lxxxiii.
3 Though twenty-four bridges now span the Thames, in 1602 the only cart and foot crossing was London Bridge, which was first constructed during the Roman occupation, its wooden structure being rebuilt in stone in 1209. Westminster Bridge, which connects Whitehall to the south bank, opened in 1750.
4 Jacobus Voragine, *The Golden Legend*, ed. Eamon Duffy, reprint (Princeton: Princeton University Press, 2012), 629.
5 2 November was the Catholic feast of All Souls, which commemorates all the departed; though suppressed during the Reformation, the holy day was still bright in living memory.

N.B. If, as I suggest, 1.2 was the opening scene in Shakespeare's original draft of the play, how does it happen that this scene was placed second in the First Folio, our earliest and authoritative text? While it is impossible (at the moment) to answer that question with conviction, one must remember that any play – even a Shakespeare play – was and is a work-in-progress *in perpetuity*; to this day, directors are trimming, cutting, shuffling scenes, time-shifting, and heaping on physical business to evoke new meanings from his texts. If, as we're told, the house musicians would play while the auditors entered the theatre and found their places, one can see how a seamless segue into 1.1 was possible if the musicians played the 'dying fall' as Orsino and company took the stage. Some bright mind may have suggested this alteration – it worked – and it made its way into the Folio. In any case, Shakespeare was deceased seven years before the (revised) text made its appearance in print.

10

Tributes private and public

We tend to separate Shakespeare from other authors; he appears timeless, and deserves to stand apart. But Shakespeare was, after all, a writer – a great writer, of course, but he was also an infant, adolescent, lover, husband, father, and man. Weren't his own life experiences as important to him as, say, Antony's or Bolingbroke's, or more so? Weren't his friendships as dear to him as Valentine's, his loves as unquenchable as Helena's, his losses as bitter as Hamlet's? Though a multitude of commentators and biographers have judged Shakespeare an unusually secretive person, wouldn't it be stranger still if events in his own life did not colour his works?

Every fiction writer's *oeuvre* constitutes an autobiography. Though it may not be linear, cannot be literal, might intentionally obfuscate or drift into fantasizing, it is notwithstanding true. It is truer than can be any biography written by a researcher-come-lately, no matter how diligent, perceptive, and blunt. I have argued that Shakespeare's works are no exception, that his sonnets and plays are studded with local, topical, and personal allusions, many of them yet to be recovered. As I will suggest in this chapter, some of the most trenchant and revealing are the tributes he fashioned for those he mourned. Because they were written as 'private' memorials, that is, for a very small coterie among Shakespeare's auditors, they have remained completely opaque to commentators for centuries, and even now are difficult to detect and parse.

Private memorials on stage

With the writing of *King John* in 1596 (if not years before), William Shakespeare began a practice of inscribing into his texts tributes to deceased friends, family, and benefactors. The most conspicuous of these (if not to us then perhaps to his colleagues and some first auditors) was his play-length tribute to Marlowe. He also drew three portraits of Thom Nashe in *Love's Labour's Lost*, *As You Like It*, and *Twelfth Night*. Another, briefer memorial written for the deceased William Brooke, Tenth Baron Cobham and Lord Chamberlain, appears in *Henry V*.

Brooke is said to have taken umbrage at Shakespeare's adoption of the name of his famous predecessor, Sir John Oldcastle (d. 1417), for the misleader of Prince Hal in *1 Henry IV* (1596). (See the discussion of the Oldcastle contretemps in 'Shakespeare's bad timing' in Longer notes' below.) In August 1596 Brooke succeeded Henry Carey as Lord Chamberlain; he briefly held the post until his death in March 1597, at which time Carey's son, George (1547–1603), attained the post. Perhaps because of lingering enmity between the Careys and Brookes, Shakespeare waited almost two years before Falstaff's death provided the appropriate vehicle. Shakespeare also framed his tribute in such a way that only Brooke's nearest family and friends would recognize it.

In *Henry V* 2.3 Bardolph, Pistol, and their Eastcheap brothers-in-arms are preparing to join the King's expedition to France when Hostess brings word that Sir John Falstaff has died. On hearing this Bardolph declares, 'Would I were with him, wheresome're he is, either in heaven or in hell.' Hostess responds,

> Nay, sure he's not in hell. He's in Arthur's bosom if ever man went to Arthur's bosom. A made a finer end, and went away an it had been any christom child. A parted ev'n just between twelve and one, ev'n at the turning o'th' tide – for after I saw him fumble with the sheets, and play with flowers, and smile upon his finger's end, I knew there was but one way. For his nose was as sharp as a pen, and a babbled of green fields. (9–16)[1]

Hostess's speech has two thrusts. First, she assures us that, after a death as decorous as any innocent child's, Falstaff has been saved; his soul has flown directly to 'Arthur's bosom' – that is, Abraham's heavenly bosom. Given that Hostess is speaking on the eve of Henry's departure for France, 11 August 1415, Falstaff's is a remarkably early exemplar of a Protestant death and instantaneous salvation. Then again, Foxe and the Elizabethans admired the Lollard John Oldcastle as an archetypal Protestant.[2] The second element of Hostess's speech is a three-part description of the moment of Falstaff's death.

Hostess begins with (1) the hour of death, telling us that Falstaff 'parted ev'n just between twelve and one', that is, between midnight and 1 a.m. She also that noticed Falstaff died (2) 'ev'n at the turning o'th' tide'. This was the traditional hour of leave-taking, when ships left harbour and sailors said farewell to loved ones; it became proverbial for that final leave-taking, death. Non-sailors should understand that 'tide-turn' is not an instantaneous event; in the Thames the tide rose and fell almost imperceptibly in the half-hour before and after turn.[3] This seeming lack of flow is known as 'slack tide'.

Finally, Hostess tells us that (3) Falstaff 'babbled of green fields' – that is, he attempted to recite the Twenty-Third Psalm. The version in the Geneva Bible (1599) begins, 'The Lord is my shepherd, I shal not want. He maketh me to rest in grene pasture, & leadeth me by the still waters.'

So Falstaff died:

1. Between 12 midnight and 1a.m.
2. At the turning of the tide.
3. Having muttered the Twenty-Third Psalm.

I will demonstrate that these three details form a precise epitome of the death of William Brooke, whose forebear Oldcastle was sometime Falstaff.

We know from a letter of Rowland Whyte to Sir Robert Sydney that Brooke died on the night of 5–6 March; on Sunday 6 March Whyte wrote, 'About midnight my Lord Chamberlain [Brooke] died.' So both Falstaff and Brooke died (1) at the midnight hour.

The site of Brooke's death was his home at Blackfriars where the Fleet River entered the Thames. With modern oceanographic computer software it is possible to recover the time at which the tide in the Thames turned on the night of 5–6 March 1597. In fact, tide-turn at London Bridge was 12.19 a.m. – that is, nineteen minutes after midnight 'ev'n just between twelve and one'. Like Falstaff, Brooke (1) died at the midnight hour as (2) the tide turned.

Hostess also reports that Falstaff mumbled the Twenty-Third Psalm. Elizabethans who followed the liturgical calendar in the Book of Common Prayer would read or recite all 150 Psalms over the course of each month. After years of repetition many could instantly recall the evening of the month prescribed for the beloved Twenty-Third Psalm. It was the fourth – except in March, when the

Twenty-Third Psalm was prescribed for evening prayer on the fifth day of the month.[4]

So Falstaff and Brooke both died (1) at the midnight hour (2) at the turning of the tide, and (3) in association with the Twenty-Third Psalm.

Of course, these might be three coincidences. But is that likely? Particularly given the awkward association of Brooke with Oldcastle-Falstaff in *1 Henry IV*?

A better question is: who among Shakespeare's auditors could have recognized these ephemeral connections between the deaths of Oldcastle-Falstaff and Brooke? Only those persons so close to Brooke that they would have attended his death.

Family members and intimate friends who were present in the death room would certainly have noted the hour of Brooke's passing. Some of them may have made the journey to his Blackfriars residence by water, and may have had to return home by the same route; they would have been mindful of the turning of the tide. And all those who were confessing Anglican Christians may well have joined in reciting that evening's devotions including the Twenty-Third Psalm. This is just the tiny coterie audience that Shakespeare wished to reach with his encomium for his late benefactor.

Hostess's insistence that Falstaff (and Brooke) made a fine end and flew to Abraham's bosom is Shakespeare's gentle memorial for his deceased Lord Chamberlain.

How Henry Carey inspired Faulconbridge

Emrys Jones liked to caution his doctoral candidates (myself included): 'We have Shakespeare's plays, but not his mind.' That was his way of discouraging extravagant speculation about Shakespeare's meanings (doubtless, Professor Jones would have been horrified by the title of this book). One of the questions raised during those too-short tutorials in his rooms at New College concerned *King John*: was Shakespeare's play a rewrite of an anonymous (and not very good) play, *The Troublesome Reign* of *King John* (*ca.* 1589)? Or was *The Troublesome Reign* a rewrite of Shakespeare?

Though the former sequence is now widely accepted, in 1993 scholars were still divided. Early in the twentieth century Peter Alexander thought Shakespeare's the earlier; in his Arden Series 2 edition (1963) Ernst Honigmann supported Alexander's theory.[5] And twenty years later in *Shakespeare's Influence on his Contemporaries* Honigmann elaborated this mistaken idea.[6] Formidable scholars queued on both sides of the question.[7]

More than a decade passed before Kenneth Muir finally unhorsed the scurrilous notion in 1977.[8] Nowadays, the consensus rightly holds that *The Troublesome Reign* provided the template for Shakespeare's *King John*. But as late as the 1990s, the Alexander-Honigmann position had its adherents. Professor Jones also raised a corollary question: didn't it appear that Shakespeare's sole purpose in rewriting the earlier play was to create the heroic Bastard Faulconbridge?

In time I concluded that Shakespeare had created his *King John* and the character of the royal Bastard as a tribute to his recently deceased Lord Chamberlain and patron, royal bastard Henry Carey, who died on 23 July 1596. As well, I inferred that Constance's lament for her Arthur expressed the playwright's own grief at the death of Hamnet Shakespeare, buried a mere nineteen days later. As luck would have it, over lunch one summer Sunday I had occasion to offer my conclusion to Professor Jones. He took it aboard, but I've never been entirely sure he believed it.

In fact, Shakespeare wrote two memorials for Henry Carey, one in *King John*, a second in *Hamlet*. In the former play Shakespeare modelled the character of Philip Faulconbridge on Carey. Some resemblances are obvious: both were royal bastards, swashbuckling campaigners, heroic, resourceful, cynical, steadfast, and unshakably loyal. But Shakespeare's linkage of the two illegitimates runs much deeper; indeed, it may border on sedition.

Carey's claim to the English crown was every bit as good (and bad) as Elizabeth's. Born in 1533, Elizabeth had been declared a bastard by her father and Act of Parliament (1536). Carey was her senior (born *ca*. 1526) and male – either trait would have been sufficient to give him precedence in the royal succession had both their births been legitimated. Notwithstanding, Carey proved the Queen's unflaggingly loyal subject; he laboured tirelessly and heroically in Elizabeth's service in the northern wars, on her Privy Council, and as chief of her personal bodyguard during the Armada emergency of 1588. Like Shakespeare's Faulconbridge, who sought no honours beyond service, Carey (on his deathbed) refused Elizabeth's offer of an earldom.[9]

Tributes private and public 151

Carey was no fey courtier; contemporary accounts characterize him as frank, outspoken, bluff – in Sir Robert Naunton's phrase, 'He loved sword and buckler men'.[10] Throughout her reign Elizabeth relied on Carey's capabilities – and loyalty – implicitly. She sent him north in 1568 to quell the intrigues festering about Mary Queen of Scots and numberless conspiracies among the northern earls and their Scots accomplices. Though Carey's troops were vastly outnumbered, he won a series of startling victories; the Queen wrote, 'you were by God appointed the instrument of my glory'.[11] This was the stuff of legend.

By spring 1571, the northern marches were quieted. But Carey still pursued the renegade Earl of Northumberland – which led to a memorable episode. Carey 'used the threat of force to bring about the surrender of the castle [at Leith] but to no avail; the defenders hoped for succour from France while the king's party clamoured insistently for more money ... [finally] in May 1572 the Scots handed over Northumberland in return for £2000.'[12] Commodity, indeed.

Carey's magic touch in the north made him indispensable to Elizabeth for the next fifteen years. Though the Queen appointed him to her Privy Council in 1577 and handed him the Chamberlain's wand in July 1585, Elizabeth repeatedly sent Carey north when danger threatened. His final sally was in 1587. As the Armada crisis loomed Carey was abruptly recalled in April 1588 to raise musters in Norfolk and Suffolk and to serve as chief of the Queen's personal bodyguard, which implies that Carey enjoyed the Queen's perfect trust. For this service Elizabeth presented him with the magnificent Hunsdon Onyx. Carey died on 23 July 1596 and was buried in Westminster Abbey on 12 August (one day after Hamnet Shakespeare) at the Queen's expense – a fitting tribute to the extraordinary career of a royal bastard. His heirs and friends erected a monument that is, even by Westminster standards, regal.[13]

The moment in Carey's life which most strikingly embodies the royalty of spirit with which Shakespeare endued his Faulconbridge was his final hour. Carey had long sought an earldom for himself and his heirs. Perhaps because of his (unspoken) claim to the crown Elizabeth denied him this advancement. It wasn't until Carey was dying that the Queen relented. Fuller reported that

> When he [Carey] lay on his death-bed, the Queen gave him a gracious visit, causing his Patent for the said Earldom to be drawn, his Robes

to be made, and both to be laid down upon his bed; but this Lord (who could dissemble neither well nor sick) 'Madam,' said he, 'seeing you counted me not worthy of this honour whilst I was living, I count myself unworthy of it now I am dying.'[14]

If there is truth to this tale, Carey's words must have been whispered among his intimates and retainers – and more widely – within moments after they fell on the chastened ear of the Queen.

It is, I suggest, Henry Carey's fault that *King John* is considered Shakespeare's most unsatisfying play; its 'stage history in the twentieth century is a melancholy record of fewer and fewer productions'.[15] Even the handful of scholars who have written at length about *King John* find themselves sorely pressed to appreciate (or defend) its curiously hollow structure and lack of a central hero-figure.[16] Sigurd Burckhardt wrote: 'Even bardolaters have little good to say about the last two acts ... And I strongly suspect Shakespeare himself knew he was not bringing the thing off.'[17] The play's most admired Shakespearean creation is dismissed as a supernumerary: '*King John* with Faulconbridge as hero is a play without form and void, signifying nothing. He is outside the structure of the play as he is outside it historically.'[18] But the fact is, Faulconbridge and Henry Carey were the heart and soul of the play.

Our principal dissatisfaction with *King John* comes in the final act when Prince Henry makes his sudden appearance and we find ourselves convinced that the wrong man (boy) possesses the throne. In 1962, William Matchett identified the root of our discontent:

> The plot of King John is built around the question of who should be King of England and thus of what constitutes a 'right' to the throne. In the first act, three characters are shown to have particular claims to the crown. With the death of Arthur, the failure and eventual collapse of John and ... it would appear that the Bastard is being groomed to take over as rightful king. The final scenes, however, with their surprising introduction of a new claimant of unknown character and ability [Prince Henry], defeat this expectation.[19]

I believe that this disconcerting *dénouement* is precisely the effect Shakespeare was driving for when he took up *The Troublesome Reign* and created the Bastard Faulconbridge to commemorate Henry Carey, that is, the wrong heir occupies the throne. This patent sedition has never been recognized by scholars.

Shakespeare's leap to the sixteenth century

In those months immediately following Carey's death it would not have taken much to encourage the wiser sort among Shakespeare's audience to correlate his dashing Faulconbridge with the late-great, larger-than-life Henry Carey. The character's royal bastardy, outspoken manner, heroism, and selfless honour could have been sufficient to establish the connection. But Shakespeare adopted two subtle strategies to tighten the links between Carey and the Bastard. First, through time-shift signals he jogged his auditors' focus from the thirteenth to the sixteenth century.

Time-shifts were a familiar tactic for delving into contemporary subjects which might be banned by the censors. One device which Shakespeare employed in *King John* is a reference to a French '*armado*' (3.4.2).[20] Shakespeare's loaded word, *armado* does not appear in *The Troublesome Reign*; it is also Spanish in form, *armada* being the French. When Shakespeare's *French* King Philip announces that his '*armado*' has foundered some auditors could detect a link with the fate of *Spanish* King Philip's Armada of 1588.[21] Henry Carey played a heroic role during that emergency just as the Bastard will emerge to lead the armies of *King John*.

Another of Shakespeare's time-shift signals – obscure to us but resonant with Elizabethans – appears in John's diction as he defies the papal legate, Pandulph:

> What earthie name to Interrogatories
> Can tast the free breath of a sacred King?
> Thou canst not (Cardinall) devise a name
> So slight, unworthy, and ridiculous
> To charge me to an answere, as the Pope:
> Tell him this tale, and from the mouth of England,
> Adde thus much more, that no Italian Priest
> Shall tythe or toll in our dominions:
> But as we, under heaven, are supreme head,
> So under him that great supremacy
> Where we doe reigne, we will alone uphold
> Without th'assistance of a mortall hand. (3.1.147–58)

In this speech Lily B. Campbell detects 'the voice of Elizabeth' speaking through John;[22] her inference misses the mark. It is not Elizabeth speaking but her father, Henry VIII. A careful reading of

Shakespeare's words reveals a precise epitome of Henry's attacks on the power of the papacy in England.

To begin, 'interrogatories' are legal questions, usually in writing, demanded of a witness or litigant. Thomas More notes in his *Apology* that it was common practice to question suspected heretics from a written list of interrogatories; many of the questions were cleverly designed to trip the interrogatee and/or entrap him in heresy.[23] But it was also common for a secular or clerical court, when witnesses or litigants were distant, to send written interrogatories to be answered under oath in the presence of an officer. In 1533 the practice of sending interrogatories from Rome to England and vice versa was outlawed by the Act in Restraint of Appeals (24 Henry VIII, c. 12).

John's next lines ridicule the name 'Pope' and exchange it for 'Italian priest', a common epithet in Shakespeare's time. The Pope's title was officially denounced in the Ecclesiastical Licenses Act (25 Henry VIII, c. 21) of 1534, which makes repeated references to 'the Bishop of Rome, called the Pope'.

John next dismisses the Pope's power to 'tythe or toll in our dominions'. Tithing and tolling are distinct activities. In 1532, Act 23 Henry VIII, c. 20 placed a moratorium on the payment to the Pope of those tithes known as 'first fruits', that is, the first year's revenues of a newly appointed English bishop. This ban became permanent in 1534 under the Act Restraining the Payment of Annates (25 Henry VIII, c. 20). As to the Pope's power to 'toll' – that is, to levy a tax upon the kingdom of England by exacting an annual tribute of £200 known as 'Peter's pence' – this facility was suppressed by the Ecclesiastical Licences Act.

Finally, we come to John's proclamation that 'we, under heaven, are supreme head' of the church in England. The words derive from the Act of Supremacy (26 Henry VIII, c. 1) of 1534, which finally made official the break with Rome: 'the King's Majesty justly and rightfully is and oweth to be the Supreme Head of the Church of England'.[24]

Considered in this light, John's speech to Pandulph is not merely a reiteration of Protestant propaganda in England under Elizabeth. Shakespeare has written a point-by-point restatement of the antipapal statutes of Henry VIII — and very nearly ticks through them in exact chronological order. By so doing, Shakespeare contrives to make his John thunder with the voice not of Elizabeth but of Henry

VIII, father of Henry Carey. Elizabethans would not have confused the rhetoric of Henry VIII with that of Elizabeth as some scholars have done. Shakespeare's auditors knew that only Henry had been 'supreme head' of the English church; in 1559 Elizabeth became merely its 'supreme governor'.[25]

Carey and James Gournie

In addition to time-shifting the on-stage action, Shakespeare sketched into *King John* an episode linking the Bastard with Henry Carey. He contrives for his Bastard to free the captured Queen Eleanor in 3.2, a feat performed by John in *The Troublesome Reign*; this is a nod at Carey's body-guarding Queen Elizabeth during the Armada scare.

Some other instances are particularly inscrutable; overt references to the newly deceased Carey in late 1596 could have run afoul of the censor. But as ephemeral as Shakespeare's Carey–Faulconbridge links may be, they are also unmistakable. The first appears when Eleanor recognizes Faulconbridge's resemblance to a deceased king, Richard *Cordelion*:

> He hath a trick of *Cordelions* face,
> The accent of his tongue affecteth him:
> Do you not read some tokens of my sonne
> In the large composition of this man? (1.1.85–8)

Henry Carey was said to strongly resemble Henry VIII in his face, brusque manner of speaking, and 'large composition', that is, burly physique.[26] But this might have been said of any number of men.

Now comes one of Shakespeare's almost-invisible touches which link Faulconbridge with Carey: the name of Lady Faulconbridge's attendant, who does not appear in *The Troublesome Reign* but with whom Shakespeare's Bastard seems to enjoy familiar relations. The name appears as 'Gurney' in the Folio stage direction 'Enter Lady Faulconbridge and James Gurney' (1.1.219, stage direction). But the stage direction may have been a book-keeper's interpolation; Shakespeare spells the name 'Gournie' in the Bastard's speech, 'James Gournie, wilt thou give us leave a while?' (230).

As to the particularity Shakespeare lends to Gournie – who appears here and never again – Braunmuller notes that 'Shakespeare rarely names plebian characters so precisely unless there is an ulterior motive.'²⁷ Shakespeare's name, Gournie, points to France and Normandy, the ancestral home of the Careys. 'Gournie' is derived from the town of Gournay in Haute-Normandie not far from the Careys' seat, Lisieux.²⁸ Ascelin and Hugh de Gournay fought beside William the Conqueror at Hastings in 1066; perhaps some Careys of Lisieux did, too. Shakespeare's wink at the Norman Gournay or Gournie is another nod to the Careys.

Acts of recognition in *King John*

The Troublesome Reign begins with Queen Elinor importuning the barons to recognize John as a worthy successor to late King Richard (1.1–8). When Shakespeare took up the old play he deftly restructured the drama to focus attention on acts of recognition; repeatedly, these occur at critical junctures.

Shakespeare's first act of recognition may have preceded his first line of dialogue; some commentators and directors believe that *actus primus* should open with a dumb-show coronation of John.²⁹ I believe that Shakespeare's company offered a coronation pantomime preceding John's preemptory '*Now* say Chatillion what would France with us?' (1.1.1, my emphasis). The coronation dumb-show may have been repeated prior to the first line of 4.2: 'Heere once againe we sit: once again crown'd'; John has been recognized as king a second time, much to the consternation of his nobles. In 5.1 John's kingship is recognized a third time as Pandulph replaces the crown upon his head. Against this repetitious, hollow pageantry Shakespeare sets the stony reality of the citizens of Angiers, who cannot and will not recognize John (or Philip of France) as their rightful king.

For his part, the Bastard is the focus of four acts of recognition. In 1.1 Eleanor recognizes Faulconbridge as the son of Richard *Cordelion*. In 5.1, the despairing John recognizes the Bastard as the leader of the English armies, saying, 'Have thou the ordering of this present time' (80). There is a final act of recognition in the play – when the Bastard kneels before the boy-king Henry, saying, 'with all submission on my knee, I do bequeath my faithfull services And true subjection everlasting' (5.7.112–13). Shakespeare found all these acts of recognition in some form in *The Troublesome Reign*.

But Shakespeare added another act of recognition. It occurs in a scene which pre-echoes the opening of *Hamlet*. Both scenes take place in perfect darkness; the characters on stage cannot see one another's faces. *King John* 5.6 begins,

> *Hub.* Whose there? Speak hoa, speak quickely, or I shoote.
> *Bast.* A Friend. What art thou?
> *Hub.* Of the part of England.
> *Bast.* Whither doest thou go?
> *Hub.* What's that to thee?
> *Hub.* [Bas.] Why may not I demand of thine affaires,
>   As well as thou of mine?
> *Bast.* Hubert, I think.
> *Hub.* Thou hast a perfect thought. (5.6.1–7)

The moment is an eerie pre-echo of the opening of *Hamlet* Q2:

> *Bar.* Whose there?
> *Fran.* Nay answere me. Stand and unfolde your selfe.
> *Bar.* Long live the King.
> *Fran.*   Barnardo.
> *Bar.*   Hee. (1.1.1–4)[30]

In *Hamlet*, as in *King John*, a watchful soldier issues a challenge only to find himself challenged. In *Hamlet* the speakers recognize one another by voice. A few lines later the challenger in *King John* must ask, 'Who art thou?', to which the Bastard pregnantly replies, 'Who thou wilt; and if thou please Thou mayst befriend me so much as to think *I come one way of the Plantagenets*' (5.6.11–13, my emphasis).

Whereas *The Troublesome Reign*'s acts of recognition were all matters of politics, Shakespeare's 5.6 has an elusive, almost existential quality. 'Who's there?' is *the* question of identity which haunts both Faulconbridge and Prince Hamlet. Shakespeare, commencing work on the revision that became *Hamlet* Q2, remembered his memorial for Henry Carey in *King John*. The common question tying the two protagonists is *legitimacy and the right to rule* – which links both Faulconbridge and Hamlet with the Careys. One might say that *The Tragedie of Hamlet Prince of Denmarke* begins at *King John* 5.6.1. (See 'On the illegitimacy of Hamlet' in 'Longer notes' below on Hamlet's questionable legitimacy.)

Hamlet, Lamord, and the Careys

When Shakespeare undertook the draft of *Hamlet* that we have in Q2, he devised a series of emblematic moments that remember and honour Henry Carey and son George. Elsewhere I have suggested that *Hamlet* Q2 is a revised text, purpose-written in mid-to-late 1603.[31] I offered evidence that Q2 was a rewrite of a pre-existing, full-blown *Hamlet*, and proposed that Shakespeare's Q2 revision was occasioned by three events which occurred in 1603: the death of Queen Elizabeth during the night of 23–4 March 1603; the 'seven years' mind' of the death of Henry Carey in July 1596; and the death of George Carey on 9 September 1603.

A central element of Shakespeare's memorial for the Careys in *Hamlet* Q2 is the appearance in 4.7 of a mysterious Frenchman not present in the First Quarto (Q1). Suborning Laertes to Hamlet's murder, Claudius recalls:

> some two months since
> Heere was a gentleman of *Normandy.*
> I have seene my selfe, and serv'd against, the French,
> And they can well on horsebacke, but this gallant
> Had witch-craft in't, he grew unto his seate ...
> *Laer.* A Norman wast?
> *King.* A Norman.
> *Laer.*   Upon my life *Lamord.*
> *King.*   The very same.
> *Laer.* I know him well, he is the brooch indeed
> And Jem, of all the Nation. (Q2 4.769–82)

The intrusion of Shakespeare's mysterious Norman and the proper spelling of his name have eluded and tantalized scholars. Both mysteries can be solved by reference to a long-ignored incident that was a turning-point in the fortunes of the Carey family.

Henry Carey was the nominal son of William Carey, sometime Master of the Horse to Henry VIII, and Mary née Boleyn.[32] The pair married on 4 February 1520; Mary was then fourteen, Carey twenty-four. Thereafter, Mary lived at court; her first child, Catherine, was born in 1524 – after which she embarked on an affair with the King for which her husband was richly compensated.[33] Mary's royal tryst ended in July 1525, perhaps when she realized she was pregnant by the King. On 4 March 1526 she gave birth to Henry Carey. Since it was common knowledge that King Henry had enjoyed Mary as well as her sister Anne[34] – and since the boy Carey strongly resembled the King, and since the child was baptized Henry (as was the King's acknowledged bastard, Henry

Fitzroy, 1519–37) – it was then as now suspected that Henry Carey was the King's bastard son.

But if Carey were Henry's natural son, why didn't he acknowledge him as he had Fitzroy, whom he created Duke of Richmond in 1524? Because had the King done so it would have raised a diriment impediment (his prior *coitus* with Mary) and rendered his marriage to her sister Anne void and their issue illegitimate.[35] Even so, on William Carey's death (23 June 1528) the king seized two year-old Henry from his mother's care and appointed Queen Anne his guardian.[36]

Once at court the boy was well educated and popular.[37] Henry became Elizabeth's favourite cousin; shortly after coming to the throne she created him Baron Hunsdon (1559) and Knight of the Garter (1561). She also named him Master of the Hawks.[38] Carey patronized a company of players of which James Burbage was a member. Carpenter James was an impresario as well as an actor like his celebrated son;[39] in 1584 he claimed to be 'Lord Hunsdon's man'. Shortly thereafter Elizabeth named Carey Lord Chamberlain.[40]

During his lifetime Carey seemed indifferent to the rumours about his birth and held himself out as a Carey and nothing but. His father, William (*ca.* 1500–28), was a descendant of an old Norman family; from Lisieux the Carreys had migrated to Guernsey and thence to England *circa* 1066.[41] But by the reign of Henry V the English Carys had apparently fallen on hard times. Then, suddenly, their line was ennobled by the remarkable feat of arms which was the defining event in the family's fortunes. The encounter is recorded in an obscure chronicle, *Remarkable antiquities of the city of Exeter* (1681). It is a tale uncannily parallel to Shakespeare's anecdote of Lamord:

> [In] A.D. 1413 a Knight named Argonise, who in divers Countries for his Honour had performed many noble Achievements, at length visited England, and challenged many persons of his Rank and Quality to make trial of his skill in Arms, which the said Sir Robert Cary accepted, between whom was waged a cruel encounter and a long and doubtful combat in Smithfield, London; where this Mars vanquished this Argonise, for which he was by the King knighted and restored to part of his Father's inheritance.[42]

So William Carey's forebear Robert won his spurs and redeemed his family's fortunes by defeating a French champion at Smithfield under the eye of Henry V.⁴³ There is every reason to believe that the Careys of Shakespeare's era cherished the ancient victory; as the Exeter chronicler records, 'by the Law of Heraldry, whosoever fairly in the Field conquered his Adversary may fortify the wearing and bearing of his Arms ... and accordingly he [Sir Robert Cary] takes on him the Coat Armoury of the said Argonise, being Argent on a bend Sable, Three Roses of the First, and ever since borne by the name of Cary.'⁴⁴ As a consequence, the coat of arms of Argonise (Figure 8) was familiar to Elizabeth, her courtiers, and Shakespeare. It boldly adorns Carey's tomb in Westminster Abbey.

Having established the concordance between the historical Argonise and fictional Lamord, it may be possible to confirm the correct spelling of the Frenchman's name, a conundrum long debated. The difficulty arose from variants in Q2 and the Folio; whereas Q2 gives us Lamord, the Folio has Lamound – which latter spelling Rowe adopted in his edition of 1709.⁴⁵ In 1725, Pope opted for Lamond.⁴⁶ In 1821, Edmond Malone speculated that Shakespeare wrote 'Lamode' to suggest that the Frenchman was fashionable (*à la mode*).⁴⁷ In the Victorian era 'Lamond' was preferred.⁴⁸ Our contemporary editors embrace 'Lamord' unanimously,

8 Coat of arms of Argonise and Carey

beginning with Bevington (1988), and Wells and Taylor (1986).[49] In 2002 Orgel and Braunmuller footnoted with finality, 'Lamord *i.e.*, "the death" (French: *la mort*)', which put period to the debate.[50]

But in 1899 Edward Dowden had produced a singular reading of Lamord: 'I retain the Q form of the name', he wrote, 'having noticed in Cotgrave, "*Mords*, [Fr.] a bitt of a horse."'[51] Jenkins, though unaware of the tale in the Exeter chronicle, also suspected a hidden significance: 'The excessively elaborate introduction of the fencing stratagem suggests ... it had for the dramatist some ulterior significance ... many suspect a personal allusion.'[52] In fact, Dowden and Jenkins came close to the truth; Lamord's identity is a personal allusion honouring the Careys, whose line was ennobled by the defeat of a French champion.

But if this is so, how is Shakespeare's fictitious name Lamord analogous to the name Argonise? Certainly, Shakespeare must have recognized that the historical champion's name implied he came from the wooded Argonne region of France. Does Shakespeare's fictitious Lamord also have a real world geographical etymology? I will suggest it does.

Dowden's curious reading was nearly correct; 'Lamord' derives from the French for the equine bitt or bit, *mords*. But the playwright's translation was not literal; rather, he is indulging in a typical Shakespearean wordplay – on the French *mords* = bite, and its homonym, 'byght' (modern: bight). A bight is an indentation in a coastline a body of water cupped between two headlands (*OED*), of which there are several in Europe, including the Egmont Bight in Dorset and the Helgoland Bight where the British claimed a famous victory over the German navy on 28 August 1914. Lamord's Norman background identifies his bight with the Seine Bight – that bay where the Seine empties into the Channel, hard by Harfleur, where Shakespeare's Henry V delivered his memorable 'Once more' exhortation to his reluctant English tigers.[53] Argonise hailed from the Argonne region; Lamord from the Normandy's Seine Bight.

Among Norman towns south-east of the Seine Bight is Lisieux.[54] The cathedral town was home to the Carrey family, whose namesake Henry was patron of Shakespeare's company and Lord Chamberlain. If this inference is valid, a defining event in Carey family history finally certifies the spelling of Shakespeare's Frenchman's name as Lamord – and not because it is fractured French for 'the death'.

Shakespeare's Onixe and Hunsdon's Onyx

There is another passage unique to *Hamlet* Q2 which links Shakespeare's revision of his play to clan Carey. In the Folio, prior to the fencing match Claudius calls out,

> Set me the Stopes of wine vpon that Table:
> If Hamlet giue the first, or second hit,
> Or quit in answer of the third exchange,
> Let all the Battlements their Ordinance fire,
> The King shal drinke to Hamlets better breath,
> And in the Cup *an vnion* shal he throw
> Richer then that, which foure successiue Kings
> In Denmarkes Crowne haue worne ...
>   (Q2, throughlines 3727–34, my emphasis)

'Union' could mean 'marriage'. Or it could mean 'pearl'. Or it could mean both, which is marvellously apropos since pearls are known to dissolve in wine and Claudius's poisoned chalice will dissolve his marriage to Gertrude as it kills her; a husband's marriage to his wife ended at the moment of her death, a wife's marriage to her husband only once he was buried. The union-pearl in the cup is such an elegant metaphor that it's difficult to accept it as a later interpolation.[55] Indeed, in Q2 it appears in a vestigial form which leaves no doubt that the metaphor was present in a version of *Hamlet* prior to 1604 (though not in Q1) and that Shakespeare altered it in his Q2 draft; I will suggest that he did so to honour the Careys.

In Q2 the object dropped into the chalice isn't a pearl; it is an 'Onixe'. Claudius says, 'And in the cup an Onixe shall he throwe' – and, later, Hamlet says, 'Drink of this potion, is thy Onixe here?' As he worked up Q2 Shakespeare inserted 'Onixe' in the two places where the word 'union' had appeared in the pre-existing text.

But Shakespeare overlooked the single appearance in the old text of the word 'pearl'. After dropping an 'Onixe' into the cup Claudius says, 'Stay, give me drinke. Hamlet this *pearl* is thine' (my emphasis). Since the union-pearl metaphor doesn't appear in Q1, we must conclude that Q2 is a rewrite of a pre-1603 text which included a pearl but has been lost.

Which brings us to a pair of seemingly unanswerable questions. Having created his elegant union-pearl metaphor in an earlier draft of the play, why did Shakespeare disfigure it in the Q2 text? And why replace his union with, of all objects, an onyx?

Tributes private and public 163

The answer to both questions can be seen today in a small glass display case in the Elizabethan gallery of London's Victoria and Albert Museum[56] It is a fabulous and famous gem, the gift of Queen Elizabeth to a man who headed her bodyguard during the Spanish Armada emergency: her favourite cousin, Henry Carey. One can imagine how proudly Carey wore this magnificent tribute, perhaps hung about his neck on a heavy gold chain. The gem is known to historians of decorative art as 'the Hunsdon Onyx' (Figure 9).[57]

The jewel is an oriental sardonyx 3.75 inches high by 3.25 inches wide, the upper face white, the lower brown. It represents the myth of Perseus' rescue of Andromeda from imprisonment on an island. Sword in hand (left), Perseus descends from the clouds to her rescue. The piece is Italian, dated to the early sixteenth century, and in an English gold frame. Anyone spying this massive jewel on Carey's breast would recognize its portrayal of his defence of Elizabeth during the Armada emergency. For the multitude of courtiers who knew that George Carey (1547–1603) would have been King of England had Henry VIII married his grandmother instead of his great-aunt ... who remembered that the Careys fetched their coat-of-arms from a French champion named Argonise ... and who had

9 The Hunsdon Onyx

seen Henry and George wearing the magnificent Hunsdon Onyx ... Shakespeare's previously unrecognized encomium in *Hamlet* Q2 rang clear.

George Carey's last illness remembered

Lamord and Claudius's Onixe would as readily connect Shakespeare's Danish prince with George Carey as with his father. But Shakespeare may have also included in Q2 a direct and trenchant reflection on George's final illness and death. Although the younger Carey died on 9 September 1603, he had relinquished the Chamberlain's white wand to Thomas Howard, later Earl of Suffolk, on 4 May. In fact, Howard had been discharging the office since 28 December 1602 because Carey was slowly dying of a sexually transmitted disease, most likely syphilis, and the effects of treatment with mercury.

Historians continue to debate whether syphilis was present in Europe in the medieval era or imported from the New World after 1492. By Shakespeare's time the malady the English called 'the French disease' was endemic; modern investigators speculate that syphilis carried off such luminaries as Henry VIII, Charles VIII, Francis I, and Ivan the Terrible. The madness of Henry's elder daughter, Mary, is ascribed to congenital infection and/or her contact with Philip of Spain. Since the disease felled heads of state and grandees as well as the poor, the progress of syphilis had been carefully observed by physicians and was well understood in Shakespeare's England.

Syphilis develops in four stages; the primary and secondary stages may run together during the first 90 to 120 days after infection. These stages are characterized by the appearance of sores and lesions, by fever and hair loss. Then, abruptly, the sufferer's symptoms vanish and the disease enters a latent, hidden phase. This hiatus may last a year or as many as twenty. The disease's emergence from latency – its tertiary stage – is marked by virulent symptoms which may include ulceration of the skin and internal organs, cardiovascular degeneration, intense thoracic pain – which the English called 'bone-ache' – and madness. Shakespeare may be glancing at George Carey's illness in a passage in Q2 which appears in neither Q1 nor the Folio:

> There liues within the very flame of loue
> A kind of weeke or snufe that will abate it,

> And nothing is at a like goodnes still,
> For goodnes growing to a plurisie,
> Dies in his owne too much, that we would doe
> We should doe when we would: for this would changes,
> And hath abatements and delayes as many,
> As there are tongues, are hands, are accedents,
> And then this should is like a spend thrifts sigh,
> That hurts by easing; but to the quick of th'vlcer. (Q2 4.7.115–24)

This speech and its delicacy of phrasing seem wholly out of character as well as place; after all, evil usurper Claudius is suborning Laertes to Hamlet's murder. Shakespeare's catalogue of ills proceeding from 'the very flame of loue' includes pleurisy, death, sighs, hurts by easing, and ulcers; these could be symptomatic of any number of diseases. But they were symptoms of tertiary syphilis. Indeed, the reference to 'abatements and delayes' – with its sense of an opportunity missed – may refer to a syphilitic's latent stage. The Cambridge *Hamlet* editor, Philip Edwards, finds the disappearance of this passage from the Folio extraordinary.[58] But it may have been a late interpolation; Shakespeare may have been in the midst of revising his play when news of George Carey's impending death arrived, which could explain its misfit tone. And discretion may have been the motive for Shakespeare's editors to delete it from the Folio text; Carey had then been dead for twenty years.

Though opaque to us until now, the composite portrait of Henry and George Carey in *Hamlet* must have been transparent to some of Shakespeare's first auditors, and conspicuously so to one important coterie: Carey's heirs and intimates. The Careys' long service as Lords Chamberlain may also explain why Hamlet takes upon himself so many of that officer's duties, for example engaging actors, choosing a play, vetting the argument, advising the players on decorum, even writing a dozen or sixteen lines.

What do Shakespeare's memorials for his deceased son and three Lords Chamberlain tell us about the playwright?

Recovering Shakespeare's tribute to William Brooke restores the paradigm of Henry Chettle's man of civil demeanour; we can recognize that Shakespeare's supposed slights to Brooke are susceptible of other, kinder explanations. Far from being snide or petty towards this Lord Chamberlain, Shakespeare composed for Brooke a tender memorial, one which may have been cherished by his heirs.

To honour Henry Carey Shakespeare created one of his most dashing heroes – witty in speech, bold in action, royally magnanimous, loyal in life and to the death, and as humble and unselfish as Carey himself. Knowing that Henry Carey stands behind the flashing tongue and warlike arm of Philip Faulconbridge must deepen and excite anew our appreciation of the underappreciated *King John*.

And recognizing Henry and son George behind the mask of Hamlet brings new and tremendous pathos to the bastard prince's lament for the ineradicable stain on his soul. The only way a bastard could erase this stain would be to undo his birth. And that is the paradox that underlies the haunting question, 'To be or not to be ...'

Notes

1 Text and lineation from Gary Taylor, ed., *Henry V*, The Oxford Shakespeare (Oxford: Oxford University Press, 1982).
2 Oldcastle smuggled Wycliffite texts to the Continent, where they inspired Jan Hus and perhaps Martin Luther.
3 The interval between high and low tide is about 6 hours 12 minutes. But as tide-turn approaches the rate of rise or fall slows until it stops entirely and then slowly begins to move in the opposite direction. In the hours before and after high or low tide, the water level rises or falls by only a twelfth of its total.
4 The calendar of liturgical readings in the forepages of Elizabethan Bibles and Books of Common Prayer prescribed a specific clutch of Psalms to be read each morning and evening. By following this rubric Elizabethans would read or recite the entire cycle of 150 Psalms each month. In a thirty-day month the Twenty-Third Psalm was prescribed for evening prayer on the fourth day of the month. However, since February is a short month of only twenty-eight days, the order of the Psalms is altered during the three months of January, February, and March. The instruction in the Book of Common Prayer is as follows: 'And because January and March have one day above the said number [i.e. thirty-one days rather than thirty], and February which is placed between them both hath only twenty-eight days, February shall borrow of either of the months (of January and March) one day. And so the Psalter which shall be read in February must begin on the last day of January and end the first day of March.' In other words, those Psalms prescribed for the first day of a typical month were, for little February, advanced to 31 January. This caused the cycle of Psalms to run one day ahead throughout February; Psalms normally read on the second day

of a month were recited on 1 February, and the Psalms for the twenty-ninth day of a typical thirty-day month were recited on 28 February. In leap years those Psalms were again recited on 29 February. The final clutch of Psalms in the cycle – those normally assigned to the thirtieth day of the month – were recited on 1 March. As a consequence, during March the Psalm cycle ran one day behind the calendar; those Psalms normally assigned to the first day of a thirty-day month were recited on the night of 2 March. Therefore, on the evening of 5 March, the Psalms were those for the fourth day of a normal thirty-day month, including the Twenty-Third Psalm.

5 Peter Alexander, *Shakespeare's* Henry VI *and* Richard III (Cambridge: Cambridge University Press, 1929), 201 ff; Ernst Honigmann, ed., *The Life and Death of King John*, The Arden Shakespeare, Series 2 (London: Methuen, 1963), xviii ff.
6 Ernst Honigmann, *Shakespeare's Influence on his Contemporaries* (Hong Kong: Macmillan, 1983), 56–90.
7 Eric Sams thinks Shakespeare wrote both. 'The Troublesome Wrangle over *King John*', Notes *and* Queries 234 (March 1988), 41–4.
8 Kenneth Muir, *The Sources of Shakespeare's Plays* (London: Methuen, 1977), 78–85.
9 For a fuller discussion see Steve Sohmer, *Shakespeare for the Wiser Sort* (Manchester: Manchester University Press, 2008), 145.
10 *Oxford Dictionary of National Biography Online* cites R. Naunton, *Fragmenta regalia* (1649), 102. In the original 'mistress', signifying Queen Elizabeth, stands in place of my 'monarch'. See Wallace T. MacCaffrey, 'Carey, Henry, first Baron Hunsdon (1526–1596)', *Oxford Dictionary of National Biography*, first published 2004; online edition, September 2014, www.oxforddnb.com/view/article/4649?docPos=15 (accessed 21 June 2012).
11 *Calendar of State Papers Domestic, Addenda – Elizabeth*, XVII.246, 26 February 1570, https://babel.hathitrust.org/cgi/pt?id=hvd.32044106490162;view=1up;seq=12 (accessed 21 June 2016).
12 MacCaffrey, 'Carey, Henry, first Baron Hunsdon'.
13 Of alabaster and marble, gilded, swarming with heraldry, and thirty-six feet tall.
14 Thomas Fuller, *The History of the Worthies of England* (London, 1662).
15 A. R. Braunmuller, ed., *King John*, The Oxford Shakespeare (Oxford: Oxford University Press, 1998), 92.
16 See for example Julia C. Van de Water, 'The Bastard in *King John*', *Shakespeare Quarterly* 11 (1960), 137–46, and Lily B. Campbell, *Shakespeare's 'Histories': Mirrors of Elizabethan Policy* (San Marino: The Huntington Library, 1947), 126–67.

17 Sigurd Burckhardt, '*King John*: The Ordering of this Present Time', *English Literary History* 33.2 (June 1966), 133.
18 Campbell, *Histories*, 166.
19 William H. Matchett, 'Richard's Divided Heritage in *King John*', *Essays in Criticism* 12 (July 1962), 2.
20 Citations from *King John* and throughline numbers from Charlton Hinman, ed., *The First Folio of Shakespeare* (New York: Norton, 1968), VII.323–44. Modern act and scene numbers from E. A. J. Honigmann, ed., *King John* (London: Methuen, 1954).
21 Another time-shift signal – one which is clear to scholars and could not have escaped the notice of Elizabethans familiar with *The Troublesome Reign* – is the absence from Shakespeare's *King John* of the Earl of Essex, an important figure in the earlier play.
22 Campbell, *Histories*, 154.
23 St Thomas More, *Apology*, xlv, in *The Yale Edition of the Complete Works of St. Thomas More* (New Haven: Yale University Press, 1979), IX.915.1.
24 Henry's acts can be found in Gerald Bray, ed., *Documents of the English Reformation* (Cambridge: James Clarke, 1994).
25 Braunmuller, *King John*, 178n.
26 According to MacCaffrey, 'Carey, Henry, first Baron Hunsdon', Carey 'stood out in the estimate of his contemporaries by his plain speaking, forthrightness, and lack of guile'. William Brooke's biographer, David McKeen, describes Carey as 'a bluff man and a good soldier ... unpolished'. McKeen, *Memory*, II.645.
27 Braunmuller, *King John*, 133n. Braunmuller speculates that the name may have been modelled after a Hugh [de] Gourney to whom Holinshed, a favourite Shakespeare source, refers elsewhere – which tends to support my inference. Holinshed also mentions the village Gornay in John's Normandy campaign of 1202. He writes that while the English succeeded in raising the French siege of Radepont, 'Howbeit after this the French king wan [won] Gourney'. Raphael Holinshed, *Chronicles: England, Scotland and Ireland*, 6 vols (London, 1807), VI.284.
28 W. Arthur, *An Etymological Dictionary of Family and Christian Names, With an essay on their derivations and import* (New York: Sheldon, Blakeman, 1857).
29 For example L. A. Beaurline, ed., *King John*, The New Cambridge Shakespeare (Cambridge: Cambridge University Press, 1990), 63n.
30 Moments later in *Hamlet* Q2, Horatio and Marcellus will enter and declare themselves 'Friend to this ground. And Leedgemen to the Dane' (1.1.12–13), echoing Hubert's 'Of the part of England'. There are more pre-echoes of *Hamlet* in *King John*. In both plays the death (murder) of a rightful king is compared with the first murder; Constance's 'For since

the birth of Cain, the first male child, To him that did but yesterday suspire' (3.4.79–83) pre-echoes Claudius's 'From the first course [Abel], till he that died to day' (Q2 1.2.14–15). Young Prince Lewis's state of mind when he expresses his *ennui*, 'There's nothing in this world can make me joy. Life is as tedious as a twice-told tale ...' (3.4.107–11) is very like young Hamlet losing his mirth (2.2.306–15).

31 Sohmer, *Wiser Sort*, 127 ff.
32 One wonders whether Claudius' admiration for Lamord's horsemanship is a polite nod to the calling of Carey's nominal father, William, Master of the Horse for Henry VIII.
33 With manors, stewardships, and an annuity.
34 Reginald Pole reported that, in 1528, a member of Parliament accused Henry of sleeping Anne's mother as well as her sister. The flustered King replied, 'Never with her mother!' The anecdote is recounted in numerous sources. 'Mary Boleyn: Biography, Portrait, Facts & Information', http://englishhistory.net/tudor/citizens/mary-boleyn/ (accessed 22 March 2013).
35 The papal dispensation that Henry sought in 1527 to invalidate his marriage to Catherine was drafted by Cardinal Wolsey and intentionally framed in language so broad as to also sweep under the rug Henry's tryst with Mary. The document reads in part: 'In order to take away all occasion from evil doers, we do in the plenitude of our power hereby suspend ... all canons affecting impediments created by affinity rising *ex illicito coitu*, in any degree even in the first ... or of any affinity contracted in any degree even the first ...' Sir Gregory da Casale presented the petition to Pope Clement VII, who declined it; instead, he dispatched Cardinal Campeggio to England to join Wolsey in hearing the case between Henry and Catherine.
36 Mary's subsequent marriage to commoner William Stafford (1534) estranged her from her ambitious family and royal in-laws; she descended into poverty and died (19 July 1543) dependent on the kindness of strangers.
37 His tutor was Nicholas Bourbon, the French poet and Latin doggerel writer; Hamlet, of course, fancies himself poetical.
38 Which may have put those 'hawkes and handsaws' into Shakespeare's mind in *Hamlet* 2.2.397.
39 He is named among the list of the Earl of Leicester's players in a document of 7 May 1574.
40 The Carey family had close ties to other members of Shakespeare's circle. George Carey's wife and daughter, both named Elizabeth, were patrons of writers including Edmund Spenser and Nashe. George's daughter and heiress, Elizabeth, married Sir Thomas Berkeley, son and heir of Henry, Lord Berkeley.

41 They amassed land and influence, and are numerous today. In Normanville, La Courture, Guernsey, there stands an imposing house which, according to the *Livre de Perchage*, was owned in 1573 by Jean de Vic, husband of Anne Careye [sic]. See 'The History of the Carey Family of Guernsey A.D. 1393–2008', www.careyroots.com (accessed April 2012).
42 By AD 1085 there were four branches of Careys in Somerset and Devonshire. See *ibid*. The original Carey arms had been 'Gules, a chevron between three swans proper, one thereof they still retain in their crest'. Richard Izacke, *Remarkable antiquities of the city of Exeter, collected by Richard Isacke, Esquire, Chamberlain thereof* (London, 1681), 71.
43 Carey named a younger son Robert.
44 Izacke, *Remarkable antiquities*, 72. In "The History of the Carey Family of Guernsey', Paul Dobree-Carey records that 'The arms were first noted in Guernsey in documents borne by Nicolas Careye as Lieutenant of Thomas Wygmore, Bailiff of Guernsey, dated 1582 ... the arms for the English branch having been registered by the Heralds College in 1531.'
45 Nicholas Rowe, ed., *The Works of Mr William Shakespear* (London, 1709), V.245.
46 Alexander Pope, ed., *The Works of Shakespear*, 6 vols (London, 1725), VI.446.
47 Citing 'the next speech but one: "he is the brooch, indeed, And gem of all the nation"'. Edmond Malone, ed., *The Plays and Poems of William Shakespeare*, 10 vols (London, 1821), VII.452.
48 By J. P. Collier (1858), Dyce (1877), Wright (1894), Verity (1911), and Brook's and Crawford's Yale (1917). Only Craig (1905) held out for Lamord. 'This name, so suggestive of La Mort, looks the right name for the centaur-like Norman conjured up out of nowhere [and] Lamound seems more like to be a misreading of it ...' G. R. Hibbard, ed., *Hamlet*, reprint, The Oxford Shakespeare (Oxford: Oxford University Press, 2008), 315n.
49 See David Bevington and David Scott Kasdan, eds, *The Tragedy of Hamlet, Prince of Denmark* (New York: Penguin, 1988); Stanley Wells, Gary Taylor, John Jowett and William Montgomery, eds, *The Oxford Shakespeare: The Complete Works* (Oxford: Oxford University Press, 1986).
50 Stephen Orgel and A. R. Braunmuller eds, *The Complete Pelican Shakespeare*, 2nd revised edition (New York: Penguin, 2002).
51 E. Dowden, *The Plays of Shakespeare* (London, 1899), VI.179. He did, however, perceive that his proposed emendation – 'Lamords' – would be agrammatical since 'the word mords is masculine'. He attributed this

to printing-house error: 'the printer of Q may be responsible for *La*', the feminine article instead of a masculine *Le*.
52 Harold Jenkins, ed., *Hamlet*, The Arden Shakespeare, Series 2 (London: Methuen, 1982), 369n.
53 *Henry V* 3.1.1–34.
54 Le Manoir Carrey still stands in the town, the present structure being a sixteenth-century half-timbered, three-storey dwelling.
55 Consider Hamlet's cry in Q1, 'Then venom to thy union here' as he stabs Claudius.
56 Thanks to Lucy Cullen of the Department of Sculpture, Metalwork, Ceramics and Glass, Victoria and Albert Museum.
57 'The celebrated Hunsdon onyx cameo, set in an enameled gold pendant illustrates marvelously the virtuoso talents of one of the best – albeit anonymous – hardstone engravers of the Renaissance ... [and] matches the best engraving of the great cameo-cutters of ancient Greece and Rome.' Diana Scarisbrick, *Ancestral Jewels* (New York: Vendome Press, 1989), 15.
58 Philip Edwards, ed., *Hamlet*, The New Cambridge Shakespeare (Cambridge: Cambridge University Press, 1985), 209n.

Epilogue: personal Shakespeare

This book ends where it began: with echoes of Nashe and Johnson railing against close readers – those 'mice-eyed decipherers' who 'profess to have a Key for the decyphering of every thing' in a book or play. These and other shrill disclaimers tell us Elizabethans and Jacobeans read and listened to their authors as closely as modern scholars do. And those early auditors had a stupendous advantage over even the best-informed of us: they breathed in the same milieu as Shakespeare and were alert to the same events, trends, personalities, conflicts, scandals, rumours, slang, parlour games, capers, larks, and jokes. What wouldn't a modern scholar give to attend the Bankside Globe one drizzly May afternoon in 1600 to hear *As You Like It* as one of Harvey's 'wiser sort' did, with ears and eyes tuned to catch every nuance, intimation, allusion, and innuendo of London life? Shakespeare's auditors came to the theatre and thumbed his quartos with an awareness we can't share. Clearly, their efforts at deciphering were not disappointed.

What I have suggested throughout this book is that Shakespeare wrote into his plays certain passages and characters imbued with intensely personal significance, and that these were perceptible only to a few among the many; for that reason, their subtexts have eluded Shakespeare's commentators. It is also true that after four hundred years of study by legions of mice-eyed scholars, 'Eureka!' moments have become few and far between. But new opportunities for deeper understanding of Shakespeare's works (and the man) are still there if only we approach his texts with informed particularity, but also in a comprehensive way. It's not the presence of passionate shepherd Silvius or Jaques' impious '*ducdame*' or his spying on Audrey and Touchstone or even Phebe's citation from *Hero and Leander* that suddenly illuminates Marlowe behind the mask of Jaques. It's the

Epilogue: personal Shakespeare

accumulation, the accretion of Shakespeare's allusions, hints, clues, winks, and intimations that gradually reveals the face in the mosaic and the workman's technique; once the portrait is seen full-length, how much richer and deeper the colours.

King John has long been recognized as a difficult and unsatisfying play. But with Carey taking the role of Faulconbridge – and the wrong successor, an unknown Prince Henry, suddenly appearing out of nowhere to fill John's vacant throne in 5.7 – how much more pensive and politically relevant the work now seems. If Shakespeare's hopes for resurrection and reunion with his lost son Hamnet, the passing of Nashe, and the anniversary of his twins' baptism on Candlemas underlie the text of *Twelfth Night*, then his motive for ending on a note of melancholia becomes clear and appropriate for the first time.

Throughout this book I have taken one precept as a given: every fiction writer's works – whether stories, novels, poems, or plays – grow out of, are stirred by, and then are saturated with that writer's personal experience and immediate world. A play might be set in stormy Britain before the founding of Rome or in Alexandria in 30 BC or on a balcony in Verona in 1582. But whether a leading character is named Lear or Cleopatra, Cyrano or Willy Loman, Juliet or Jaques, the writer has chosen to tell this story because it illuminates his own life and times. A playwright who devotes himself to writing about, say, Napoleon isn't so much writing about Napoleon as exploiting the Emperor to interrogate a question-issue-event that is dogging his writer's mind. There are persons who write about Napoleon for Napoleon's sake. They are historians.

Simply put, Shakespeare's plays are more personal than we have recognized. He has populated them with his friends, lovers, enemies. I have cited only a handful: Christopher Marlowe and Thomas Nashe, Emilia Bassano Lanier, Gabriel Harvey, William Brooke, the Careys, and Hamnet Shakespeare. But the personal associations in Shakespeare's plays remain a dimension less than well understood. Perhaps that was why the playwright remained inscrutable to Thomas Carlyle, and why Sidney Lee found his art '*Impersonal*'. But once Henry Carey's likeness is called to our attention we recognize how much of that royal bastard is in Philip Faulconbridge just as we may now perceive how much of Thom Nashe invests Feste. We waited 378 years for a commentator to recognize Gabriel Harvey in Malvolio. And for decades we may go on quibbling over whether Emilia Lanier is the one-and-only dark lady of the sonnets. (But isn't she an impeccable model for Jessica?) And what about Marlowe as Jaques? Perhaps we're not yet ready to swallow that whole. But aren't we a bit more hesitant to push the dish aside? As for *Twelfth Night*, this book has presented it as what it really was: a play into which Shakespeare poured friends, enemies, his most bitter loss, and his hopes for heaven.

At the outset I cautioned that not every reader will be satisfied with the inferences I draw, or with my solutions to Shakespeare's cruces. Yet I hope the reader will recognize that those presented here are the best we have. Fifty years ago in his preface to *Shakespeare's Meanings* Sigurd Burckhardt wrote:

> I believe that when we read Shakespeare, we are – ultimately – reading his mind; the question is only how well or badly, how scrupulously or wilfully we go about reading. Shakespeare not only abides our questions, he tells us which questions to ask; he took infinite pains to be precisely understood. I am convinced that he can be understood much more truly than he has been.[1]

I hope we now better understand Shakespeare's best-known, best-loved comedy as a more personal play – and Shakespeare as a more personal writer – than we have imagined.

Note

1 Sigurd Burckhardt, *Shakespeare's Meanings* (Princeton: Princeton University Press, 1968), vii.

Longer notes

These longer notes treat with topics relevant to this text which have been subjected to intensive scholarly interest and lively debate, but have so far eluded consensus.

Why the bishops burned the books

The bishops' book-burning of June 1599 is extensively investigated in Cyndia Susan Clegg's *Press Censorship in Elizabethan England*.[1] Clegg relates the Nashe-Harvey ban to the suppression of John Hayward's *The First Part of the Life and Raigne of King Henrie IV*, twice confiscated and burned in 1599, the second instance concurrent with the bishops' action of 1–4 June.[2] Hayward's book was seen to have touched (perhaps seditiously) on matters of 'State'. It was dedicated to Robert Devereux, Second Earl of Essex (1565–1601), and detailed the deposition of Richard II by Bolingbroke; anecdotally, Elizabeth is said to have identified with poor Richard, and the Earl was believed to harbour royal pretentions. Perhaps Hayward's intentions were to encourage Essex in that direction. But why would the same net sweep up a sundry group of satirists, pamphleteers, and epigrammatists? Clegg's suggestion that certain of the latters' doggerels could be closely read as comments on Essex's desultory military campaign in Ireland and/or his royal ambitions only tends to emphasize the scattershot nature of the bishops' ban.

A more reasonable explanation could be that Elizabeth, incensed by her own and others' interpretations of Hayward's *Henrie* and its link to Essex, baited her bishops into a radical act of suppression. After both Queen and Essex were dead, Francis Bacon published an *Apologie, in Certain imputations concerning the late Earle of Essex*, which included this tale: 'For her Majesty being mightily incensed with that booke which was dedicated to my Lord of Essex ... thinking it a seditious prelude to put into the people heads boldnesse and faction, said she had good opinion that there was treason in it, and asked me if I could not find any places in it, that might be drawne within case [lead to a prosecution] of treason.'[3] Bacon claims he laughed the old Queen out of it, telling her he found no treason in Hayward's book, only theft (plagiarism) from Tacitus. That Elizabeth even contemplated a formal prosecution illuminates the height of her dudgeon. Indeed, Hayward – 'an unlikely traitor and a victim of "strong" reading'[4] – was interrogated in Star Chamber, threatened with the rack, and slapped into prison.

Given the tenor of Elizabeth's response to the book, it's certainly possible that she could have prodded her bishops to (a) order the dedication to Essex removed (February 1599)[5] and (b) confiscate and destroy the dedication-free second edition (after 28 May). Either as cover for these acts, or in the bishops' desire opportunistically to make a one-time clean sweep, they issued their ban on 1 June which netted Harvey, Nashe, *et al.*, and lit their conflagration. In any case, the ban was an extraordinary act of censorship, one bound to be remembered by London writers for years to come.

Shakespeare's bad timing

Bad timing may be the simple explanation for Shakespeare's Oldcastle–Falstaff gaffe. When Henry Carey died on 23 July 1596 he had been patron of Shakespeare's company for two years and Lord Chamberlain for a dozen. Carey's son George inherited the former distinction and politicked hard for the latter; he was disappointed. On 8 August 1596 Elizabeth gifted the lucrative and influential post to William Brooke, member of the Privy Council and Warden of the Cinque Ports. But young Carey did not brood long; Brooke died after only seven months in office and George received the white wand on 14 April 1597. In the interim, so we're told, Shakespeare levelled two broadsides at Brooke.

The first appears in *1 Henry IV* (1596), wherein Shakespeare imprudently lampooned Brooke's illustrious ancestor, Sir John Oldcastle. In 1409, Sir John had assumed the title Baron Cobham on his marriage to widowed Joan, the Baroness. Shakespeare may have found licence for exploiting Oldcastle's famous name in the old play *The Famous Victories of Henry the Fifth* (*ca.* 1588), in which Sir John is cast as the misleader of Prince Hal's youth. Apparently Shakespeare's caricature of Oldcastle created a flap; some months after the debut of *1 Henry IV* Shakespeare altered the name 'Oldcastle' to 'Falstaff' and appended a disclaiming Epilogue to its sequel, *2 Henry IV* (1597?). In his edition of 1709 Nicholas Rowe explained: 'some of the family being then remaining, the Queen was pleased to command him to alter it; upon which he made use of Falstaff.'[6] We have only Rowe's word for this, and his single-source intelligence is viewed by some with scepticism.

What is held out as Shakespeare's second swipe at Brooke appears in *The Merry Wives of Windsor* (1597) via the character of foolish Ford, a husband who cloaks himself in the alias 'Brooke' while soliciting his own cuckolding (2.2.152–3). This play is thought to have been purpose-written for the occasion of George Carey's induction as a Knight of the Garter. If so, the merrymaking lords may have received Ford's alias as a bit of fun at the expense of Carey's deceased rival. Curiously, the name 'Brooke' in *Merry Wives* also underwent an Oldcastle-like transformation; when the play appeared in the Folio the impertinent 'Brooke' had become an everyday 'Broome'.

One cannot but wonder why a man of Shakespeare's admired discretion would intentionally — and so very publicly — twit a powerful court official upon whose good will his own career and the fortunes of his acting company depended.

A more likely explanation for Shakespeare's Oldcastle-Falstaff gaffe is that *1 Henry IV* was written and staged prior to Henry Carey's death on 23 July 1596 – and Brooke's appointment as Lord Chamberlain came as an awkward surprise to Shakespeare as it did to George Carey. Regarding the 'Brooke' alias in *The Merry Wives of Windsor*, if (as we've been told) this play was written in haste for performance on St George's Day, 23 April 1597, well, by that date Brooke had been dead six weeks, that is, no harm, no foul.

Brooke's death and the quarrel of Pistol and Nym

Recovering Shakespeare's link between of the deaths of Falstaff and Brooke casts a new, dark light on the rivalry between Pistol and Nym in *The Life of Henry V*. As Falstaff lies dying the pair come near to violence over the hand of Nell Quickly and the lordship of her tavern-whorehouse – two dubious prizes. Their squabbling may have been inspired by events surrounding the death of Brooke. The Chamberlain's last illness was bruited from at least mid-February; on 18 February 1597 Rowland Whyte reported, 'My Lord Chamberlain is sayd to be very ill ... My Lord of Hunsdon [George Carey] is thought shalbe Lord Chamberlain by his death, or by resignation if he live, for his body is to weake to brave the burden of the place [post].'[7] London society – certainly including Shakespeare and company – were keenly aware that, as Brooke lay dying, swarms of noblemen and arrivistes were shamelessly politicking for the right to succeed to his offices and emoluments. The opportunists included the Earl of Essex, young Brooke, George Carey, Sydney, Whyte, and others. Whyte's letters amply convey their ugly machinations. Shakespeare's Eastcheap rivals personify their venality.

On 21 February, Whyte writes to Sydney that Cecil 'went on Saturday to blackfriars [sic] to see my Lord Cobham' in his illness while Henry Cobham is reported to be daily pleading with the Queen for his father's offices. On 25 February: 'The physicians vary in their opinion of [the survival] of Lord Cobham.' On 28 February: 'My Lord Chamberlain grows weaker; his eldest son earnestly sues [the Queen] to be Lord Warden of the Cinque Ports.' On 1 March Whyte's letter begins, 'This day a speach was at Court that my Lord Chamberlain cannot live', and the following day, 'It is now held certain Lord Cobham cannot live.' On 4 March, Essex writes to Sydney, 'I do believe now that my Lord Chamberlain will dy.' On that day Whyte reports: 'Mr. Hen. Brooke, Sir Ed. Wooton and the two Lords Buckhurst and Hunsdon do stand for [have declared their candidacy for warden of the] Cinque Ports.' On 6 March Whyte reports the death of Brooke and notes: 'The Court is full of who shall have this and that office; most say Mr. Harry Brooke shall have Eltham and the Cinque Ports ... Lord Hunsdon is named for Lord Chamberlain.'[8]

No small miracle: the twice-striking clock in *The Comedy of Errors*

Though commentators have gamely struggled to divine the meaning of Shakespeare's clock twice striking one o'clock in *The Comedy of Errors*, none has cracked (or even dented) this crux. But the extraordinary time-event – the phenomenon of a clock moving backwards – could have suggested only one antecedent to Elizabethans who knew their Bible. Of course, the best-known instance of God playing with time occurs in the Book of Joshua, during the Israelites' conquest of the Amorites (10:12–15). But stopping the Sun is not the same as causing it move backwards in the heavens. That silent but extraordinary miracle occurs only once – in 2 Kings – and concerns an elderly and ailing Hezekiah, a youngish Isaiah, and 'the sundial of Ahaz'. Both prophets were well known to Elizabethan Christians because both had predicted the coming of the Messiah.

Hezekiah, sometime King of Judah (*ca.* 715–686 BC), was a religious zealot and reformer. In 2 Kings 20, he is sick to death. Young Isaiah prophesies that God will cure Hezekiah on the third day and give him fifteen more years of life. Hezekiah finds his prophecy incredible and demands a sign. Isaiah replies, 'This signe shalt thou haue of the Lord ... Wilt thou that the shadowe [on the sundial] goe forwarde ten degrees, or go backe ten degrees? And Hezekiah answered, It is a light thing for the shadowe to passe forward ten degrees: not so then, but let ye shadow go backe ten degrees. And Isaiah called vnto the Lord, and he brought againe the shadowe ten degrees backe by the degrees by the degrees whereby it had gone downe' (2 Kings 20:8–11).

The function of Shakespeare's clock twice striking one o'clock is to convey to his auditors that it's not some pagan Destiny but the divine hand of the Old Testament God that is moving the play's characters like pieces on a chessboard and giving them the time they need to sort themselves and save Egeon's life. The motor that drives Shakespeare's plot in *Errors* is exactly what Paul promised the Ephesians: the hand of God will lead those cast asunder back to a loving reunion. It is Paul's great Doctrine of Comfort.

Shakespeare's Nashe in *Love's Labour's Lost*

In *A Cup of News*: *The Life of Thomas Nashe*, Charles Nicholl makes a spirited argument for Nashe as Moth:[9] 'The whole portrait [of Moth] catches Nashe's physical presence: small, skinny, mercurial, piquant. Moth is a *bolde wagg, a handfull of wit, a deere imp*: he is *little, voluable, quick, acute, well-educated*[10] Then there is Armado's epithet for Moth, *my tender Iuvenall* (1.2.7–8). The name is repeated three times in the next few lines, and again in Act III, where Moth is *a most acute Iuvenall*. This clearly echoes the nick-name Greene gave Nashe in the *Groats-worth of Wit, young*

Iuvenall, that byting Satyrist, punning on juvenile and Juvenal, the Roman satirist. Shakespeare had doubtless lingered on this passage in *Groats-worth*, since young Iuvenall is one of the scholers Green warns about upstart players like William Shake-scene.'[11]

Having satisfied himself with the Thom–Moth connection, Nicholl recognizes Harvey behind the mask of Don Adriano de Armado. 'If Moth is Nashe, his master, the ridiculous Armado, is surely Harvey ... At every turn we recognize Gabriel's "singuler giftes of absurditie and vaineglory". Armado the braggart is the Harvey whom Nashe calls a "professed poeticall braggart", a "vaine Braggadochio", notorious for "intolerable boasting" and "horrible insulting pride". Holofernes calls Armado "thrasonicall", referring to the bragging soldier, Thraso, in Terence's *Eunuchus*. Nashe also calls Harvey "this Thraso" in *Strange News*, and speaks of "his Thrasonisme" in *Have with you [to Saffron-Walden]*.'[12] Throughout the play, Armado repeatedly reveals himself as a pretentious buffoon and poseur. Boyet describes him as 'a Phantasime, a Monarcho, and one that makes sport To the Prince and his Book-mates'. And Holofernes declares: 'He draweth out the thred of his verbositie finer then the staple of his argument. I abhorre such phanatical phantasims, such insociable and point-devyse companions' (5.1.18–19).

Anyone who has troubled to read Harvey's published work can recognize this style as his, whether in one of his attacks on Greene or Nashe, or his *G. Harvei gratulationum Valdensium libri quatuour* (1578). When Armado enters in 5.1 he greets Holofernes, Sir Nathaniel, and the others with the word 'Chirrah!', a corruption of the Greek 'hello' or 'good-day', *chaere*. This may be a wink at *Gratulationes*, which begins '*Gabrielis Harveii χάἱςε, vel Gratulationes Valdinensis Liber Primus*'. But why a Spanish Harvey? Perhaps this is Shakespeare's discretion at work. Nicholl describes Harvey's appearance as having a 'Mediterranean cast he was so proud of after the Queen had told him he looked "something like an Italian"'[13] Shakespeare may have translated Harvey's Italianate appearance to Spanish so as to avoid sailing too close to the imperial wind.

On the illegitimacy of Hamlet

Elsewhere I have noted that *Hamlet* Q2 contains a passage written for a coterie audience with specialized knowledge:[14] those and only those who have read law. As a consequence, the passage has been a source of frustration (and despair) to centuries of commentators. It would not be extravagant to say that Hamlet's monologue in 1.3 is among the least well understood in the entire canon; directors who don't get it cut it, as in David Farr's 2013 production at the Royal Shakespeare Company. In fact, the speech may be intentionally opaque to avoid a possible charge of *lèse-majesté*; Shakespeare's meaning would have been obscure to the mass audience and transparent only to those who had read law and remembered *De Laudibus Legum Angliae* of Sir John Fortescue.

In *Hamlet* Q2 1.3 Shakespeare provided the prince with a long meditation which appears in neither Q1 nor the Folio. It occurs as Hamlet anticipates a confrontation with the Ghost of his father. As the scene begins, Hamlet, Horatio, and Marcellus stand shivering on the platform. The night is shattered by the trumpets and ordnance of the king's rouse. Horatio asks, 'Is it a custom?' and Hamlet replies, 'Ay marry is't, But to my mind, though I am native here And to the manner born, it is a custom More honoured in the breach than the observance'[15] (13–38). In Q1 and the Folio Hamlet's speech ends here and 'observance' provides a weak cue for the Ghost's entrance. But in Q2, having commenced with the allusion to his birth, Hamlet continues with a speech about 'particuler men' – a glancing reference to himself. We know that Hamlet is a 'particuler' man from a prior exchange with Gertrude:

Ham: I Maddam, it is common.
Quee: If it be
    Why seems it so perticuler with thee? (Q2 1.2.74–6)

In case we missed that particular–Hamlet connection, the Ghost will threaten to make 'each particuler haire [on Hamlet's head] to stand an end, Like quils upon the fearfull Porpentine' (1.5.19–20). Hamlet's meditation begins:

So oft it chaunces in particuler men
That for some vicious mole of nature in them
As in their birth wherein they are not guilty,
(Since nature cannot choose his origin)
By the ore-grow'th of some complextion
Oft breaking downe the pales and forts of reason,
Or by some habit, that too much ore-leavens

> The form of plausive manners, that these men
> Carrying I say the stamp of one defect
> Being Natures livery, or Fortunes starre,
> His vertues els be they as pure as grace,
> As infinite as man may undergoe,
> Shall in the generall censure take corruption
> From that particuler fault: the dram of eale
> Doth all the noble substance of a doubt
> To his own scandle. (1.5.23–38)

Hamlet alleges that 'some vicious mole of nature … in their birth' predisposes 'particuler men' to ungovernable appetite ('complextion') or ugly 'habit' which inevitably brings them to ill repute. Yet the man polluted by this 'vicious mole' is 'not guilty' since he 'cannot choose his origin', that is, his parentage or the circumstances of his conception and birth. Notwithstanding his innocence, the 'vicious mole of nature' pollutes him with 'one defect' so virulent that were all his other virtues 'pure as grace', nevertheless he 'Shall in the generall censure [the Last Judgement] take corruption From [be damned by] that particuler fault'.

What form of obloquy could cause a man *in utero* to forfeit any hope of salvation? To the minds of Elizabethans there was such a stain — only one — and it is described in Deuteronomy, an Old Testament book closely read in Henry VIII's time.[16] Deuteronomy 23:2 declares: 'A bastard shal not entre into the Congregacion of the Lord: even to his tenth generacion shall he not entre into the Congregacion of the Lord.'

When Shakespeare wrote this speech 'vicious' had not achieved its modern savage sense; rather, 'vicious' alluded to vice – 'depraved, immoral, bad' (*OED*). Applied to persons, it meant 'addicted to vice or immorality … profligate, wicked'. The word 'mole' signifies a 'spot or blemish on the human skin … a fault.' But it also identifies the familiar small mammal, in which sense *OED* finds it applied to persons who exhibit 'mole-like' qualities, that is, 'whose (physical or mental) vision is defective' or those who labour in darkness. We know the identity of the 'mole' in *Hamlet*; in Q2 1.5.161 the prince addresses the Ghost of his father beneath the stage as 'olde Mole'. Hamlet declares the stain of bastardy to be as unshirkable as livery, indelible as Fortune's star (destiny); Elizabethans believed bastardy could not be expunged from a newborn infant, not even by the sacrament of baptism. Hamlet's meditation on illegitimacy concludes with the lines Harold Jenkins nominated as 'the most famous crux in Shakespeare'[17] 'the dram of eale Doth all the noble substance of a doubt To his own scandale' (Q2 1.4.33–5). The 'noble substance' of the offspring is tainted with 'doubt' and scandalized by the injection of the 'dram' – that is, a sixteenth of an ounce – of the mysterious 'eale'. What fluid in such a small quantity could exert this defining power over a man's character? 'Scandale' points to a fault of sexual incontinence; *OED* cites, 'O God, that one borne noble should be so base, His generous [engendering] blood to scandall all his race.'[18] Shakespeare's 'dram of eale' is surely a recondite reference to semen, an ill-placed dollop of which can render an otherwise noble man a bastard.

One needs to remember that Hamlet is replying to Horatio's question about the king's rouse; his cue is excessive drinking, and Hamlet's diction is drawn from associated jargon. Elsewhere, Shakespeare uses 'dram' in its senses of both avoirdupois weight and a measure of fluid.[19] He also quibbles with the word in an ethical sense: dram = scruple = compunction (*2 Henry IV* 1.2.130; *Twelfth Night* 3.4.79). But at the close of Hamlet's speech Shakespeare is using 'dram' in the sense of a fluid measure and quibbling on an unspoken word: 'bastarde'.[20] In addition to the familiar meaning of 'bastard', 'born out of wedlock, illegitimate,' its homonym 'bastarde' identified a 'sweet kind of Spanish wine, resembling muscadel; sometimes any kind of sweetened wine' (*OED*), including Falstaff's favourite, sack.[21] Shakespeare uses the word in this sense in *1 Henry IV*: 'Score a pint of bastarde in the Half-moon' (2.4.30).[22]

Bastarde wines differ from varietals by what the French call *dosage*, wherein wine is adulterated by the addition of a foreign substance, usually sugar or honey, as an aid to fermentation. A wine thus adulterated forfeits its varietal appellation, loses its 'name', and is left nameless – that is, a 'bastard(e)'.[23]

As to the etymology of the mysterious 'eale', the word is a variant of 'ealdren', an obsolete dialectical form of 'elder' (*OED*) signifying the elder tree. Elders produce the elderberry, from which wine has been fermented in England since ancient times.[24] Owing to the low sugar content of elderberries, winemakers invariably 'bastardized' the fermenting juice by adding honey. Elderberry wine – eale – is always a bastarde.[25]

Shakespeare would have known that the elderberry had another close association with Denmark, Danes, and the Danelaw – those areas of eastern England from York to London ruled by Danish invaders, first from AD 867 to 954 and again from 1016 to 1035; Shakespeare's source, Saxo Grammaticus's tale of Amelth, is set during this period. The English vernacular names for the elder tree – 'Danewort' and 'Bloodwort' – derived from a tradition that the elder sprang up in places where Danes slaughtered Englishmen or vice versa[26] The name 'elder' derives from the Old English word 'ellfrn' (*OED*). Clearly, Shakespeare understood the connections between elders, bastard(e) elderberry wine, eale, and Danes – and so would certain members of *Hamlet*'s first auditors, particularly those who enjoyed a tipple and had read law.

But if four centuries of scholars have found Hamlet's 'dram of eale' speech inscrutable, who among Shakespeare first auditors could have understood it? The answer is: those who had read law and remembered *De Laudibus Legum Angliae* (*In Praise of the Laws of England*), written *circa* 1470 by Sir John Fortescue (1394?–1476?). The Chief Justice of the King's Bench composed his treatise for the instruction of Edward, Prince of Wales and son of the deposed king Henry VI.[27] The book was long received as a definitive treatise on English law. It was first printed during the reign of Henry VIII (1509–47), and a translation from the Latin by Robert Mulcaster was reprinted six times between 1573 and 1672.[28]

In Fortescue's discussion of the laws of inheritance and succession, he explains that a child conceived out of wedlock forever carries the stigma of bastardy, even if the parents subsequently marry:

> [To] the childe borne out of matrimonye, the lawe of Englande alloweth no succession, affirmynge it [the child] to be naturall onely and not lawfull [because] the sinne of the firste carnal accion [premarital *coitus*] ... is not purged by the matrimonie ensuynge ... whiche doth not onelye judge the childe so gotten to be illegittimate but also prohibiteth it to succede in the parents inheritance.[29]

Fortescue then asserts the intransigent stain of bastardy in language that reads like a prose paraphrase of Hamlet's 'dram of eale' speech:

> If a bastard bee good, that cometh to him by chance, that is to wytte, by speciall grace but if he be evil that commeth to him by nature. For it is thought that the base child draweth a certein corruption and stayne from the synne of his parentes, without his owne fault ... Howbeit the blemish which bastards by the generation do receave ... thereof is

immortall: for it is knowen with god and with men ... whom nature in her gyftes severeth, markynge the natural or bastard chyldren as it were with a certein privie mark in their soules.[30]

This passage shares an extraordinary run of vocabulary with Hamlet's speech: 'chance', 'grace', 'nature', 'corruption', 'fault', 'stayne' and 'blemish', without his own fault, known with God ('generall censure'), 'nature ... markynge' ('Nature's livery'), and the notion that bastards carry 'a certein privie mark in their soules'. Indeed, Hamlet's speech reads like Shakespeare's poetical précis of Fortescue.[31]

What does this tell us about Hamlet's right to royal succession? In that part of his treatise which deals with bastardy and inheritance, Fortescue explains that although Roman civil law does not permit a child born out of matrimony to succeed to his parents' estate, children may succeed who were conceived out of wedlock but legitimated by the subsequent marriage of the parents: 'The Civile law doth legittimate the childe borne before matrimonie aswell as that which is borne after: and geveth untoo it succession in the parents inheritance'.[32]

But English law differs significantly from Roman civil law. Under English law a child conceived out of wedlock continues to carry the stigma of bastardy, and *may not succeed even if the parents subsequently marry*. The 'naturall onely' status of a child born out of matrimony brings a terrific irony to the Ghost's challenge to Hamlet to revenge his murder: 'If thou hast nature in thee beare it not' (Q2 1.5.81).

Fortescue explains that a bastard cannot inherit because, under law, a bastard child has no father and is nameless. To support his legal arguments Fortescue quotes a miserable doggerel:

To whom the people father is, to him is father none and all.
To whom the people father is, well fatherless we may him call.[33]

It makes perfect sense to Fortescue that a latter-born sibling – either born in wedlock to the same parents or, in the event of the death of either partner, born of the remarriage of either father or mother – should take precedence in heritance over a firstborn natural child:

It were therefore unreasonable that a child afterwarde borne in the same wedlock, whose generation cannot be unknown shoulde be disherited, and that a childe whiche knoweth no father should be heire to the father & mother of the other, specially in the roialme of England where the eldest sonne only enjoieth the fathers inheritance.³⁴

By this logic, any child born in wedlock to Claudius and Gertrude would take precedence over Hamlet in the Danish succession. This may explain why Hamlet didn't succeed to the throne of Denmark on the instant of his father's death; by immediately marrying Gertrude, Claudius 'popped in between th' election and my [Hamlet's] hopes' (5.2.64).³⁵ The 'o'er-hasty marriage' of Claudius and Gertrude had rendered her marriage to Old Hamlet childless. Denmark was without either a ruler or an heir – a perilous condition for a state, and one long prevailing in Shakespeare's England under the childless Elizabeth.

Though opaque to generations of playgoers and commentators, to those among Shakespeare's first auditors who read and remembered Fortescue, Hamlet's soliloquy is unmistakable as a meditation on his bastardy. But why did Shakespeare present Hamlet's patrimony in language so obscure? Again, his consideration may have been to avoid any hint of *lèse-majesté*. Two of England's previous monarchs – Mary and Elizabeth Tudor – had been declared bastards, and controversy surrounded the patrimony of Elizabeth's most likely successor, James VI of Scotland. Royal legitimacy was not a subject any Elizabethan playwright wished to interrogate openly.

Notes

1 Cyndia Susan Clegg, *Press Censorship in Elizabethan England* (Cambridge: Cambridge University Press, 1997), 198–224.
2 John Hayward, *The First Part of the Life and Raigne of King Henrie IV* (London: John Wolfe, February and April–May 1599).
3 Francis Bacon, *Sir Francis Bacon His Apologie, in Certain imputations concerning the late Earle of Essex* (London, 1604), 36.
4 Clegg, *Press Censorship*, 221.
5 Essex himself seems to have sensed the danger and demanded the dedication removed.
6 Nicholas Rowe, ed., *The Works of Mr. William Shakespear* (London, 1709), I.ix.
7 C. L. Kingsford, ed., *Report on the Manuscripts of Lord de l'Isle and Dudley Preserved at Penshurst Place* (London: HM Stationery Office, 1925–66), II.240.
8 *Ibid.*, 246.

9 Charles Nicholl, *A Cup of News: The Life of Thomas Nashe* (London: Routledge & Kegan Paul, 1984), 203 ff.
10 *Ibid.*, 212.
11 *Ibid.*
12 *Ibid.*, 214.
13 *Ibid.*, 183.
14 Steve Sohmer, *Shakespeare's Mystery Play and the Opening of the Globe Theatre 1599* (Manchester: Manchester University Press, 1999), 217 ff.
15 Jenkins' note on 'to the manner born' is useful: 'Not merely familiar with the custom from birth, but committed to it by birth. It is part of his [Hamlet's] heritage.' Harold Jenkins, ed., *Hamlet*, The Arden Shakespeare, Series 2 (London: Methuen, 1982), 208.15n.
16 Deuteronomy 25:5, the law of the Levirate which required a brother to marry his dead brother's wife, provided one basis for Pope Julius II's dispensation (26 December 1503) which allowed Prince Henry to become betrothed to Catherine of Aragon, recently widowed by his brother Arthur. Two decades later, Deuteronomy 24:1, which requires a husband to divorce a wife in whom he finds 'uncleanesse', formed a pillar of Henry's appeal to Pope Clement VII to let him put Queen Catherine away. The King claimed to be haunted by Leviticus 20:21: 'And if a man shall take his brother's wife, it is an unclean thing: he hath uncovered his brother's nakedness; they shall be childless.'
17 Jenkins, *Hamlet*, 449.
18 *Nobody and Somebody* (London, 1592), E2b.
19 *Cymbeline* 1.4.135; *The Winter's Tale* 2.1.138.
20 See M. M. Mahood's *Shakespeare's Wordplay* (London: Methuen, 1968) for other examples of Shakespeare's unspoken puns.
21 The quibble on alcoholic beverages has an after-echo at 1.4.40 when Hamlet speculates whether the Ghost is a 'spirit of health'.
22 There are numerous references to bastarde wines in medieval and Renaissance literature, e.g., 'The fellows of Merton ... purchase some bastard in 1399.' James E. Thorold and Arthur George Liddon Rogers, *A history of agriculture and prices in England* (London, 1866), 1.xxv.619.
23 'Bastards ... seeme to me to be so called because they are oftentimes adulterated and falsified with honey.' Charles Estienne, Jean Liébault, Gervase Markham, and Richard Surflet, *Maison rustique, or, The countrey farme* (London, 1616), 642.
24 The name of the familiar elder tree, *Sambucus nigra*, derives from the Old English word 'ellfrn' (*OED*). It is also related to the Danish 'hyld' or 'hyldetrf'. The elder is typically a low tree or shrub, and its young branches are filled with pith.

25 *OED* citation: '1398 Trevisa Barth. De R., xvii. cxliv. (1495) 700, "The Ellern tree hath vertue Duretica."'
26 *OED* cites: '1538 Turner Libellus; *an annoymous Herbal of 1568*, and 1578 Lyte Dodoens, iii. xlv. 380: "This herbe is called ... in Englishe Walwort, Danewort, and Bloodwort."'
27 Fortescue fought at the battle of Towton (1461) and was subsequently attainted by the victorious Edward IV. In the aftermath, Fortescue 'followed Queen Margaret to Flanders, and remained abroad, living in poverty, with her and the Prince of Wales.' Brian Bond, 'Fortescue, Sir John William (1859–1933)', *Oxford Dictionary of National Biography*, first published 2004; online edition, October 2007, www.oxforddnb.com/view/article/33213?docPos=17 (accessed 22 February 2014). During their exile, Fortescue undertook the education of the Prince. His *De Laudibus* is a dialogue between the Prince and Fortescue, who offers many illustrations of the superiority of English Common Law over the Roman civil law.
28 These citations are from the London edition of 1599. Sir John Fortescue, *De Laudibus Legum Angliae* (London, n.d. [*ca.* 1515]), 90r–94r.
29 *Ibid.*, 96r–97v.
30 *Ibid.*, 90r.
31 For reasons unfathomable, the editors of the Arden Series 3 *Hamlet* saw fit to ignore Fortescue as a source of (and key to) Hamlet's 'dram of eale' speech.
32 Fortescue, *De Laudibus Legum Angliae*, 93r.
33 *Ibid.*, 94r.
34 *Ibid.*, 34r.
35 Though the kingship of Denmark was nominally elective, it was rare that the heir apparent was denied.

Bibliography

Manuscripts

Baines, Richard, 'A note containing the opinion of on[e] Christopher Marly concerning his damnable Judgment of Religion, and scorn of Godes word', British Library, London, Harley MS 6848,

Cecil, William, 1st Baron Burleigh, 'Memorial Concerning Dr. John Dee's Opinion on the Reformation of the Calendar', British Library, London, MS Lansd. No. 39, Art 14, Orig.

Forman, Simon, Diaries, Bodleian Library, Oxford, MS Ashmole 200.

Grindal, Edmund, Archbishop of Canterbury, Letter to Queen Elizabeth, 6 March 1583, British Library, London, Add. MS 32092.

Privy Council, Letter to the Fellows of Cambridge University, 29 June 1587, The National Archives, Kew, Privy Council Registers PC2/14/381.

Reference works

Dix, Morgan, ed., *The Book of Common Prayer 1549*, facsimile (New York: Church Calendar Press, 1881).

The Geneva Bible (London, 1599).

The Oxford English Dictionary, 2nd edition, version 4.0, CD-ROM (Oxford: Oxford University Press, 2009) (*OED*).

Other works

Acheson, Arthur, *Mistress Davenant* (London: Bernard Quaritch, 1913).

Adelman, Janet, *Blood Relations: Christian and Jew in* The Merchant of Venice (Chicago: University of Chicago Press, 2008).

Aiello, Ilona, 'Rethinking Shakespeare's Dark Lady', in Michael Schoenfeldt, ed., *A Companion to Shakespeare's Sonnets* (Oxford: Blackwell Publishing, 2007), 291–303.

Alexander, Peter, *Shakespeare's* Henry VI *and* Richard III (Cambridge: Cambridge University Press, 1929).

Anon., *Nobody and Somebody* (London, 1592).
Aquinas, Thomas, St, *Summa theologica*, www.newadvent.org/summa/ (accessed 11 August 2011).
Arber, Edward, *A Transcript of the Registers of the Company of Stationers of London*, 5 vols (London and Birmingham, 1875–94).
Arlidge, Anthony, *Shakespeare and the Prince of Love: The Feast of Misrule in the Middle Temple* (London: Giles de la Mare Publishers, 2000).
Arthur, W., *An Etymological Dictionary of Family and Christian Names, With an essay on their derivations and import* (New York: Sheldon, Blakeman, 1857).
Asquith, Clare, *Shadowplay* (New York: Public Affairs, 2005).
Astington, John H., *English Court Theatre 1558–1642* (Cambridge: Cambridge University Press, 1999).
Bacon, Francis, *Sir Francis Bacon His Apologie, in Certain imputations concerning the late Earle of Essex* (London, 1604).
Baldwin, T. W., *The Organization and Personnel of the Shakespeare Company* (Princeton: Princeton University Press, 1927).
Barbee, C. Frederick, and Paul F. M. Zahl, eds, *The Collects of Thomas Cranmer* (Cambridge: W. B. Eerdmans, 1999).
Baring-Gould, Sabine, *Early Reminiscences 1834–1864* (New York: Dutton, 1922).
Bate, Jonathan, *Shakespeare and Ovid* (Oxford: Oxford University Press, 1993).
Beard, Thomas, *The Theatre of God's Judgments* (London, 1597).
Beaurline, L. A., ed., *King John*, The New Cambridge Shakespeare (Cambridge: Cambridge University Press, 1990).
Bevington, David, 'A.L. Rowse's Dark Lady', in Marshall Grossman, ed., *Aemelia Lanier: Gender, Genre, and the Canon* (Lexington, KY: University Press of Kentucky, 1998), 10–27.
—— ed., *As You Like It* (First Folio), Internet Shakespeare Editions, http://internetshakespeare.uvic.ca (accessed 11 November 2014).
Bevington, David, and David Scott Kasdan, eds, *The Tragedy of Hamlet, Prince of Denmark* (New York: Penguin, 1988).
Billon, Thomas, *Les presages d'bon-heur du Roy, et de la France* (Paris: A. Savgrain, 1617).
Blackburn, Bonnie, and Leofranc Holford-Strevens, *The Oxford Companion to the Year* (Oxford: Oxford University Press, 1999).
Bond, Brian, 'Fortescue, Sir John William' (1859–1933)', *Oxford Dictionary of National Biography*, first published 2004; online edition, www.oxford dnb.com/view/article/33213?docPos=17 (accessed 22 February 2014).
Boose, Lynda, 'The 1599 Bishops' Ban and Renaissance Pornography', in Richard Burt and John Michael Archer, eds, *Enclosure Acts: Sexuality,*

Property, and Culture in Early Modern England (Ithaca, NY: Cornell University Press, 1994), 191–9.
Booth, Stephen, *Shakespeare's Sonnets* (New Haven: Yale University Press, 1978).
Braunmuller, A. R., ed., *King John*, The Oxford Shakespeare (Oxford: Oxford University Press, 1998).
Bray, Gerald, ed., *Documents of the English Reformation* (Cambridge: James Clarke, 1994).
Brink, Jean R., 'Domesticating the Dark Lady', in Jean R. Brink, ed., *Privileging Gender in Early Modern England*, Sixteenth Century Essays & Studies 23 (1993), 93–103.
Brissenden, Alan, ed., *As You Like It*, The Oxford Shakespeare (Oxford: Clarendon Press, 1993).
Browne, Thomas, *Pseudodoxia Epidemica or Enquiries into very many received tenets and commonly presumed truths* (London, 1646).
Browning, Robert, 'At the "Mermaid"' (1876), in *The Works of Robert Browning*, Riverside Edition, 6 vols (Boston: Houghton, Mifflin), V.333.
Bruce, John, ed., *Diary of John Manningham, of the Middle Temple, and of Bradbourne, Kent, Barrister-at-Law, 1602–1603* (Westminster: J. B. Nichols and Sons, 1868).
Bullough, Geoffrey, *Narrative and Dramatic Sources of Shakespeare*, 7 vols (New York: Columbia University Press, 1975).
Burckhardt, Sigurd, '*King John*: The Ordering of this Present Time', *English Literary History* 33.2 (June 1966), 133–53.
—— *Shakespeare's Meanings* (Princeton: Princeton University Press, 1968).
Burgess, Clive, '"By Quick and by Dead": Wills and Pious Provision in Late Medieval Bristol', *English Historical Review* 102.405 (1987), 837–58.
Burns, Edward, ed., King *Henry VI, Part 1*, The Arden Shakespeare, Series 3 (London: Bloomsbury, 2000).
Burns, Margie, 'Odd and Even in *As You Like It*', *Allegorica* 5.1 (1980), 119–40.
Calendar of State Papers Domestic, Addenda – Elizabeth, XVII.246, 26 February 1570, https://babel.hathitrust.org/cgi/pt?id=hvd.32044106490 162;view=1up;seq=12 (accessed 21 June 2016).
Calvert, Hugh, *Shakespeare's Sonnets and Problems of Autobiography* (London: Merlin Books, 1996).
Calvin, John, *Institutes of the Christian Religion* (Paris, 1536).
Campbell, Lily B., *Shakespeare's 'Histories': Mirrors of Elizabethan Policy* (San Marino: The Huntington Library, 1947).
Capell, Edward, ed., *Mr. William Shakespeare his Comedies, Histories, and Tragedies, set out by himself in quarto, or by the players his fellows in folio, and now faithfully republish'd from those editions in ten volumes*

octavo; with an introduction, 10 vols (London: P. Leach for J. and R. Tonson, [1767–68]).
Carlyle, Thomas, *Essays on Goethe* (London: Cassell, 1905).
Chambers, E. K., *The Elizabethan Stage*, 4 vols (Oxford: Clarendon Press, 1923).
Chettle, Henry, *Kind-Hart's Dreame* (London, 1592).
Clegg, Cyndia Susan, *Press Censorship in Elizabethan England* (Cambridge: Cambridge University Press, 1997).
Conrad, Hermann, 'Was ihr wollt', *Preussische Jahrbücher*, July–December 1887 (Berlin: George Reimer, 1887), 1–33.
Cook, David, ed., *Dramatic Records in the Declared Accounts of the Treasurer of the Chamber, 1558–1642*, Malone Society Collections 6 (Oxford: Malone Society, 1962).
Cox, Lee Sherman, 'The Riddle in *Twelfth Night*', *Shakespeare Quarterly* 13 (1962), 360.
Darlow, Biddy, *Shakespeare's Lady of the Sonnets* (London: Palantype Organization, 1974).
Daugherty, Leo, *William Shakespeare, Richard Barnfield, and the Sixth Earl of Derby* (London: Cambria Press, 2010).
Davies, John, *Epigrames and Elegies* (London, n.d. [*ca.* 1599]).
Donno, Elizabeth Story, ed., *Twelfth Night or What You Will*, The New Cambridge Shakespeare (Cambridge: Cambridge University Press, 1985).
Dowden, E., *The Plays of Shakespeare* (London, 1899).
Duncan-Jones, Katherine, '"They say a made a good end"', *The Ben Jonson Journal* 3 (1996), 1–6.
—— ed., *Shakespeare's Sonnets*, The Arden Shakespeare (London: Bloomsbury, 2010).
Dusinberre, Juliet, ed., *As You Like It*, The Arden Shakespeare, Series 3 (London: Bloomsbury, 2006).
Dymock, Tailboys ('Thomas Cutwode'), *Caltha Poetarum* (London, 1599).
Edmondson, Paul, and Stanley Wells, eds, *Shakespeare's Sonnets* (Oxford: Oxford University Press, 2004).
Edwards, Philip, ed., *Hamlet*, The New Cambridge Shakespeare (Cambridge: Cambridge University Press, 1985).
Elam, Keir, *Shakespeare's Universe of Discourse: Language Games in the Comedies* (Cambridge: Cambridge University Press, 1984).
—— ed., *Twelfth Night*, The Arden Shakespeare, Series 3 (London: Bloomsbury, 2009).
Estienne, Charles, Jean Liébault, Gervase Markham, and Richard Surflet, *Maison rustique, or, The countrey farme* (London, 1616).
Everett, Barbara, '*Or What You Will*', *Essays in Criticism* 35 (1985), 294–314.
Fleay, F. G., *Shakespeariana* (London, 1884).

Fortescue, Sir John, *De Laudibus Legum Angliae* (London, n.d. [*ca.* 1515]).
Fuller, Thomas, *The History of the Worthies of England* (London, 1662).
Garber, Marjorie, *Shakespeare After All* (New York: Pantheon Books, 2004).
Gillett, Charles Ripley, *Burned Books: Neglected Chapters in English History and Literature*, 2 vols (New York: Columbia University Press, 1932).
Goddard, Harold C., *The Meaning of Shakespeare*, 2 vols (Chicago: University of Chicago Press, 1960).
Green, Martin, 'Emilia Lanier IS the Dark Lady', *English Studies* 87.5 (October 2006), 544–76.
Greenblatt, Stephen, *Will in the World* (New York: Norton, 2004).
Grosart, Alexander Bulloch, ed., *The Complete Works of Thomas Nashe*, 6 vols (London: privately printed, 1883–84).
—— *The Works of Gabriel Harvey* (London: privately printed, 1884–85).
Guilpin, Edward, *Skialetheia* (London, 1598).
Haffenden, John, *William Empson*, 2 vols (Oxford: Oxford University Press, 2005).
Hall, Joseph, *Virgidemiarum*, 2 vols (London, 1597–98).
Halliday, F. E., *A Shakespeare Companion 1550–1950* (New York: Funk and Wagnalls, 1952).
—— *A Shakespeare Companion 1564–1964* (Baltimore: Penguin, 1964).
Halliwell-Phillipps, J. O., *Shakespeariana* (London, 1841).
Hanks, Patrick, Kate Hardcastle, and Flavia Hodges, *A Dictionary of First Names*, 2nd edition, Oxford Paperback Reference (Oxford: Oxford University Press, 2006).
Harris, Frank, *Shakespeare and his Love* (London: Frank Palmer, 1904).
—— *The Women of Shakespeare* (New York: Mitchell Kennerley, 1911).
Harrison, G. B., *Shakespeare at Work* (London: Routledge, 1933).
Harvey, Richard, *Theological Discourse of the Lamb of God* (London, 1590).
Hassel, R. Chris, Jr., *Faith and Folly in Shakespeare's Romantic Comedies* (Athens, GA: University of Georgia Press, 2011).
Hattaway, Michael, ed., *As You Like It*, The New Cambridge Shakespeare (Cambridge: Cambridge University Press, 2009).
Hayward, John, *The First Part of the Life and Raigne of King Henrie IV* (London: John Wolfe, February and April–May 1599).
Heminges, John, and Henry Condell, eds, *Shakespeare: The First Folio* (London: Jaggard, 1623).
Hibbard, G. R., *Thomas Nashe* (London: Routledge and Kegan Paul, 1962).
—— ed., *Hamlet*, reprint, The Oxford Shakespeare (Oxford: Oxford University Press, 2008).

Hinman, Charlton, ed., *The First Folio of Shakespeare* (New York: Norton, 1968).
'The History of the Carey Family of Guernsey A.D. 1393–2008', www.careyroots.com (accessed April 2012).
Holinshed, Raphael, *Chronicles: England, Scotland and Ireland*, 6 vols (London, 1807),
Honan, Park, *Christopher Marlowe, Poet and Spy* (Oxford: Oxford University Press, 2005).
Honigmann, Ernst, *Shakespeare's Influence on his Contemporaries* (Hong Kong: Macmillan, 1983).
Honigmann, E. A. J., ed., *King John* (London: Methuen, 1954).
—— *The Life and Death of King John*, The Arden Shakespeare, Series 2 (London: Methuen, 1963).
Hopkins, Lisa, *Christopher Marlowe, Renaissance Dramatist* (Manchester: Manchester University Press, 2011).
Hotson, Leslie, *The Death of Christopher Marlowe* (London: Nonesuch, 1925).
—— *The First Night of* Twelfth Night (London: Macmillan, 1954).
Hunt, Maurice, 'Christian Numerology and Shakespeare's *The Tragedy of King Richard the Second*', *Christianity and Literature* 60.2 (Winter 2011), 247–75.
—— 'Thomas Nashe, *The Unfortunate Traveller*, and *Love's Labour's Lost*', *Survey of English Literature* 54 (Spring 2014), 297–314.
Hunter, Joseph, *New Illustrations of the life, studies, and writings of Shakespeare* (London, 1845).
Hutson, Lorna, 'Lanier [*née* Bassano], Emilia (*bap.* 1569, *d.* 1645)', *Oxford Dictionary of National Biography*, rev. first published 2004; online edition, January 2012, http://dx.doi.org/10.1093/ref:odnb/37653 (accessed 16 March 2013).
Izacke, Richard, *Remarkable antiquities of the city of Exeter, collected by Richard Isacke, Esquire, Chamberlain thereof* (London, 1681).
Jenkins, Harold, ed., *Hamlet*, The Arden Shakespeare, Series 2 (London: Methuen, 1982).
Jerome, St, *The Vulgate Preface to Paul's Letters*, trans. Kevin P. Edgecombe, www.tertullian.org/fathers/jerome_preface_pauls_letters.htm accessed 4 August 2011).
Jonson, Ben, *Bartholomew Fair* (London, 1605).
—— *Epistle to the two universities, Volpone; or, The Fox* (London, 1605).
—— *Apologetical Dialogue* (London, 1616).
—— *The Works of Beniamin Ionson* (London: William Stansby, 1616).
—— *The Works of Ben Jonson* (London: Hodgkin, 1692),
Jusserand, Jean, *Le roman au temps de Shakespeare* (Paris: Asnières, 1887).
Kafka, Franz, *The Complete Stories* (New York: Schocken E-Books, 1971).

Kermode, Jenny, *Medieval Merchants: York, Beverley and Hull in the Later Middle Ages* (Cambridge: Cambridge University Press, 2002).
Kingsford, C. L., ed., *Report on the Manuscripts of Lord de l'Isle and Dudley Preserved at Penshurst Place* (London: HM Stationery Office, 1925–66).
Kinney, Arthur F., *Shakespeare by Stages: An Historical Introduction* (Oxford: Blackwell Publishers, 2003).
Knowles, Richard, ed., *As You Like It*, A New Variorum Edition of Shakespeare (New York: MLA, 1977).
Lanier, Aemilia, *Salve Deus Rex Judaeorum* (London, 1611).
Latham, Agnes, ed., *As You Like It*, The Arden Shakespeare, Series 2 (London: Methuen, 1975).
Lee, Sidney, *The Impersonal Aspect of Shakespeare's Art*, address before the English Association, London, 11 June 1909 (Oxford: Oxford University Press, 1909).
Leimberg, Inge, '"M.O.A.I.": Trying to Share the Joke in *Twelfth Night* 2.5 (a Critical Hypothesis)', *Connotations* 1.1 (1980), 78–95.
Lodge, Oliver W. F., 'Shakespeare and the Death of Marlowe', *Times Literary Supplement*, 14 May 1925.
Logan, Robert A., *Shakespeare's Marlowe: The Influence of Christopher Marlowe on Shakespeare's Artistry* (Aldershot: Ashgate Publishing, 2007).
Lothian, J. M., and T. W. Craik, eds, *Twelfth Night, or What You Will*, The Arden Shakespeare, Series 2 (London: Thomson Learning, 1975).
Luther, Martin, *That Jesus Christ was Born a Jew* (Wittenberg: Cranach & Doring, 1523).
—— *Small Catechism* (St Louis: Concordia, 2008).
MacCaffrey, Wallace, T., 'Carey, Henry, first Baron Hunsdon (1526–1596)', *Oxford Dictionary of National Biography*, first published 2004; online edition, September 2014, www.oxforddnb.com/view/article/4649?docPos=15 (accessed 21 June 2012).
Mahood, M. M., *Shakespeare's Wordplay* (London: Methuen, 1968).
Malone, Edmond, ed., *The Plays and Poems of William Shakespeare*, 10 vols (London, 1821).
Marston, John, *The Metamorphosis of Pigmalion's Image and Certaine Satyres* (London, 1598).
—— *The scourge of vilanie* (London, 1598).
'Mary Boleyn: Biography, Portrait, Facts & Information', http://english history.net/tudor/citizens/mary-boleyn/ (accessed 22 March 2013).
Matchett, William H., 'Richard's Divided Heritage in *King John*', *Essays in Criticism* 12 (July 1962).
McCabe, Richard, 'Elizabethan Satire and the Bishops' Ban of 1599', *Yearbook of English Studies* 11 (1981), 188–93.

McDuffie, Felecia, 'Augustine's Rhetoric of the Feminine in the Confessions: Women as Mother, Woman as Other', in Judith Stark, ed., *Feminist Interpretations of Augustine* (New York: Pennsylvania State University Press, 2007), 97–118.
McKeen, David, *A Memory of Honour*, 2 vols (Salzburg: Universität Salzburg, 1986).
McKerrow, Ronald B., ed., *The Workes of Thomas Nashe*, 5 vols (London: Sidgwick & Jackson, 1904–10, repr. Oxford: Basil Blackwell, 1958).
Meres, Frances, *Palladis Tamia: Wit's Treasury* (London, 1598).
Middleton, Thomas, *Microcynicon* (London, 1598).
Miller, William E., 'The Hospitall of Incurable Fooles', *Studies in Bibliography* 16 (1963), 204–7.
More, Thomas, St, *Apology*, in *The Yale Edition of the Complete Works of St. Thomas More*, 15 vols, IX (New Haven: Yale University Press, 1979).
[Morgan, T.?] *The Copy of a Letter, Written by a Master of Art of Cambridge. Leycesters Common-wealth: Conceived, Spoken and Published with Most Earnest Protestation of All Dutifull Good Will ... Towards this Realm, Etc. Sometimes Wrongly Attributed to Robert Person* (Paris, 1584).
Muir, Kenneth, *The Sources of Shakespeare's Plays* (London: Methuen, 1977).
Nashe, Thomas, *The Unfortunate Traveler, or the Life of Jack Wilton* (London, 1594).
Nicholl, Charles, *A Cup of News: The Life of Thomas Nashe* (London: Routledge & Kegan Paul, 1984).
Nichols, John, *Illustrations of the literary history of the eighteenth century: Consisting of authentic memoirs and original letters of eminent persons; and intended as a sequel to the Literary anecdotes* (London, 1817).
Norman, Marc, and Tom Stoppard, *Shakespeare in Love*, undated draft, www.imsdb.com (accessed 21 June 2016).
O'Connor, Garry, *William Shakespeare: A Life* (London: Houghton & Stoddard, 1991).
Orgel, Stephen, and A. R. Braunmuller eds, *The Complete Pelican Shakespeare*, 2nd revised edition (New York: Penguin, 2002).
Patterson, Annabel, *Censorship and Interpretation* (Madison: University of Wisconsin Press, 1984).
Pogue, Kate Emery, *Shakespeare's Friends* (Westport, CT: Praeger, 2006).
Pont, Robert, *A Newe Treatise of the Right Reckoning of Yeares and Ages of the World, and Mens Liues, and of the Estate of the last decaying age thereof, this 1600 year of Christ (erroneously called a Yeare of Iubilee), which is from the Creation the 5548 yeare; containing sundrie singularities worthie of observation, concerning courses of times and revolutions of the Heaven, and reformation of Kalendars and Prognostications, with*

a Discourse of Prophecies and Signs, preceding the last daye, which by manie arguments appeareth now to approach (Edinburgh: Robert Walde-grave, 1599).

Pope, Alexander, ed., *The Works of Shakespear*, 6 vols (London, 1725).

Prior, Roger, and David Lasocki, *The Bassanos: Venetian Musicians and Instrument Makers in England, 1531–1665* (Menston: Scolar Press, 1995).

Puttenham, George, *The Arte of English Poesie* (London, 1589).

Quiller-Couch, Sir Arthur, and J. Dover Wilson, eds, *As You Like It*, The New Shakespeare (Cambridge: Cambridge University Press, 1926).

Rawlinson, George, ed. and trans., *The History of Herodotus*, 9 vols (New York: D. Appleton, 1885).

Reyher, Paul, 'When a Man's Verses cannot be Understood', *Times Literary Supplement*, 9 July 1925.

Richmond, Hugh, 'The Dark Lady as Reformation Mistress', *The Kenyon Review* 8.2 (1986), 91–105.

Ridley, M. A., ed., *As You Like It*, The New Temple Shakespeare (London: J. M. Dent and Sons, 1934).

Riggs, David, *The World of Christopher Marlowe* (London: Faber and Faber, 2004).

Righter, Anne, *Shakespeare and the Idea of the Play*, Penguin Shakespeare Library (London: Penguin,1967).

Rowe, Nicholas, ed., *The Works of Mr. William Shakespear* (London, 1709).

Rowse, A. L., *Shakespeare's Sonnets* (New York: Harper & Row, 1963).

—— *Shakespeare, the Man* (New York: Harper Collins, 1973).

—— *The Poems of Shakespeare's Dark Lady* (New York: Clarkson N. Potter, 1979).

Sage, John, and Thomas Ruddiman, eds, *The Works of William Drummond of Hawthornden* (Edinburgh: James Watson, 1711).

Salingar, L. G., 'The Design of *Twelfth Night*', *Shakespeare Quarterly* 9 (1958), 117–39.

Salkeld, Duncan, *Shakespeare among the Courtesans* (Farnham: Ashgate, 2012).

Sams, Eric, 'The Troublesome Wrangle over *King John*', *Notes and Queries* 234 (March 1988), 41–4.

Sayle, Charles, ed., *Letters written by Lord Chesterfield to his Son* (New York: Walter Scott, 1900).

Scarisbrick, Diana, *Ancestral Jewels* (New York: Vendome Press, 1989).

Schimmel, Annemarie, *The Mystery of Numbers* (Oxford: Oxford University Press, 1993).

Schoenbaum, Samuel, *Shakespeare's Lives* (Oxford: Clarendon Press, 1991).

Seaton, Ethel, 'Marlowe, Robert Poley, and the Tippings', *Review of English Studies* 5 (1929), 273–87.
Shapiro, James, *Shakespeare and the Jews* (New York: Columbia University Press, 1997).
—— *A Year in the Life of William Shakespeare: 1599* (New York: HarperCollins, 2005).
Smith, Bruce, *Homosexual Desire in Shakespeare's England* (Chicago: University of Chicago Press 1991, 2nd edition 1994).
Smith, Peter, '*M.O.A.I.:* "What should that alphabetical position portend?" An Answer to the Metamorphic Malvolio', *Renaissance Quarterly* 51 (1998), 1199–1224.
Sohmer, Steve, *Shakespeare's Mystery Play and the Opening of the Globe Theatre 1599* (Manchester: Manchester University Press, 1999).
—— *Shakespeare for the Wiser Sort* (Manchester: Manchester University Press, 2008).
—— '"Mention my name in Verona": Is Cassio Florentine?', in Frank Occhiogrosso, ed., *Shakespeare Closely Read* (Lanham, MD: Rowman & Littlefield, 2011), 69–80.
Spevack, Martin, *The Harvard Concordance to Shakespeare* (Cambridge, MA: Belknap Press, Harvard University Press, 1973).
Tasso, Ercole and Torquato, *The xv ioyes of marriage* (London, n.d. but ca. 1598).
—— *Of Marriage and Wyvinge* (London, 1599).
Taylor, Gary, 'The Canon and Chronology of Shakespeare's Plays', in Stanley Wells, Gary Taylor, John Jowett, et al., eds, *William Shakespeare: A Textual Companion*, 2nd edition (New York, London: W. W. Norton, 1987), 69–144.
—— 'Shakespeare and Others: The Authorship of *Henry the Sixth Part One*', *Medieval and Renaissance Drama in England* 7 (1995), 145–205.
—— ed., *Henry V*, The Oxford Shakespeare (Oxford: Oxford University Press, 1982).
Tertullian, *On the Apparel of Women*, www.newadvent.org/fathers/0402.htm (accessed 5 May 2013).
Thesaurus Linguae Romanae & Britannicae, tam accurate congestus, ut nihil pene in eo desyderari possit, quod vel Latine complectatur amplifimus Stephani Thesaurus, vel Anglice, totes aucta Eliotae Bibliotheca; opera et industria Thomae Cooperi Magdalenensis (London: Bertheleti, 1565).
Thorold, James E., and Arthur George Liddon Rogers, *A history of agriculture and prices in England* (London, 1866).
Tobin, J. J. M., 'Gabriel Harvey in Illyria', *English Studies* 61 (1980), 318–28.
Turner, Henry S., 'Nashe's Red Herring: Epistemologies of the Commodity

in *Nashes Lenten Stuffe* (1599)', *English Literary History* 68.3 (2001), 529–61.
Tyler, Thomas, *Shakespeare's Sonnets* (London: Thomas Nutt, 1890).
Van de Water, Julia C., 'The Bastard in *King John*', *Shakespeare Quarterly* 11 (1960), 137–46.
Verity, A. W., ed., *As You Like It*, The Pitt Press Shakespeare for Schools: (Cambridge: Cambridge University Press, 1899, repr. 1932).
—— *Twelfth Night, or What You Will*, The Pitt Press Shakespeare for Schools, repr. (Cambridge: Cambridge University Press, 1961).
Voragine, Jacobus, *The Golden Legend*, ed. Eamon Duffy, reprint (Princeton: Princeton University Press, 2012).
—— *The Golden Legend*, 6 vols, ed. F. S. Ellis, Temple Classics (London: J. M. Dent, 1900, repr. 1922, 1931).
Warren, Roger, and Stanley Wells, eds, *Twelfth Night, or What You Will*, The Oxford Shakespeare (Oxford: Oxford University Press, 1994).
Weis, René, *Shakespeare Unbound: Decoding a Hidden Life* (New York: Henry Holt and Company, 2007).
Wells, Stanley, Gary Taylor, John Jowett and William Montgomery, eds, *William Shakespeare: The Complete Works* (Oxford: Oxford University Press, 1986; 2nd edition, 2005.)
Wickham, Glynne, Herbert Berry, and William Ingram, eds, *Theatre in Europe: A Documentary History* (Cambridge: Cambridge University Press, 2000).
Wilson, John Dover, *An Introduction to the Sonnets of Shakespeare* (Cambridge: Cambridge University Press, 1964).
Wilson, Katherine M., *Shakespeare's Sugared Sonnets* (London: Allen and Unwin, 1974).
Wilson, Richard, *Secret Shakespeare: Studies in Theatre, Religion and Resistance* (Manchester: Manchester University Press, 2004).
—— '"Worthies away": The Scene Begins to Cloud in Shakespeare's Navarre', in Jean-Christophe Mayer, ed., *Representing France and the French in Early Modern English Drama* (Newark, DE: University of Delaware Press, 2008), 93–109.
Woods, Susanne, *Lanier: A Renaissance Woman Poet.* (Oxford: Oxford University Press, 1999).
—— ed., *The Poems of Aemilia Lanier: Salve Deus Rex Judaeorum* (New York: Oxford University Press, 1993).

Index

Aaron *TA*, 47
Abraham, 147, 149
Acheson, Arthur, 55, 71, 189
Acts, Book of, 14, 24, 104, 111, 116, 156, 190
Adam *AYLI*, 19, 21, 30, 50–1, 61, 127
Adelman, Janet, 68, 74, 189
Advent, 86
Aemilius *TA*, 65
Aeneas and Dido, 66
Agincourt *H5*, 81
Aguecheek, Andrew *TN* 8
Ahaz, The Sundial of, 179
Aiello, Ilona, 54–5, 71, 189
Alcazar, The Battle of, 22, 47
Alexander, Peter, 149–50, 167, 189
Alexandria, 90, 174
Alexandrine, 84
Almanac, Almanacke, viii, 79–80, 97
Almond for a Parrat, 118
Alphonsus, King of Aragon, 47
Amelth, 184
A Midsummer Night's Dream, 66, 80
Amiens *AYLI*, 24, 26–7, 30–1, 36
Amores, Ovid's, 13, 15–16, 52
anagram, x, 28, 77, 89–91, 92, 94–6, 112, 126–7
anagrammatic, 126
anagrammatical, 92
Anagrammatist, 90

anagrammatize, -ing, 8, 28, 116
anagrams, 7, 9, 77, 89–92, 94, 97, 144
Andrew *TN*, 8, 83, 89, 95–8, 107–8, 119, 141, 144
Andromeda, 163
Anglican, 28, 46, 78, 81, 149
Anglicans, 46
Annates, 154
Antonio *TN*, 65, 140, 143
Antony *A&C*, 52, 110, 146
Apolonius and Silla, 102–3, 120
Apostle, 104, 107, 111, 116
Aquinas, St. Thomas, x, 73, 94, 190
Ardennes, 51
Argonise, viii, 159–61, 163
Argonne, 161
Arion *TN*, 135–6
Ariosto, 53
Arlidge, Anthony, 78, 86–7, 190
de Armado, Don Adriano *LLL*, 112, 179–80
Armin, Robert, 51, 125
Asquith, Claire, ix, xii, 190
Astington, John, 87, 190
Astrophil and Stella, 57
atheism, atheist, 27–8, 30, 49
Athens, 124, 193
Audley End, 27, 127–9
Audrey *AYLI*, 23, 32–3, 36, 39, 43, 114, 172
August, 16–17, 47, 73, 87, 124–5, 144, 147, 151, 161, 176, 190, 194

Augustine, Saint, 61, 73, 197
Avon, River, 22, 101, 143

Babylonia, 19, 69
Bacon, Francis, 175–6, 187, 190
Baines Note, 35, 50, 189
Baldwin, T.W., 51, 190
Baltimore, 70, 193
Bamber, Jeremy, 78
Bancroft, Bishop Richard, 6, 16
Bandello, Fr. Luigi 63, 104
Bankside, 42, 54, 71, 136, 172
Baptista *Shrew*, 65
Baptiste *MV*, 54, 62, 64, 67
Bardolph *1–2H4, H5*, 147
Baring-Gould, Sabine, 14, 129
Barnabas, 116
Barnaby Bright, 53, 102–3
Barnardo *HAM*, 157
Barnes, Barnabe, 53
Barnfield, Richard, 53, 70, 192
Bartholomew Fair, 13, 194
Barton, John, 87
Bassanio *MV*, 64
Bassano, x, 54, 57, 62, 64–5, 67–8, 70–1, 72, 73, 174, 194, 197
Bassianus *TA*, 65
bastard, 50, 64, 68, 73, 150–3, 155–7, 158–9, 166, 173, 182–6, 188, 199
bastarde, 183, 188
Bate, Jonathan, 50, 190
Beaufort, Bishop*1–2H6* 51
Belmont *MV*, 65–7
Berlin, 88, 192
Beroune *LLL*, 9
Berry, Herbert, 14, 199
Bertie, Countess Susan, 62–3
Bevington, David, 44, 59, 64, 72–3, 161, 170, 190
Bible, 12, 14, 17, 50, 79, 107–8, 148, 179, 189
biblical, 37, 60, 68
Bight, 31, 49, 161
Binneman, Henry, 130
bishops, 6, 14, 16, 41, 45, 144, 175–6, 190, 195
Blackfriars, 149–50, 179

Bodleian Library, viii, 73, 128, 189
Boleyn, Anne, 158, 169, 195
Bolingbroke, Henry, 51, 146, 175
Bologna, 123
Booth, Edwin, 55, 71, 191
Boyet *LLL*, 180
Bracciano, Duke Orsini, 86
Bradbrook, Muriel, 125
Bradley, William, 30
Braunmuller, A.R., 156, 162, 167–8, 170, 191, 196
Bray, Gerald, 168, 191
Brissenden, Alan, 44, 50, 191
Bristol, 18, 46, 191
Britain, iv, 132, 173
Britannicae , 132, 198
British, iv, viii, 50, 88, 161, 189
Britons, 130
Brook *MWW*, 142, 170
Brooke, William Baron Cobham, 147–8, 165, 168, 173, 176–7
Broome *MWW,* 177
Browne, Thomas, 18–19, 191
Browning, Robert, ix, xi, 191
Brownist *TN,* 118
Bruce, John, 14, 86, 191, 198
Brutus *LUC,* 51
Bullough, Geoffrey, 109, 191
Burbage, Richard, 51, 58, 94, 159
Burby, Cuthbert, 112
Burckhardt, Sigurd, 152, 168, 174, 191
Burgess, Anthony, 18, 46, 191
Burleigh, William Cecil, Baron, 88, 189

Caesar, Julius, 20, 36, 42, 45, 51–2, 80, 84–5, 88, 97, 99, 127
calendar, viii, 46, 78–9, 84–6, 88, 92, 96–9, 105–6, 142–4, 149, 166–7, 189, 191
calendrical, 77, 84, 141
Calvin, John, 46, 90–1, 191
Cambridge, 3, 14–15, 22, 26–8, 46, 122–3, 128, 165
Campbell, Lily B., 153, 167–8, 191
Campeggio, Lorenzo Cardinal, 169

Index

Candlemas, 78, 81–2, 86, 95, 100–1, 144, 173
Canterbury, 5–6, 22, 27, 30, 36, 44, 52, 88, 189
Capell, Edward, 15, 44, 191
Cardano, Girolamo, 96, 98
Carey, Catherine, 158
Carey, Henry and George, viii, 54, 62–6, 73, 83, 147, 149–53, 155, 157–70, 173, 176–8, 194–5
Careye, Carrey, etc. 156–63, 165, 170–1, 173, 192, 194
Carlyle, Thomas, v, ix, xi, 173, 192
Casca *JC*, 126
Cassio, Michael *OTH*, 98, 198
Cassius *JC*, 51
Catechism, 46, 195
Catholic, 28, 46, 78–9, 81, 85, 102, 145
Catholicism, ix, 26, 49
Caxton, William, 17
Cecil, William, 8, 88, 178, 189
Celia *AYLI*, 16, 23, 34
censor, censorship, ix, 4–6, 12–13, 153, 155, 175–6, 187, 192, 196
Cesario *TN*, 82, 103, 114, 119, 140
Chamberlain, Lord 50, 54–5, 59, 78, 83, 147–51, 159, 161, 164–5, 170,176–8, 194
Chambers, E.K., 13, 192
Chapman, George, 53
Chatillion *KJ*, 156
Chaucer, Geoffrey, 3, 31, 66
Chesterfield, Lord, 85, 96, 99, 144, 197
Chettle, Henry, 72, 165, 192
Christian, 46, 51, 61, 64, 69, 74, 88, 92, 106, 109, 113–15, 123, 168, 189–91, 194
Christianity, 51, 105, 107, 113, 194
Christians, 18, 107, 110–11, 116, 148, 179
Christie, Agatha, 56

Christmas, 48, 77–8, 80, 83, 96–7, 123
Cicero, Marcus Tullius, 127
Circumcision, Feast of, 116
Claudio *ADO*, 102
Claudius *HAM*, 158, 162, 164–5, 169, 171, 186
Clavius, Christopher, 98
Clegg, Cyndia Susan, 175, 187, 192
Clement, Pope, 169, 187
Cleopatra *A&C*, 52, 55–6, 68, 110, 173
de Clerkenwell, Abbess, 56
Cobham, Lord, 147, 176, 178
Columbia, 14, 74, 109, 191, 193, 198
comedies, 44, 51–2, 108, 124, 132
comedy, 5–6, 15, 40, 43, 45, 47, 51, 55, 63, 74, 77, 83, 97, 102–4, 108, 120–1, 127, 143, 174, 178
Comedy of Errors, 18, 51, 55, 74, 86, 102–4, 108, 178–9
Conrad, Hermann, 84, 88, 192
Cordelion, Richard, 155–6
Corin *AYLI*, 23, 41–3
Corinth, 105, 106–7
Corinthian *H5*, 106
Corinthians, 103–5, 107–11, 115–17, 121
Corkine, William, 30
Cotgrave, John, 161
Cox, L.S., 126, 132, 192
Craig, William James, 170
Craik, Katherine A., 126, 132, 136, 145, 195
Cranach, Lucas, 74, 195
Cranmer, Thomas, 48, 190
Crawford, Jack, 170
Cressida *T&C*, 53, 66, 115
cuckolding, cuckoldry, 43, 177
Curio *TN*, 117, 139
Cybele, 92
Cydnus, 110
Cymbeline, 187
Cyprus *OTH*, 104
Czech, 11

Dalmatian, 105
Damascus, 68, 111, 123
Danelaw, 183
Danes, 183–4
Danewort, 184, 188
Daniel, Samuel, 53
Danish, 164, 184, 186, 188
Darlow, Biddy 56, 71, 192
Davenant, Richard, 54–5, 71, 189
Davies, John, 13, 192
Deceived, The 103
December, viii, 77–80, 85, 96–7, 135, 138, 164, 187, 192
decipherers, mice-eyed, vii, 3–5, 7, 9, 10–11, 13, 53, 61, 127, 172
Dee, John, 85, 88, 189
Defoe, Daniel, 124
Dekker, Thomas, 124
de Medici, Catherine, 90
Denmark, 157, 162, 170, 183, 186, 188, 190
Deptford, 32, 44–5, 49
Deuteronomy, Book of, 64, 182, 187
Devereux, Robert, Earl of Essex, 130, 168, 175–6, 178, 187, 190
Diana *MV*, 67
Dido, Queen of Carthage, 32, 40, 43, 66
Digges, Thomas, 85
Diomede *T&C*, 66
Dix, Morgan, 46, 52, 189, 196
Dogges, Isle of, 7, 41, 112, 123
Donne, John, 47
Donno, Elizabeth, 126, 132, 192
Dowden, Edward, 161, 170, 192
Drayton, Thomas, 53
Drummond, William, 91–2, 97, 197
Ducdame, 24, 27–8, 52, 172
Duffy, Eamon 144, 199
Duma, 13
Duncan, King *MAC,* 54, 58, 70–2, 113, 124, 192, 197
Dusinberre, Juliet, 31, 44, 48–50, 192

Dutton, Richard, 14, 190
Dymock, Tailboys, 14, 192

ealdren, 183
eale, 127, 182–4, 188
Eastbridge, 36
Eastcheap, 135, 147, 178
Easter, 49, 83–4
Edgecombe, 123, 194
Edinburgh, 46, 97, 197
Edmondson, Paul, 54, 71, 192
Edwards, Philip, 165, 171, 192
Egeon *CE,* 103, 179
Egmont Bight, 161
Egypt, 28, 42
Egyptian, 68, 88
Elam, Keir, 109, 124–5, 132, 192
Elderberry, 183–4
Eleanor, Queen *KJ,* 26, 155–6
Elegies, 13, 40, 44, 113, 192
Elinor, Queen *TR,* 156
Elizabeth I, Queen, vii, 32, 54–6, 64, 75, 77–8, 80–2, 84–6, 88–94, 96–8, 102, 104, 105, 110, 111, 113, 115, 117, 119–21, 123, 125–33, 135–6, 139, 141, 143–5, 148, 150–6, 158–60, 162–4, 166–70, 174–6, 186, 189, 191–2
Elizabethan, 3–6, 11, 13, 16, 18–19, 22, 26–7, 29–30, 34, 39, 42–3, 45, 58–9, 61, 72, 83, 87, 89, 92, 94, 105, 163, 166–7, 175, 179, 186, 191–2, 195
Elizabethans, 7–9, 16, 19, 28, 42–3, 69, 78–9, 87, 89, 93, 105, 107–8, 128, 142–3, 147–8, 153, 155, 166, 168, 172, 178, 182
ellfrn, 184, 188
Eltham, 178
Elysian, 144
Elysium *TN,* 100, 108
Embankment, 136
Emperor, 84, 105, 173
Empson, William, 3, 13, 193
Enclosures, 14, 42, 52, 190

England, ix, 5, 9, 14, 18, 35, 47, 58, 62, 68, 72, 77, 79–80, 85–6, 89, 97, 124, 129, 144, 152–5, 157, 159, 163–4, 167–9, 175, 183–4, 186, 189, 191–4, 197–8
English, xi, 14, 17, 26–8, 31, 45–6, 49–50, 52–3, 60, 68, 71, 78, 81–3, 85–7, 89–90, 97, 104, 124–5, 142, 150, 154–6, 159, 161, 163–4, 168, 170, 184–6, 188–91, 193–5, 197–9
Englishmen, 17, 27, 77, 184
Englishwoman, 60
Ephesians, Epistle to, 103–4, 180
Ephesus, 102–4, 108
Epicoene, or The Silent Woman, 92
Epicures, 49
Epicurisme, 30, 49
Epidamnum *CE*, 103
Epigrames, 13, 192
epigrammatists, 175
epillyon, 58
Epistles of Saint Paul, 14, 98, 102–3, 110, 111, 116, 123, 124, 194
Equinoctial of Eusebius, 84–5, 95–6, 108, 144
Equinox, 84–5, 88
Estienne, Charles, 189, 193
Europe, 14, 27, 85, 161, 164, 199
Eusebius, Bishop, 84–5, 95–6, 98, 144
Evans, Richard, 47
Everett, Barbara, xi, 84, 88, 192
Exeter, 8, 81, 159–1, 170, 194

Fabian *TN*, 105, 107, 144
Fabio *Gl'ingannati*, 103
Fabrizio *Gl'ingannati*, 103
Falstaff, Sir John, *1–2H4, H5,* 51, 124, 147–9, 176–7, 183
Faulconbridge, Philip *KJ*, 149–3, 155–7, 166, 173
Faustus, Dr. Faustus, 36, 38

February, 77–8, 81–2, 87–8, 95, 101–2, 144, 158, 166–7, 176, 178, 187–8, 190–1, 193
Feste, x, 28, 77, 86–7, 89, 93–8, 107–18, 120–4, 144, 173
Feste-Nashe, 111, 123
Ffrezer (Frizer, Freize), 31
Fiennes, Joseph, 134–5
First Part of the Life and Raigne of King Henrie IV, The, 175
Fitton, Mary, 54
Fitzroy, Henry, 159
Flamminio *Gl'ingannati*, 103
Fleay, Fredrick, 126, 132, 192
Fleet Prison, 119–20
Fleet River, 148
foetor Judaicus, 68
folly, 26, 29, 31, 41, 115, 117, 124, 131, 193
fool, 10, 16, 24–8, 35, 29, 41, 50, 77, 87, 93–5, 98, 108, 110–11, 114–17, 124, 196
foolerie, 16, 41, 111, 115, 127
fooling, 89, 94–5, 111, 144
foolish, 16, 28, 94, 111, 116, 121–2, 177
foolishness, 69, 95, 111, 117
Ford *MWW*, 177
Forman, Simon, 59, 62–3, 65, 73, 189
Fortescue, Sir John, 181, 184–6, 188, 190, 193
fourscore, 21, 65
fourteen, 36, 61, 108, 116, 131, 158
France, 9, 45, 90, 97, 115, 124, 133, 147, 151, 156, 161, 190, 199
Francis I, King, 164
Freemasons, xi
French, 45, 49, 51–2, 64, 90, 93–4, 98, 103, 153, 158–9, 161, 163–4, 168–9, 183, 199
Frenchman, 35, 158, 160–1
Fuller, Thomas, 151, 167, 193

Galatians, Epistle to, 107, 113, 116, 123

Gamaliel, Rabbi, 110
Ganymede *AYLI*, 32, 34, 36, 40, 43
Garber, Marjorie, 21, 46, 193
garlic, 68
Garter, Knights of, 159, 177
Gaveston *Edward III*, 26
Genesis, Book of, 12
Geneva Bible, 12, 14, 43, 73, 107, 117, 148, 189
Genoa, 17, 65
Georgia, 124, 193
German, 69, 98, 161
Gertrude *HAM*, 162, 181, 186
Getae AYLI, 33
Ghost *HAM*, 81, 181–2, 185, 187
Globe Theater, 34, 42, 52, 136, 172, 187, 198
Goddard, Harold C., 21, 46, 193
Goethe, v, ix, xi, 192
Gospels, 81, 95, 98, 102, 105, 109, 113
Grammaticus, Saxo, 184
Gratiano *MV*, 66
Gratulationes Waldenensis, 130, 180
Greek, 27–8, 66, 90–1, 116, 132, 136, 180
Greenblatt, Stephen, ix, xii, 193
Greene, Robert, 26–7, 47–8, 129, 179–80
Gregorian Reformed Calendar, viii, 78–81, 85, 87, 92, 96–7, 144
Gregory, Pope, 85, 96–7, 99, 144, 169
Grigorius, Pontifex, 95, 96, 144
Grindal, Archbishop, 85, 88, 189
Grosart, Alexander Bulloch, 14, 125, 133, 193
Grossman, Marshall, 72, 190
Guernsey, Isle of, 159, 170, 194
Guildenstern *HAM*, 135
Guilpin, Edward, 13, 193
Gundello AYLI, 27, 35, 48
Gurney, Gornay, Gournie, 155–6, 168

Hacket, William, 125
Haffenden, John, 13, 193
halitosis, 69
Hall, Joseph, 14, 87, 193
Halliday, F.E., 56, 70, 72, 193
Halliwell-Phillipps, J.O., 126, 132, 193
Hamlet, 8, 24, 36, 45, 51, 80, 115, 124, 127, 135, 146, 150, 156–8, 162, 164–6, 168–71, 180–8, 193, 192–4
Hanmer, Thomas, 27–8, 44
Hardcastle, Kate, 98, 193
Harfleur, 161
Harrington, Sir John, 126
Harris, Frank, 71, 193
Harrison, G.B., 54, 56, 71, 193
Harvard, 45, 198
Harvey, Gabriel, vii, x, 5–6, 13, 16, 27, 41, 53, 111, 112, 114, 116, 118–25, 127–33, 144, 172–3, 175–6, 180, 193, 198
Hassel, R. Chris, Jr., 124, 193
Hastings, Battle of, 156
Hatcliffe, William, 53
Hathaway, Anne, 186
Hattaway, Michael, 42, 45, 47, 51–2, 193
Hawthornden, 91, 97, 197
Hayward, Thomas, 5, 175–6, 187, 190
Helena *AWW*, 48, 146
Helgoland Bight, 161
Hell, 17–18, 61, 74, 108, 147
Helliott, Nicholas, 30
Heminges, John 4, 13, 20, 51, 193
Henrie, 176, 187, 193
Henry VII, King, 57, 168–9, 187
Henry VIII, King, 93–4, 117, 153–5, 158, 163–4, 169, 182, 184
Herbert, William 14, 53–4, 199
Hero and Leander, 15, 21–2, 35, 40, 43, 47, 49, 172
Herodotus, 35, 50, 197
Herriot, Thomas 85
Hezekiah, Prophet, 104, 179
Hibbard, G.R., 124–5, 170, 193

Hinman, Charles 168, 194
Hodges, Flavia, 98, 193
Holinshed, Raphael, 168, 194
Hollford-Strevens, Leofranc, 87, 190
Holofernes *LLL*, 180
Honan, Park, 48, 50, 194
Honigmann, Ernst, 151, 167–8, 194
Hopkins, Lisa, xi, 47–50, 194
Horatio *HAM*, 168, 181, 183
Hotson, Leslie, 15, 44, 53, 56, 78, 82, 86–7, 94, 126, 132, 194
Howard, Thomas, 128, 164
Hubert *KJ*, 157, 168
Hughes, Willy, 53
Hunsdon, Henry Baron, viii, 54–5, 58–9, 73, 151, 159, 162–4, 167–8, 171, 178, 195
Hunt, Maurice, 51, 124, 194
Hutson, Lorna, 71, 194

Iago *OTH*, 98
Illyria, vii, 97, 100–5, 106–8, 111, 112, 114, 116, 118, 120, 122, 124–5, 135, 140, 143–4, 198
Illyrians, 103, 105
Illyricum, 103, 105, 111
Gl'ingannati, 64, 86, 103, 144
Inns of Court, 77, 81, 95, 101–2, 138, 144
Ireland, 168, 175, 194
Isabella, 103
Isacke, 170, 194
Isaiah, Prophet, 104, 179
Israel, 19, 68, 81
Israelites, 68, 179
Italian, 26–7, 58, 63–4, 73, 83, 86, 93–4, 103–4, 120, 129–32, 153–4, 163, 180
Italy, 27, 48, 63, 73, 90, 115, 124
Ithaca, 14, 191
Ithamore *JM*, 47
Izacke, Richard, 170, 194

Jacobean, 5, 19, 58, 172
Jacques, 29
Jakes, 48, 127

James I, King, ix, xii, 23, 45, 54, 69, 74, 82, 94, 97, 106, 155, 159, 168, 186, 188, 190, 197–8
January, viii, 30, 71, 77–9, 81–2, 87, 94, 97, 105–6, 166, 194
Jaques, x, 15, 20–1, 23–38, 40–2, 48, 51, 172–4
Jenkins, Harold, 161, 171, 183, 187, 194
Jerome, Saint, 116, 123, 194
Jerusalem, 8, 81, 105, 107, 110, 116
Jessica *MV*, x, 62, 64–7, 69, 73, 174
Jesus, 48–9, 69, 74, 81–2, 87, 90, 93, 95, 108, 110, 195
Jew, 15, 22, 44, 47, 62, 64, 66, 69, 74, 110, 189, 195
Jewish, 63–4, 67–8, 81, 116
Jews, 19, 64, 68–9, 74, 189, 198
Johnson, Samuel, 27–8, 45, 172
Jones, Emrys, xi, 54, 58, 70–2, 100, 113, 124, 149–50, 192
Jonson, Ben, 5, 7, 9–14, 50, 53, 92, 109, 113–14, 123–4, 132, 192, 194
Jowett, John, 51, 73, 170, 198–9
Judah, 179
Judaicus, 68
Judaism, 64
judge, 43, 184
judging, judgement, 11, 16–17, 20, 49, 50, 55, 59, 102, 129, 182, 189, 190
Judith, 73, 101, 196
Julian, viii, 78–81, 84–7, 92, 96–7, 99, 137
Juliet, 44, 52, 56, 80, 135, 173, 192
July, xi, 3, 44, 73, 84, 128, 150–1, 158, 168–9, 176–7, 192, 195, 197
June, xi, 6, 13, 16, 26, 44, 48, 62, 73–4, 113, 144, 159, 167–8, 175–6, 189, 191, 195–6
Jusserand, Jean, 124, 194

Juvenal, 180
juvenile, 114, 180

Kafka, Franz, 11–12, 14, 194
Kalendars, 46, 196
Kalends, 142
Kasdan, David Scott, 170, 190
Katherine, Queen, 54, 57, 65, 70–2, 113, 124, 192, 199
Kay, Dennis, xi, 52
Kemble, Charles, 136
Kent, Countess of 62, 66, 70, 86, 191
Kentucky, 72, 190
Kermode, Jenny, 46, 195
Kingsford, C.L., 189, 195
Kinney, Arthur, 7–8, 14, 195
Kinsmen, 74
Kipling, Rudyard, xi
Kit' Marlowe, 29
Knowles, Richard, 45–6, 48, 50, 195
Knox, John, 61, 73

Laertes *HAM*, 158, 165
Lamord, Lamode, Lamond, 157–61, 164, 169–70
Lanier, Alfonso, 62–3, 65, 67
Lanier, Emilia Bassano, x, 54–60, 62–4, 67, 70–4, 173–4, 190, 193–5, 199
Laroque, Francois, 45
Lasocki, David, 57, 72, 197
Latham, Agnes, 33, 50, 195
De Laudibus Legum Angliae, 181, 184, 188, 193
King Lear, 8, 51, 173
Leicester, Earl of, 52, 128–30, 169
Leila *Gl'ignannati*, 103
Leimberg, Inge, 127, 133, 195
Leith, 151
Lenten Stuffe, Nashe's, 9, 14, 41, 112, 115, 118, 199
Leo the Great, Pope, 28, 70, 192
Leonard, Saint 94, 141–3, 144
Leontes *CYM*, 102
Levirate, 188
Leviticus, Book of, 188

Leycesters Common-wealth, 52, 197
Lichfield, Richard, 122
Liébault, Jean, 188, 192

MacCaffrey, Wallace T., 73, 167–8, 195
Madonna, 82, 93, 109, 118
Magdalene, Mary, 3
Magdalenensis, 133, 198
Magi, 81–2
Mahood, Molly, 100, 187, 195
Malone, Edmond, 45, 53, 87, 160, 170, 192, 195
Malta, 15, 22, 44, 47
Malvolio *TN*, x, 82, 86, 89, 95, 97, 106–8, 110, 114, 118–21, 123, 125–8, 131, 133, 141, 173, 198
Manningham, John, 77, 86, 191
Manus Osculatione, 129–32
Marcade *LLL*, 45
Marcellus *HAM*, 168, 181
March, 71, 84–6, 88, 147–8, 158, 166–7, 169, 178, 189, 194–5, 197
Margaret *H6, R3*, 26, 188
Maria *TN*, 82, 90, 107, 111, 114, 117–19, 130–2
Markham, Gervaise, 53, 188, 192
Marlowe (Marlin, Marley), Christopher, x–xi, 5, 13, 15–17, 19–53, 83, 98, 114, 144, 147, 172–4, 189, 194–5, 197–8
Marprelate, 33, 44
Marripodi, Michele, 73
Marston, John, 10, 13, 126, 195
Mar-text, Sir Oliver *AYLI*, 43–4
Massacre, 22, 45, 47–8
Matchett, William, 152, 168, 194
Matthew, Saint, 28, 36
Mayer, Jean-Christophe, 45, 199
McCabe, Richard, 45, 195
McDuffie, Felicia, 73, 196
McKeen, David, 168, 197
McKerrow, Ronald B., 14, 48, 98, 124–5, 133–96

Medawar, Jocelyn, xi, 45, 51
Menaechmi, 86, 102
Menaphon, 26
Merchant of Venice, The, vii, x, 53, 55, 57, 59, 61–5, 67, 69, 71, 73–4, 80, 189
Meres, Frances, 30, 49, 56, 72, 196
Mermaid Inn, xi, 109, 191
Mermidons, 107, 109
Messaline, 101
Messiah, 125, 179
Metamorphoses, Ovid's, 33, 50
Metamorphosis, 13, 127, 195
Microcynicon, 13, 196
Middlesex, 7
Middleton, Thomas, 13, 196
Miller, William E., 125, 196
Montgomery, William, 73, 170, 199
Much Ado about Nothing, 80, 101
Muir, Kenneth, 150, 167, 196
Mulcaster, Robert, 184

Nashe, Thomas, vii, x, 4–14, 9, 16, 22, 27, 29, 33–4, 39–41, 44, 48, 53, 77, 93, 95, 98, 110–25, 127–33, 144, 147, 169, 172–3, 175–6, 179–80, 187, 193–4, 196, 198, 199
Nathaniel *LLL,* 180
Naunton, Sir Robert, 73, 154, 167
Navarre *LLL,* 45, 97, 199
Nest of Ninnies, 125
Nicaea, 84–5, 96
Nicaean, 85, 95
Nicholl, Charles, 6, 13, 93, 98, 124, 179–80, 187, 196
Nicholls, Constable Allen, 30
Nichols, John, 86–7, 196
Nicot, Charles, 35
Nicuola and Lattantio, 64, 104
Norman, 134, 144, 156, 158–9, 161, 170, 196
Normandy, 156, 158, 161, 168
Northumberland, 154
November, viii, 5, 46, 88, 141–4, 190

Nunn, Trevor 142
Nuttall, Anthony, xi
Nym, *H5, MWW,* 177

Occhiogrosso, Frank, 99, 198
O'Connor, Garry 54, 59, 71–2, 196
October, 8, 30, 36, 59, 71, 85, 93, 96, 112–13, 190, 194
Ogden, C.K., 3
Oldcastle, Sir John, 4, 8, 147–9, 166
Oliver *AYLI,* 15, 23, 33, 38, 44, 195
Olivia *TN,* 81–2, 86–7, 92–5, 98, 104, 106, 108, 111, 115, 117–18, 138–44
Onyx *HAM,* viii, 151, 162–4, 171
Orlando *AYLI,* 29–30, 32, 34–6, 38, 42–3, 50–1, 126
Orsini, Duke Virginio, 80, 82–3, 86, 135
Orsino, Count *TN,* 82, 111, 114, 116, 135–6, 138–43, 145
Osculatione Manus, 129–32
Osric *HAM,* 8
Oswald *LEAR,* 8
Othello, 65, 98
Ovid, 13, 15–16, 32–3, 40, 44, 50, 52, 190
Ovidian, 127
Oxfordians, 28

Palladis Tamia, 49, 72, 196
Pandarus *T&C,* 115
Pandulph *KJ,* 153–4, 156
Paris, xi, 22, 45, 47–8, 52, 97, 124, 190–1, 194, 196
Parker, Archbishop Matthew, 28, 35–6, 48
Parliament, 85, 96, 150, 169
Patterson, Annabel, 5, 13, 196
Paul, Saint, vii, x, 13, 15, 44, 48, 54, 71, 94, 98, 100–5, 106–9, 110–12, 115–17, 122–4, 144, 169, 178, 186, 189, 191–3, 195–6
Pauline, 110–11, 113–15, 117

Pavia, 96, 98, 144
Peele, George, 22, 47
Pembroke, Earl of, 70, 128
Pennsylvania, 73, 196
Penshurst Place, 187, 195
Peter, Saint, 87, 112, 116, 127, 133, 143, 149, 154, 167, 189, 198
Petruchio *SHREW*, 65
Phebe *AYLI*, 15, 21–2, 39–40, 43, 50, 172
Philemon, Epistle to, 33
Philip, King of France, 153, 156
Philip, King of Spain, 164
Philippians, Epistle to, 116
Pierce Pennilesse, 33, 118–19
Pierce's Supererogation, 119
Pigrogromitus, 77, 86, 95
Pigrogronitus, 95–6, 108, 144
Pistol *2H4, H5, MWW* 147, 177
Pitcher, John, xi Plautus, 86, 102–3
Poetaster, 10
Pogue, Kate Emery, 61–2, 73, 196
Poley, Richard, 50, 198
Polonius *HAM*, 36
Pontius Pilate, 60, 61, 90
Portia *JC*, 65, 73
Prague, 11, 73
Preussische Jahrbücher, 84, 88, 192
Prior, Roger, 56, 72, 87, 98, 197, 199
Protestant, 17–18, 27, 71, 102, 147, 154
Proteus *TGV*, 139
Psalms, 102, 142, 148–9, 166–7
Pseudodoxia Epidemica, 18–19, 191
Purgatory, 17–18
Puttenham, 28, 49, 89–92, 97, 197
Pyramus *MND*, 66

Quaritch, Bernard, 71, 189
Queubus, 95, 98, 107
Quiller-Couch, Arthur, 15, 44, 197
Quinapalus, x, 77, 86, 94

Rabelais, 90–1
Raleigh, Sir Walter, 20–1, 35, 47
Raphael, 168, 194
Rawlinson, 50, 197
Reformation, 17–18, 36, 71, 88, 145, 168, 189, 191, 197
Reimer, Thomas, 88, 192
Renaissance, 14, 47, 72, 126–7, 133, 171, 188, 190, 194, 198–9
resurrection, 92, 100, 102, 108–9, 111, 116, 123, 136, 173
reunion, 100–2, 104, 109, 143–5, 173, 179
Reyher, Paul, 15, 44, 197
Rheims, 26
Riche, Barnaby, 102–4, 120, 144
Richmond, 71, 159, 197
Riddles, 52, 84, 123, 126–7, 130, 192
Ridley, M.A., 44, 197
Riggs, David, 36, 45, 48–52, 197
Rogers, A.G.L., 188, 198
Roman, 22, 23, 26, 33, 50, 52, 84, 111, 116, 119, 124, 144, 180, 185, 188, 194
Rome, 22, 103, 105, 112, 154, 171, 173
Romeo *R&J*, 56, 63, 80, 135, 139
Rosalind *AYLI*, 7, 21, 23, 26–7, 32, 34–6, 40, 43, 48, 50, 56, 83
Rosencrantz *HAM*, 135
Rowe, Nicholas, 160, 170, 177, 187, 197
Rowley, Samuel, 124
Rowse, A.L., 53–4, 56–9, 62, 70–2, 190, 197
Ruddiman, Thomas, 97, 197

Saffron, 27, 53, 115–22, 128–9, 131–3, 180
Salanio *MV*, 65
Salic Law, 52
Salingar, L.G., 83, 87, 197
Salkeld, Duncan, 71, 197

Index

Salve Deus Rex Judaeorum, 58, 60–3, 72, 195, 199
Salzburg, 196
Samuel, Prophet, ix, xi, 53, 124, 197
Saturday, 178
Saul, King, 111–12
Sayle, Charles, 99, 197
Schimmel, Annemarie, 18–19, 46, 197
Schoenbaum, Samuel, ix, xi, 197
Schoenfeldt, Michael, 71, 189
Scotland, 168, 186, 194
Scots, 91, 151
Scripture, 69, 90, 98, 102, 114, 144
Scythian, 35, 48, 50
Seaton, Ethel, 50, 198
seauenteene, 21
seauenth, 37
seauentie, 21
Seaven, 53
seaven, 20
Sebastian *TN*, 28, 81–2, 100–1, 104–5, 107, 116, 141, 143, 144
Segal, Rabbi Arthur, 74
Seine River, 49, 161
Senior, Duke *AYLI*, 24, 29–31, 34, 36, 38, 41, 43, 51
September, 30, 130, 158, 164, 167, 195
Septenaries, 19
seven, 3–4, 15–21, 24, 30–1, 34, 36–40, 45, 51, 54, 78, 83, 139–40, 145, 158, 176
sevenfold, 19
seventeen, 20, 23
seventeenth, 18, 28, 45, 101, 126, 131
seventh, x, 15, 17–20, 38, 42, 57
seventy, 19, 60, 111
sex, 3, 58–9, 61, 73
sexual, 6, 13–14, 43, 55, 58–9, 61, 104, 183, 190
sexuality, 43
sexually, 164
Shakespeare, Edmund, 94

Shakespeare, Hamnet, 101, 143–4, 150–1, 173, 186
Shakespeare, Judith, 101
Shakespeare, William i, iii, vii-1, 3–4, 6–10,12–24, 26–36, 38–48, 50–74, 77–84, 86–9, 91–5, 97–105, 107–25, 127, 131–2, 134–6, 138–47, 149–62, 164–74, 176–87, 189–99
Shakespearean, 45, 84, 93, 118, 134–5, 152, 161
Shakespeariana, 132, 192–3
Shaw, G.B., 71
shepherd, 7, 15, 20–3, 40, 42–4, 47, 52, 148, 172
shepherdess, 22, 40, 114
shipwreck, 104, 134, 140, 143
Shoreditch, 30, 94, 136, 141–2
Shylock *MV*, 64–5
Sidney, Sir Robert, ix, xi, 8, 173, 195
Siena, 103
Silvio *Appolonius*, 104
Silvius *AYLI*, 23, 38, 172
Simeon *Appolonius*, 81
Skialetheia, 13, 194
Smith, Bruce, 14, 127, 133, 198
Smithfield, 10, 159
Sohmer, David, 45
Sohmer, Steve, iii-iv, xi, 51–2, 73–4, 167, 169, 187, 198
Sommer, Summer(s), Will, 77, 93–5, 112–13, 117–18, 124–5, 130, 144, 150
Sonnets, x, 23, 53–7, 59, 60–4, 67–9, 70–2, 74, 129, 146, 189, 191–2, 197, 199
Sosigenes, 88
Southampton, Earl of, 53, 56, 59
Southwark, 136, 138
Spain, 48, 115, 164
Spanish, 22, 47, 153, 163, 180, 183
Spenser, Edmund, 169
Spevack, Marvin, 45, 198
spy, 26–7, 31–5, 48, 50, 163, 172, 194

stanzo *AYLI,* 24, 26, 36
Steinbeck, John, 22
Stoppard, Tom, 134–6, 145, 196
Strange Newes, 8, 13, 41, 44, 92, 98, 111–12, 118, 129–30, 140, 144, 165, 179–80, 187, 196
Stratford, 22, 55, 80, 101
Stubbes, Thomas, 5
Sunday, 78–9, 85, 148, 150
Surflet & Markham, 188, 192
Sydney, Sir Philip, 57, 130, 148, 178
syphilis, 164–5
Syria, 68

Tacitus, 176
Tamburlaine, 22, 35–6, 40, 47–8
Taming of the Shew, The, 51, 65
Tarlton, Richard, 94
Tarsus, 110
Tasso, Torquato, 13, 198
Taylor, Gary, 22
Tempest, The, 63
Terence, 181
Tertullian, 18, 61, 72, 124, 194, 198
Testament, Old and New, 19, 93, 104, 110–11, 120, 179, 182
Thames, 49, 136, 138, 145, 148
theatre, 5, 14, 24, 30, 32, 39–40, 42, 49, 52, 58, 71, 74, 87, 94, 97, 136, 145, 172, 187, 190, 198–9
theatrical, 16, 34, 39–40, 47
Theobald, Lewis, 84
Thisbe *MND,* 66
Thorpe, Thomas, 53
Thraso, 128, 180
tide, 147–9, 166
tideturn, 148
time, 4, 12, 18–22, 24, 30, 52, 58, 81–2, 86–7, 92, 96, 104–5, 112, 114, 116–17, 124, 129, 135–6, 138, 140–7, 147–8, 150, 153–6, 164, 168, 173, 176, 178–9, 182, 191

times, x, 11, 19–20, 37, 46, 68, 90, 97,105, 111, 123, 127, 129–30, 159, 173, 179, 183–4, 196
Titus Andronicus, 22, 51–2, 65
tobacco, 35
Tobin, J. J. M., 118–20, 124–5, 132, 198
Toby *TN,* 8, 77, 82–3, 87, 95–7, 107, 114, 119, 144
Topas, Sir *TN,* 120
Touchstone *AYLI,* x, 15–16, 21, 23, 27, 29, 32–4, 37–41, 43, 46, 51, 111, 113, 172
touchstone, 12, 51
Towton, Battle of, 188
Trimming, 122, 125
Troilus *T&C,* 53, 66, 115
Trojan *T&C,* 66
Trollope, Frances, 12
Troublesome Reign of King John, The, 149–50, 152–3, 155–7, 167–8, 197
Tubal *MV,* 65
Tudor, viii–ix, 5, 18, 137, 169, 186, 195
Twelfth Night, vii-viii, x, 8–9, 28, 64, 70, 75, 77–105, 108–15, 117–29, 131–3, 135–6, 138–41, 143–5, 147–8, 150, 152, 154, 156, 158, 160, 162, 164, 166, 168, 170, 173–4, 183, 192, 194–5, 197, 199
Tyler, 71, 199
Tyrwitt, 53
tythe, 153–4

Ulysses *T&C,* 51
Unfortunate Traveller, The, 98, 111, 124–5, 194, 196
Union (pearl), 162, 171

Valdensium, Valdinensis, 129–30, 180
Valentine *TGV,* 78, 94, 140–1, 146
Vapians *TN,* 95–6, 108
Variorum, 27, 45–6, 50, 84, 195

Venetian, 54, 62–6, 72, 197
Venice, vii, x, 53, 55, 57, 59, 61–5, 67, 69, 71, 73–4, 104, 189
Venus and Adonis, 70, 92
Vere, Francis, 8
Verity, A.W., 45, 122, 125, 170, 199
Vernal Equinox, 84–5
Vernon, Elizabeth, 56
Verona, 51, 63, 98, 173, 198
Veronese, 98
Victoria Embankment, 136
Victoria & Albert Museum, viii, 163, 171
Viola *TN*, x, 81–2, 92, 100–3, 108–9, 114–15, 117, 119, 134–6, 138–44
virginals, 62, 70, 74
Virginio, 82, 86, 135
vnion, 162
Volpone, 9, 14, 194
Voragine, Jacobus, 17, 46, 142, 145, 200
Vulgate, 124, 191
Vultu, Vultum, Vultus, 129, 131, 133

Walden, 27, 53, 118–22, 128–9, 131–3, 180
Wales, 184, 188
Walsingham, Francis, 26, 32
Warburton, William, 84
Warren, Roger, 87, 98, 199
Warwickshire, 39, 42, 51, 80
Watson, Thomas, 30, 97, 197
Wells, Stanley 51, 54, 71, 73, 87, 98, 161, 170, 192, 198–9

Westminster, 86, 135, 145, 191
Westminster Abbey, 151, 160
Westport, 73, 196
Whitehall, 82, 102, 136, 138, 145
Whitgift, Bishop, 6, 16, 93, 112
Whyte, Rowland, 8, 148, 178
Wickham, Glynne, 14, 199
Wilde, Oscar, 53
William (young Shakespeare) *AYLI*, 39–40
Wilson, Richard, ix, xii, 15, 44–5, 57, 70, 72, 80, 87, 197, 199
Wilton, Jack, The Unfortunate Traveler, 98, 111, 122, 125, 196
Windsor, 47, 177
Wittenberg(e), 8, 74, 195
Wolfe, John, 119, 187, 193
Wolsey, Cardinal, 169
Woods, Susanne, 57–8, 72–3, 199
Wooton, 178
wordplay, vii, 89, 91, 93, 95, 97–9, 109, 144, 161, 181, 195
Worthies, 45, 167, 193, 199
Wroithesley, 53
Wycliffite, 166
Wygmore, Thomas, 170

Yarmouth, 9, 41, 111, 123
Yeats, William Butler, 22
Yonkers, 58
York, xii, 14, 45–6, 50–1, 58, 70–4, 99, 109, 168 170–1, 184, 193, 199

Zahl, 48, 190
Zeus, 32, 43

EU authorised representative for GPSR:
Easy Access System Europe, Mustamäe tee 50,
10621 Tallinn, Estonia
gpsr.requests@easproject.com

www.ingramcontent.com/pod-product-compliance
Lightning Source LLC
Chambersburg PA
CBHW070352240426
43671CB00013BA/2476